ROOSEVELT, CHURCHILL, *and the* WORLD WAR II OPPOSITION

ROOSEVELT, CHURCHILL, *and the* WORLD WAR II OPPOSITION

A Revisionist Autobiography

George T. Eggleston

with Illustrations

The Devin-Adair Company
Old Greenwich

For information address The Devin-Adair Company,
143 Sound Beach Avenue, Old Greenwich, Conn. 06870.

Library of Congress Catalog Card Number: 79-1727
ISBN: 0-8159-5311-9

Manufactured in the United States of America

I know of no country in which there is so little independence of mind and real freedom of discussion as in America . . . In America the majority raises formidable barriers around the liberty of opinion; within these barriers an author may write what he pleases; but woe to him if he goes beyond them. Not that he is in danger of an auto-da-fé, but he is exposed to continued obloquy and persecution. His political career is closed forever, since he has offended the only authority (i.e. majority opinion) which is able to open it.

— ALEXIS DE TOCQUEVILLE (1835)

Table of Contents

Illustrations follow pages 82 and 194

Publisher's Preface

This is the story of a man who tried to keep America out of the 1939 European War — and of what happened to him as a result.

It is a carefully researched look at the determination of FDR and Churchill to get America into that war against the many-times-established wishes of over 80 percent of the American public to stay out of it.

The mendacity and deceit that were used by the Roosevelt government at that fateful time established a precedent that has been unsurpassed by later administrations for its record of secrecy and coverup.

In 1940 the America First Committee, representing the grass roots of America, had become effective under the leadership of General Robert Wood, Colonel Charles Lindbergh, and others, including George Eggleston, who had been appointed editor of a conservative magazine, *Scribner's Commentator*, dedicated to keeping the U.S. out of the second "War to end War."

With the bombing of Pearl Harbor, America was in — by the back door, as Henry Stimson put it — and the America First Committee was dissolved. So too was *Scribner's Commentator*. Eggleston volunteered for the Navy and went to Quonset, Rhode Island, for officer training. But FDR and those around him had neither forgotton nor forgiven certain individuals who had opposed U.S. entry into the war. Lindbergh was called a copperhead, his commission was canceled, and his services volunteered were declined. Overnight the hero became a pariah, not to the vast American Public, but to those running the war.

In George Eggleston's case the revenge was even rougher. From the day he received his commission as a naval officer he was subjected to a systematic hounding by a New Deal prosecutor who swore he was going to have Eggleston before a grand jury for the rest of his life.* That story of perjury in high places is told here for the first time after a lapse of almost forty years. It is a powerful story — one it is hard to believe actually happened.

DEVIN A. GARRITY

*As final pages of this book were being prepared for the printer the author wrote to the Navy asking for clarification of his discharge status. He received this statement from the office of the Chief of Naval Personnel, Washington, D.C.:

A careful review of the record of subject officer indicates that his period of service was characterized as Honorable. No further action by the Chief of Naval Personnel is considered required in this case.

Foreword

As AMERICA APPROACHES the last decades of the twentieth century it becomes increasingly clear that U.S. entry into the second Anglo-German war succeeded only in upsetting the balance of power in Europe and fostering a new arms race. Certainly in June, 1941, when Hitler's forces marched into Russia and England was demonstrably safe from invasion, it was not necessary for America to enlarge the conflict. The hopes and aspirations of tens of millions of Americans — 83 per cent, if the Gallup Poll is to be believed — at that time expressed the single-minded desire that America stay out and help arrange a negotiated peace between England and Germany.

In a letter to me from Switzerland in 1972, two years before his death, Charles Lindbergh wrote:

> In preparing *Wartime Journals* for publication I often thought of you and the men and women we worked with in the attempt to keep our country from entering the war. I feel as strongly as ever that we were right in the position we took, and I believe this is becoming more evident with each passing year.

Unfortunately none of us in the 1940-41 movement to keep America out of the war knew how cleverly the cards had been stacked against us in those pre-Pearl Harbor months. Only as the papers and writings of prominent Englishmen have come to light do we have the true record of some of the deceits practiced on the American people and the U.S. Congress.

For example, in a speech in Philadelphia in late 1940 Mr. Roosevelt declared:

> There is no secret treaty, no secret understanding in any shape or form, direct or indirect, with any other government or any other nation in any part of the world to involve this nation in any war.

But to the British these words were soon to be discounted as strictly campaign oratory. Winston Churchill's memoirs reveal that in January, 1941 — almost a full year before Pearl Harbor — Harry

Hopkins brought to 10 Downing Street this top-secret pledge from the White House:

> The President is determined that we shall win the war together. . . He has sent me here to tell you that at all costs he will carry you through.

British historian Ronald Lewin has disclosed in *Churchill as War Lord* that immediately following the Hopkins mission of January, 1941, Churchill sent a secret military mission to Washington to work out plans for an Anglo-American invasion of Europe. This group, comprising an air commodore, a major general, and two rear admirals, was registered with U.S. Immigration as a "Purchasing Commission," and its members were under orders from London to dress as civilians.

Roosevelt apologists have been unanimous in the assertion that FDR had to deceive the American people for their own good. The apologists claim that it would eventually be seen that the end had justified the means. So what was the end?

Britain's eminent military analyst, Sir Liddell Hart, concluded the final chapter of his *History of the Second World War* with this observation:

> This catastrophic conflict, which ended by opening Russia's path into the heart of Europe, merely produced the looming fear of another war.

Another eminent British military analyst, Major General J.F.C. Fuller, expressed himself in stronger language, which Gen. Albert C. Wedemeyer quoted in his 1958 book, *Wedemeyer Reports*:[1]

> The second crusade ended even more disastrously than the first, and this time the *agent provocateur* was not the German Kaiser, but the American President, whose abhorrence of Nazism and craving for power precipitated his people into the European conflict and so made it world wide.

There are some who have defended the President by saying that of course it was the Japanese attack on Pearl Harbor that forced the U.S. to enter the war. This was challenged by still another Briton, The Rt. Hon. Oliver Lyttelton, a member of Churchill's war cabinet, who declared in an address to the American Chamber of Commerce in London on June 24, 1944:

> America provoked Japan to such an extent that the Japanese were forced to attack Pearl Harbor. It is a travesty of history to say that America was forced into the war.

In America in 1940-41, with the opinion polls showing such a vast majority of the people against entering the war, it seems incredible that the White House would not listen to the message and honor it. And with the leadership of the noninterventionist movement in the hands of such men as Senators Taft, Byrd, Vandenberg, Wheeler, Lodge, Nye, Bennett Champ Clark—and Generals Wood, Dawes, Summeral, Johnson, MacNider, ex-President Hoover, Colonel Lindbergh, and Captain Rickenbacker — one would think it incredible that the Administration would ignore the overwhelming opposition to involvement.

But the proponents of noninvolvement were not for long ignored. They soon found that the imperial Presidency would stop at nothing to silence and, if possible, punish dissidents.

Introduced for the first time in U.S. history was a Presidential program of electronic bugging, as well as manipulation of the grand jury system, in the attempt to intimidate and silence all critics of FDR's maneuvers to involve America in another European war.

The following pages, while largely autobiographical, will, I hope, convey some of the atmosphere of the pre-Pearl Harbor days and demonstrate some of the attempts by the Roosevelt Administration to destroy the reputations and careers of certain individuals who were considered effective at the time in their efforts to prevent our becoming involved in World War II, the "war to end all wars."

G.T.E.

I

Discovering New York

THE PRESIDENTIAL ELECTION of 1928, in which Herbert Hoover won a landslide victory over Alfred E. Smith, was to go down in history as the peak point of America's record year of abundance. Never had the U.S. enjoyed such a twelve-month cycle of prosperity. Optimism over the Wall Street highs had cast a spell of euphoria over everyone. Stocks were to continue to go up, up, and up. Everyone shared the feeling that there was never to be another war. Good fun and laughter were abounding.

The editor in chief of the satirical magazine *Life* (not to be confused with the later Luce publication) was Robert E. Sherwood, ably assisted by Robert Benchley and Dorothy Parker. In May, 1928, just prior to the nominating conventions of both the Democratic and Republican parties, Sherwood had the bright idea that *Life* should attempt a large-scale spoof — the magazine would sponsor its own candidate for President, none other than Will Rogers.

Will Rogers was easily the best-loved character in the U.S. at the time. He was the gum-chewing vaudeville-trained, cowboy philosopher who poked fun at Presidents, yet was always a welcome guest at the White House. He was definitely a national institution — a sort of court jester to official Washington. Although Rogers had been only an infrequent contributor to *Life*, he had been a longtime friend of Sherwood. When Sherwood offered him the nomination, he immediately approved the idea and suggested that they call his ticket the Anti-Bunk Party. Echoing Coolidge's famous statement, "I do not choose to run," Rogers took the slogan, "He chews to run."

Remuneration played no part in Rogers's arrangement with *Life*. Although Rogers was already one of the highest paid performers in the entertainment field, he agreed to write several "political pieces" for Sherwood at the magazine's usual rates.

In the announcement issue, with a caricature of Rogers on the cover, the magazine declared editorially that their man was the first candidate for President in history who was intentionally funny. In Rogers's acceptance message he wrote: "*Life*'s offer has left me dazed — if I can stay dazed, I ought to make a perfect candidate. Now, let us be honest. We want the wet vote and we want the dry vote. Our plank hereby endorses wine for the rich, beer for the poor, and moonshine liquor for the prohibitionist." Thousands of campaign buttons were distributed coast to coast, and when a New York radio station offered to give the new political party free time on the air, such guest stars as Eddie Cantor, Amelia Earhart, and Leon Errol enthusiastically gave of their talents in endorsement of the Anti-Bunk candidate.

On polling day such was the nation's mood for fun that many a ballot, coast to coast, was invalidated because of the large number of write-in votes for Rogers. In addition to the headliners of Broadway and Hollywood who endorsed Rogers, many prominent citizens unabashedly went on record in his behalf. In a letter to *Life* Henry Ford, Sr., wrote: "The joke of Will Rogers' candidacy for President is that it is no joke. It is a serious attempt to restore American common sense to American politics."

In 1928 and 1929 the national mood, which glorified spoof and fun, was quite naturally reflected in the colleges of the U.S. This was the heyday of the campus comic magazine, and almost every college in the country had its fun sheet. The Harvard *Lampoon* had been the first of the genre. During the Roaring Twenties the *Lampoon* had a hundred imitators, including such successful publications as the Cornell *Widow*, the Princeton *Tiger*, the Columbia *Jester*, the Dartmouth *Jack o' Lantern*, the Michigan *Gargoyle*, the Wisconsin *Octopus*, and the Stanford *Chaparral*.

At the University of California we had the *Pelican*, and in 1929 I became its editor. The *Pelican* had been founded at Berkeley in 1903, with Rube Goldberg as its first editor. At the turn of the century only a few women were enrolled on the Berkeley campus. As these damsels tended to be bespectacled and homely, they were referred to by campus wags as pelicans — hence the name of the new magazine.

The *Pelican* had long been a successful publishing venture. During the year of my tenure of office it was the proud boast of our business manager that we had a larger circulation and carried more advertising than any other college magazine. The business manager and I considered ourselves fortunate to draw down the modest salaries allotted to us.

In the twenties there were no big-business scouts checking the campuses for graduates who might be wooed into today's high-salaried world of computers. In fact, few of my classmates, aside from those who entered law school, had any idea what they intended to do to earn a living. But all were optimists and expected to achieve their idea of the American Dream — a good job, marriage and family, a car in every garage and a chicken in every pot.

Some of us in journalism on the campus had reasonable grounds to feel that there might be a future in our chosen field. Seniors who had held down top posts editing the campus paper, *The Daily Californian*, had little difficulty signing on as reporters on the San Francisco and Oakland newspapers. One especially brilliant managing editor of the "Cal" was handpicked by the *Wall Street Journal* to be a West Coast correspondent.

We on the *Pelican* staff were avid followers of Robert Sherwood's *Life,* and of *Vanity Fair, Judge,* and *College Humor.* The *New Yorker* had not as yet attracted attention on the campus. James Thurber was later to describe the early issues of that magazine as "the devil-may-care comic weekly of the 1920s, irreverent, understaffed, with little on its mind and going nowhere in particular."

During the last semester before commencement both *College Humor* and *Judge* held cartoon contests in which undergraduates from all over the U.S. were invited to enter samples of their work. I won a first prize from *Judge,* a check for $300, and a second prize from *College Humor,* $500 plus a Gruen watch (which I still treasure). With the awards came letters from each of the editors ending with the almost identical words, "If you are in the East some time, do come by our office and say hello."

Upon receipt of the letters I decided not to wait for commencement. (My diploma was mailed to me later.) After I finished my last examination paper, I put what savings I had into traveler's checks, and with a financial assist from my parents boarded an eastbound train for Chicago and New York. Proudly wearing my new watch, I stopped off a day in Chicago and visited the *College Humor* offices, where I was warmly received by its editor, H.N. Swanson, and publisher, J.M. Lansinger. The magazine occupied a small office building the company owned at 1050 North La Salle Street. The reception room, where I waited a few minutes before being received, was decorated with framed covers of the magazine — reproductions of pastel portraits of beauteous young models done by the outstanding pretty-girl artist of the period, Rolf Armstrong. Several framed posters announced some of the talent appearing in the magazine at the time: "A new novel by Percy Marks, author of *The Plastic Age* — Sports articles by Grantland Rice, Knute Rockne, Westbrook Pegler, Bob Zuppke, and many others! — Humorous features by Frank Sullivan and S.J. Perelman — Illustrations by Ralph Barton and Russell Patterson." All this was to my mind a very lively bill of fare.

It developed during our conversation that Mr. Lansinger also owned the nearby Lansing Hotel, as well as a dude ranch out in Colorado. There was a feeling of prosperity around the place, and I was duly impressed when Mr. Lansinger sent me back to the railroad station in his chauffeur-driven Cadillac. In parting it was suggested by Editor Swanson that perhaps after I had seen a bit of New York I might like to return to Chicago; there might be a job opening on the magazine at a later date.

On the ride down Michigan Boulevard to the station I recall asking the chauffeur the meaning of the laurel wreaths that decorated two of the traffic kiosks. "They're for the two policemen who were shot here last week," he said.

As might be anticipated, I marveled at finding myself in New York. I arrived on a Sunday morning when the streets were clean and lifeless, and the city so quiet that as I walked the long canyons gawking upward at the fabulously high buildings, I wondered if I could ever feel at home in such overpowering surroundings. I found a neat, small room in the Fraternity Clubs building a couple of blocks from Grand Central Station. The Fraternity Clubs operation was one of the Allerton House hotels, which, by special arrangement with a group of college fraternities, slanted its advertising toward the college trade. The ceiling of the foyer of the building was studded with the coats of arms of various fraternities, and I was pleased to see the shield of mine, Kappa Alpha, surrounded by those of Deke, Phi Delt, Sigma Chi, Zeta Psi, and others. The room rent was sixty-eight dollars a month.

During my first week in New York I did all the things one would expect. I rode the double-decker buses up and down Fifth Avenue.

I rode the elevated to Harlem. I took the subway to the Battery and visited the Statue of Liberty. I walked around Wall Street and joined a group of tourists in a tour of Trinity Church. I of course spent almost a full day wandering through the Metropolitan Museum. The immediate vicinity of my new address was endlessly fascinating. I never tired of walking across 42nd Street to Times Square — and especially at night of gaping at the wildly flashing signs on Broadway and reading the news in lights that ceaselessly paraded around the top of the *Times* Building.

On almost every corner from Grand Central Station to the Square there were flacks selling gadgets from open suitcases mounted on easels in such a way as to be quickly folded up upon the approach of the police. One memorable character I watched for several minutes before he packed up and fled had an ingenious routine. His open suitcase was lined with black velvet, upon which was displayed a dazzling array of wristwatches. In his left hand he held several watches that he waved before the eyes of the gathering crowd. In his right hand he held a watch he pressed to the ears of a couple of his henchmen in the crowd. "Every one goes," he repeated again and again as his stooges piously listened to the ticking, nodded, and bought one with a crisp dollar bill. Instantly there were dollar bills flashing all over the place as the man delivered dozens of watches, all from his pocket. Then in a flash he snapped his suitcase shut and was gone. It all happened so fast that the dollar bill I tried to press on the man never reached its mark. In the aftermath most of the sheepish purchasers faded away. Two or three remained to examine with curses what they had bought — children's imitation watches from the Five-and-Ten.

Perhaps the greatest boon for any young man in Manhattan in 1929 who had to be careful with his budget was the Automat restaurant chain. There were two in the Grand Central area, and the quality of the food, especially the pot of home-style baked beans that appeared in answer to two nickels in a slot, was excellent. By eating mostly in the Automats and only occasionally patronizing one of the sumptuous Longchamps restaurants I managed to keep my cost of living within reasonable bounds.

With the letter from the editor of *Judge* in my pocket, I decided to make my first call on the editor of *Life*. I figured that if I first called at *Judge* and sold none of my wares there, I might be a bit discouraged. Whereas if I first had a rebuff from *Life*, I still had my letter to bolster up my courage for the visit to *Judge*.

Life magazine at the time was America's glamorous opposite number to England's *Punch*. The campaign for Will Rogers of the year before had brought the magazine more than its share of national attention. It was a famous institution. As I alighted from the elevator to enter the editorial offices of *Life* on the ninth floor of the bank building at 598 Madison, I felt so self-conscious that if the elevator doors had not closed behind me I would surely have bounded out again to descend to street level.

The elevator opened directly onto the *Life* reception room, dominated by stained glass panels. A large horizontal panel that occupied most of the wall behind the receptionist's desk was a replica in leaded glass of *Life*'s well-known masthead decoration, a knight on horseback chasing a bat-winged devil across the landscape. The knight's shield was labeled *Life,* and his leveled lance was a long quill pen. The panel was lighted from behind, which brought out the colors in the fashion of the Tiffany lampshades of the Gay Nineties.

Other glass back-lighted panels were enlarged segments of political cartoons that had run in the magazine. Several framed Maxwell Parrish covers adorned the rest of the wall space. A bronze cupid about six times life size stood on a pedestal in the center of the room. The cupid held a bronze quill pen in one hand and a scroll in the other. I was surprised and not a little flustered that I was the only caller in the room. I wondered for a few moments if I was out of bounds. Truth was that this was a Monday. Regular contributors, and hopeful beginners as well, were supposed to call on Wednesdays from ten to twelve.

Oh, how wonderful at such a time and in such a place to find a smiling, friendly receptionist! I told the attractive young lady at the desk my name and asked if I might see someone in the editorial department. Her name, I learned later, was Kay Corbett. She was one of the great receptionists of New York. She actually made me feel as though I had an appointment and was expected. After a quick phone call, she told me to go through the door to the right marked "Editorial." Beyond the first door was another door, the editor's. The stained glass of this door depicted the dome of the nation's Capitol opened up so several legislators could dip their large spoons inside and ladle out the gravy.

Life's editor in chief in 1929 was Norman Anthony, a blond, balding man with a ready grin and a highly animated personality.

He had but recently been brought over to *Life* from *Judge*. At *Judge* he had succeeded Harold Ross as editor when Ross left *Judge* to become founder of the *New Yorker*.

Robert Sherwood had been separated from *Life* some six months earlier, when the management decided he was spending too much of his time writing plays. Getting fired from *Life* at the age of thirty-two was probably the best thing that ever happened to Sherwood. By devoting all his energy to writing plays he turned out half a dozen hits, including *Reunion in Vienna, The Petrified Forest, Idiot's Delight, Abe Lincoln in Illinois,* and *There Shall Be No Night.* Each of the last three plays won a Pulitzer Prize. In 1940 he switched his talents to politics and became President Roosevelt's chief speechwriter. It is hard to believe, in retrospect, that the brilliant Sherwood was actually fired and did not resign of his own account. But his biographer, John Mason Brown, in telling of the incident, wrote that Sherwood was quite shaken by the dismissal and very much worried financially at the time by his cutoff from the regular paycheck. According to Brown, Sherwood had enjoyed editing the magazine, especially during the Will Rogers campaign for President. At the height of the electioneering ballyhoo he had written facetiously to his mother: "We'll get Will in the White House yet, and then it's the Court of St. James for me!"

Norman Anthony quickly took the manila envelope from my grasp and shook out a dozen of my rough pencil sketches on his desk. I shall be everlastingly thankful to him for what happened next. He picked up the sketch on top of the heap, studied it for a moment, then let out a roar of laughter. One by one he looked at the lot, laughed some more, and okayed four for me to take along and finish for publication. In the first sketch, the one that broke the ice, a well-groomed young man with suitcase in hand was about to register at a hicktown hotel out West. (A cowboy in chaps and Stetson was lounging in the lobby.) The young man was addressing the room clerk: "I'm traveling for my father's health."

My visit to the *Judge* office was even more productive. *Judge* was located in a modern office building at 18 East 48th Street. The *Judge* offices were strictly bare and workmanlike. Editor Jack Shuttleworth, a short, handsome man in his mid-thirties, shook my hand warmly and took only a few moments to look over my sketches. He selected three and scribbled his okay on them, then called in his art director, Phil Rosa, and introduced me. Rosa, who was a warm-blooded Latin type about twice the size physically of the editor, picked up one of the okayed sketches and said, "Jack, I think this would make a cover."

A Cover! I tried to keep my composure. A Cover! Oh well, I thought, they will probably buy my sketch and turn it over to one of their regular artists to finish. Again Rosa put his oar in: "Let's let him try a finish on this and see how it comes out."

With six pencil sketches to finish in India ink and a seventh to render in full color, I staggered back to my room at the Fraternity Clubs in a mild daze.

The calendar then stood at mid-June, and the thermometer stood in the nineties. In those days before air-conditioning, New York City during a heat wave was about as enervating as a Turkish bath. I bought an electric fan, but found it useless during daylight hours. Working in my room while the sun shone was impossible. I did all my finished drawings during the late night hours, stripped to my shorts and sopping up perspiration with a towel, in spite of the feeble efforts of my fan to keep the air moving in from the open window.

During that month in New York I sold six-hundred-dollars worth of drawings to *Life* and *Judge*, and at month's end I had the satisfaction of seeing my *Judge* cover appear on the newsstands around town. The cover drawing was an atrocious pun. A ship-wrecked mariner was pictured wading ashore on a tiny tropical coral islet where a grass-skirted houri was standing under a coconut tree. "I won't mind this atoll" was the caption. I suppose this was my contribution to the early demise of *Judge*. It may also have been a premonition of my later weakness for tropical islands.

II

Year of the Market Crash

AFTER I HAD CASHED my first checks from *Life* and *Judge* I had such a feeling of solvency that I decided to call on a couple of friends of my undergraduate days who had recently come East to enter the newspaper business. One was William Randolph Hearst, Jr. — Bill to his friends — who had been sent by his father to understudy various departments of Hearst's *New York American*. (He was to rise to editor in chief of the Hearst papers and share a Pulitzer Prize for his dispatches from Moscow.) The other had come to New York to work as young Bill's assistant. He was Roger (Red) Friend, who had been Bill's roommate in the Phi Delt house at the University of California.

Neither Bill nor Red had at this particular point in their careers become very seriously involved in their chosen profession. It was thanks to them, however, that I saw a bit of the world of news-gathering as it existed in the bygone age of Hecht, MacArthur, and "The Front Page."

Just a block from the *New York American* building on Cherry Street was a speakeasy called the Rain House. Here every Friday afternoon around five o'clock a group of Hearstlings met in a back room to partake of beer and often stronger stuff whilst playing penny ante. The stakes were purposely low, because reporters in those days were very low-salaried. For this I was grateful. Besides a scattering of reporters, there were always three regulars on hand at these Rain House gatherings. Two were famous editorial cartoonists of the day, Winsor McKay and Nelson Harding. The other was Harry Acton, who wrote a popular column for the *American* called "The Gang Plank." It was Acton's job to meet all the great ocean liners docking in the city, carrying famous personalities from all over the world.

Another friend from college days with whom I lunched occasionally was Albert L. Furth. Bill Furth had been an editor of the *Daily Californian* at Berkeley and had recently been hired by Henry Luce to be a writer for *Time* magazine. Over the years there have been many anecdotes bandied around about *Time*'s practice of assigning writers to jobs they know nothing about in order to get a fresh slant on a subject. Furth's experience was one of the first of the kind. When Furth was hired, his interview with Henry Luce had been very brief. Luce asked Furth what he knew about sports. When Furth said he had never played in any sport, had never been interested in any sport, and in fact disliked all sports, the response was "That's fine, you're just the man to write sports." Furth did a lot of boning up on sports in old newspaper files and managed to survive the ordeal. He was to wind up later as managing editor of *Fortune*.

As a young actor who has landed a few bit parts suddenly begins dreaming of playing Hamlet, I found that during my second month in New York my ambition had soared to the extent that I wanted to be an editor. I wrote a note to H.N. Swanson in Chicago asking if there was an opening on *College Humor*. He replied by inviting me to come out and be an associate editor at a starting salary of seventy-five dollars a week.

During my second month in New York I had discovered that instead of selling six sketches out of a dozen submitted to editors, my average had fallen abruptly, so that if I sold one or two a week I was doing about as well as I could hope for. The payment for finished drawings was twenty-five and thirty-five dollars at the time. With the pay offered by *College Humor* equaling a sale of two or three drawings a week, I decided that the move to Chicago was definitely a sound one from a financial standpoint.

Although I had found the humidity in New York almost unbearable, Chicago in that summer of 1929 seemed to me not only the hottest city I had ever been in but the dirtiest. I used to keep a change of linen in my office drawer because the things I wore to work each morning were usually soot-encrusted by mid-afternoon.

My chores on *College Humor* included a first reading of unsolicited manuscripts and a daily search through the piles of campus comic magazines for material to reprint. I also did a page of cartoons and comment for each issue called "Campus Patter."

Living costs in Chicago were wonderfully moderate at the time. You could get a good lunch for sixty-five cents and one of the best dinners in town for a dollar fifty. Only the speakeasy was an expensive luxury of the period. But for those of us earning seventy-five dollars a week there was little danger of becoming habitués of these gin palaces, where a drink cost as much as a good dinner elsewhere.

There was evidence on every hand that Chicago was deserving of its worldwide reputation as the crime capital of the U.S. Gangland killings dominated the headlines of almost every newspaper. Those were the days when the Capone and O'Banion hoods were locked in a deadly struggle for control of the hundred-million-dollars-a-year shakedown racket in the city. Just a few months prior to my arrival in Chicago seven O'Banion stalwarts had been machine-gunned to death in the so-called Valentine Day Massacre.

With so much crime in the air, it was inevitable that there was a ready market for detective magazines. A room on the third floor of the *College Humor* building housed John Lansinger's contribution to this market, a money-making little magazine called *Real Detective*. The editor of *Real Detective* was a middle-aged, billiard-ball bald man named Fred Baird. Baird looked like the type of chief of detectives always pictured in the movies of the thirties. Sometimes, when tired of reading manuscripts, I climbed the stairs to Baird's office and spent half an hour chatting about his all-abiding interest, the solution of crime.

One of the reasons the detective magazine made money was that the operation was a one-man affair. I never saw a secretary or any other kind of help around Baird. He sat behind a desk loaded with manuscripts and pecked out his letters and copy on an ancient typewriter at his elbow. On the desk in front of him, the only feature aside from the piles of manuscript, was a large wooden bowl full of Bull Durham. Baird smoked an endless chain of self-rolled cigarettes. He could roll a perfect-looking cigarette with one hand, a trick I had often tried during my college days without a glimmer of success.

The highlight of my visits to Baird came one morning when for the first time I found his door closed. In response to my knock he opened the door upon a darkened room and said in a low whisper, "There's something going on across the way." His room was stifling — he had all his blinds down — with only the crack of one window up about an inch from the bottom. "Look through there," he said, "and you will see what I mean." Peeking out, I looked directly across an alleyway where there was a similarly shaded window opened to a crack at the bottom immediately on my line of vision.

Baird explained that for several days he had been positive that he was being spied upon from the apartment house window opposite his office. He also said he was quite sure he was being followed each day on his walks between his lakefront apartment and the office. Baird was convinced that his life was endangered because of a series of articles he was running in his magazine "exposing" the operations of the Capone gang. To put it in Baird's words, he was being "tailed because these birds would like to see that I am rubbed out before any more installments of the story appear." When Baird put his problem before the boss, he was so convincing and so apparently shaken and unfit for work that it was decided he must be given police protection. Lansinger also went a step beyond this and hired an investigator from a private detection agency to look into the situation.

For almost a week the whole work force of the Collegiate World Publishing Company was caught up in speculation as to the odds on Baird's future life-span. He became noticeably more nervous and paler each day, and lost considerable weight. He confessed to me that he wanted most of all to go away to parts unknown. But the security police insisted that he stay around so they could get a line on who was shadowing him.

The flurry of excitement subsided when the private eye hired by Lansinger discovered that Baird had been under surveillance all along by none other than a team of sleuths hired by his wife. Mrs. Baird had suspected, and with good reason, that her husband was dallying with a lady friend. When all the facts came to light and became office gossip, Baird seemed thenceforth a very sheepish and indrawn man. It was understood that Mrs. Baird had given her husband such a severe dressing down that the poor fellow's spirit was all but broken. I had met Mrs. Baird once. She was all of twenty years older than Baird and was reputed to be an heiress, a rumor their lavish Gold Coast apartment seemed to bear out.

June, July, and August of 1929 marked the golden summer of the Bull Market. It was my good fortune at this point in my life that I had no money to invest in anything. Success stories abounded of sales clerks and taxi drivers getting rich overnight on the ever rising market. More than three hundred million shares of stock were held on margin when the crash came in October, making tens of thousands of big and little speculators suddenly penniless.

Despite the crash, to all outward appearances the Collegiate World Publishing Company continued to prosper. It was known that Mr. Lansinger's personal fortune had shrunk considerably. But the circulation figures of *College Humor* and *Real Detective* continued healthy. The chauffeur-driven Cadillac was still a symbol of affluence at 1050 North La Salle Street.

My two years in Chicago were pleasant ones. My chores under Swanson and Lansinger were generously rewarded, considering the fact that I was still in my early twenties. In the fall of 1931 my status in the company took a sudden spurt upward, quite by accident. By way of kidding the college Greek letter system a bit, I introduced into my page of Campus Patter a fraternity I called Rho Dammit Rho. For some silly reason the thing caught on, and Rho Dammit Rho chapters were soon established on over a thousand campuses. Yale, Harvard, Dartmouth, and West Point each had two chapters of the "fraternity." *College Humor*'s promotion department ordered charters and membership cards printed, and, finally, silver-plated pins were produced. In all, over thirty thousand applications for membership were received. The mail rooms at 1050 North La Salle were glutted with Rho Dammit Rho fan mail for weeks on end.

In early summer, 1932, the company decided to set up an editorial office in New York, and I was appointed to be in charge of it. My job was to scout for fiction and article material and keep in close touch with as many literary agents as possible.

The summer heat that often lay like a blanket over New York and seemed so oppressive during the weeks of my early siege of the city did not bother me nearly so much upon my return. For one thing, I managed to lease comfortable quarters in Tudor City, where the air off the East River kept things reasonably cool on warm June nights. The greatest contribution to my comfort, however, was thanks to *College Humor*'s cover artist Rolf Armstrong and his wife Louise, who opened their guest room to me each weekend at Bayside. Bayside, Long Island, in the early 1930's, before it was destroyed by creeping urbanization, was an active yachting center. The Armstrong studio-house of fieldstone and weathered timbers was an enlarged version of a Basque fisherman's dwelling. The Armstrong dock and boathouse fringing the property on the bay shore provided easy access to the water for the artist's collection of sailing craft. In the boathouse were three sailing canoes and two day sailers. On a mooring a hundred yards offshore was Rolf Armstrong's annual entry in Larchmont's Race Week, the 40-foot Q-class sloop *Amourette*. I am forever indebted to the Armstrongs for introducing me to the joys of sailing. The sailing bug, once it bites the receptive novice, bites deep and delivers a virus that lasts a lifetime.

III

The Original Life Magazine

MY NEW OFFICE WAS in the Graybar Building on Lexington Avenue just off 42nd Street. A near neighbor in the building was the Condé Nast organization, publishers of *Vogue, House and Garden,* and *Vanity Fair*. Fred Dayton, sales manager of the Nast Press, had noted the newly arrived *College Humor* representative on the directory in the Graybar lobby and invited me to lunch.

Fred Dayton's multifaceted personality suggested many things other than the successful salesman. At fifty-five he looked, in his well-tailored dark suit and black Homburg, very much like a British elder statesman. He was never without a large cigar in his mouth, and he always wore his hat in the office. I learned some time later that he had invited me to lunch because the owners of *Life* had asked him to help them find a new editor. When I was ushered into his office at the appointed hour, he rose behind a huge desk piled high with books and greeted me with a vigorous handshake. Hat, cigar, and heavy tortoise-rimmed glasses were so impressive as to be almost overwhelming. But only momentarily. He waved me to a chair, offered me a cigar, which I politely declined, and nodded toward the stacked books. "Reference works on the Connecticut River Valley," he said. He explained that he had been working for several years on a history of the Connecticut River. *Steamboat Days*, a book he had written about the era of packet boats on the river, had been published recently. He then asked me if I had any relatives living around Essex. "I've run across the name Eggleston in several Connecticut genealogies," he said. I replied that according to family records my forebears had settled in Connecticut in the early 1630's. Fred Dayton chuckled. "Could be that we're related," he said. "Daytons have been scattered along the river towns from Hartford to Saybrook for ten generations."

Our luncheon destination was the Players at 16 Gramercy Park. A visit to the Players in the 1930's was a never-to-be-forgotten experience for any newcomer to New York. The old mansion had been deeded to the club by Edwin Booth in 1888. When Booth founded the club with a group of his close friends, he had a special purpose in mind. He had long felt that actors were too prone to lead a cloistered life. He thought they mingled too much with fellow actors. The club was organized to include a modest portion of actors. But the majority of members were to come from the ranks of artists, editors, and writers. An occasional businessman was acceptable if he could qualify as a "Patron of the Arts." Early membership rolls included such names as Joseph Jefferson, James Russell Lowell, President Grover Cleveland, Mark Twain, Augustus St. Gaudens, Stanford White, John Singer Sargent, George Horace Lorimer, Charles Dana Gibson, and the first Cornelius Vanderbilt.

Preceding lunch my host seated himself and me in the highchair gallery facing the play at the pool table, opposite the bar lounge in the club's basement floor. On the wall nearby was a portrait of Mark Twain, and next to it hung his billiard cue over an inscribed plaque. As the lunch hour drew near, we soon had two processions passing our highchairs, one heading for the bar and the other for the washroom. I had to admit to feeling thoroughly flabbergasted as Fred Dayton nodded to many and ticked off the names in asides to me: "Don Marquis, Walter Hampden, Otis Skinner, Heywood Broun, Harold Ross, James Thurber, John Barrymore, Ernest Hemingway, Ring Lardner, Norman Bel Geddes, Vincent Astor." If I hadn't recognized most of these persons from their photos, I would have been positive that my friend was pulling my leg.

I am sure we had a splendid lunch. The Players boasted a fine chef in those days. But such was the impact on me of the surroundings and the personalities that I didn't know whether I was eating filet of beef or cornflakes.

Fred Dayton lunched at the Players almost every working weekday year round—always using the same taxi driver he had ridden with for a decade. After he had taken me to the club several more times, he called me into his office and drew a sheet of paper out of a desk drawer.

"I have here a list of names," he began, "a list of a dozen chaps who are being considered for editor of *Life*." He lit a fresh cigar and laughed. "I happen to know that none of these fellows are available for one reason or another. Some want too much money. Some are under contract in their present jobs. I purposely put a couple of talented oddballs on the list, who were promptly vetoed by the *Life* management. A couple of weeks ago I put your name in with a short note to Clair Maxwell, *Life*'s president. I expect he will call you one of these days."

A call soon came through from Mr. Maxwell's secretary suggesting that I meet Mr. Maxwell for lunch a couple of days hence at the Hotel Chatham. Before our meeting I had the benefit of another visit with Mr. Dayton, who told me something of the background of the situation. *Life*, as well as many other magazines, had had two rather bad years because of the depression. But *Life* had enjoyed a long history of profitable years, and there was every reason for optimism about the magazine's future.

The ownership of *Life* had been acquired in 1920 by Charles Dana Gibson, the magazine's most famous contributor. During the next ten years the magazine earned over a million dollars in profits for Mr. Gibson. When, in 1930, *Life* showed a loss, for the first time, of $37,000, Mr. Gibson decided that at age sixty-three he would retire with his savings intact and relinquish the ownership of the company to his advertising manager, Clair Maxwell, and his business manager, Henry Richter. Maxwell and Richter were presently in the process of converting the magazine from a weekly to a monthly publication. To obtain necessary working capital, Maxwell had sold a block of *Life* stock to his friends Fred and Louise Francis of St. Augustine, Florida. Mrs. Francis was Louise Flagler before her marriage and had inherited a portion of the Henry Flagler fortune.

Mr. Dayton had known many of the *Life* people personally over the years. But beyond a friendly interest there was also a frankly financial interest in a valued customer. *Life* was printed on the Condé Nast presses.

Clair Maxwell was in his late thirties. After graduating from the University of Chicago, he had joined the Air Force and gone overseas just before the 1918 armistice. His countenance was handsome and rugged, and tanned from many hours spent on the golf course. He was well known and well liked in Madison Avenue circles, where two of his brothers were advertising executives. Another brother, Lee Maxwell, was president of Crowell-Collier.

My lunch with Mr. Maxwell apparently went off well. I answered a number of questions that seemed to convince him I knew something about putting a monthly magazine together. He asked me how soon I could arrange my affairs with *College Humor* and come over to *Life*. I replied that since I was no longer part of the daily operation in Chicago, I thought Mr. Lansinger would give me a friendly release any time I wished. What about salary? I said that I realized there was a depression on and would accept what he thought was fair, trusting that if I did a good job I would be rewarded in due course. A hundred dollars a week was all right with me until I could prove myself to be worth more.

I phoned Chicago, and Lansinger's reaction was warm congratulations and good luck. Swanson was in California at the time and sent his good wishes later.

On the following Monday morning at 9:00 A.M. I stepped out of the elevator on the twelfth floor of the Lincoln Building to report to my new boss. *Life* had recently moved its offices from the 59th Street building to new and larger quarters in the sixty-story Lincoln Building on East 42nd Street. I was pleased to note that the famous old *Life* reception room had survived the move, with all of its Tiffany glass paneling and the large bronze cupid intact. To complete the picture, my favorite receptionist, Miss Corbett, was on hand with her heartwarming smile. And she remembered me after the two-year interval since my last call. "I'm sorry, the editor is not in this morning," she said. "Would you like to see someone else?"

When I explained that I hadn't come to see the editor, but had an appointment with Mr. Maxwell, she phoned the boss's office to check, and soon showed me in.

The Maxwell office was a large corner one, lined with bound volumes of *Life*. He greeted me cordially, then took me down a passageway to a smaller office, where I was introduced to the business manager, Henry Richter. Mr. Richter was a rather tall, thin man, clean-shaven, with light blond hair, friendly blue eyes, and a generous mouth that easily broke into a smile. Like Mr. Maxwell, he was in his late thirties.

Henry Richter's background was quite different from Maxwell's. He had started work at *Life* as an office boy in 1902. He later attracted the attention of *Life*'s founder, John Ames Mitchell, who sent him through several night schools to emerge as a qualified auditor and accountant. After Mr. Mitchell's death in 1920, Richter served the Gibson ownership as treasurer and business manager for the next highly profitable decade.

Next we were outside the editor's door, with its stained glass cartoon of congressmen ladling out graft from under the Capitol dome. Here I was introduced to Mrs. Mary Hughes, editorial secretary, and her assistant. Both were smiling rather self-consciously, and I realized that they could not help wondering whether or not I was going to make things difficult for them. Mr. Maxwell pointed to a paste-up dummy on Mrs. Hughes's desk. "There is the upcoming issue," he said. "You have about four days to look it over before we go to press." "Sorry, Mr. Maxwell, but final okay is due tomorrow," said Mrs. Hughes.

Inside the editor's office I experienced a series of surprises, pleasant and otherwise. On the desk that was now to be mine was a very large basket of flowers. "We sent a notice of your appoint-ment out to the Associated Press last night — and it seems that a few of your friends saw it." I felt a hot tinge of blush creeping up the back of my neck. I had the instant embarrassing thought that my mother might have wired the floral offering from California. But I was soon relieved when I untied a large red ribbon from the attached envelope and found a message of best wishes from the *College Humor* staff in Chicago. Clair Maxwell shortly left me on my own, and I tried out my swivel chair and whirled around in it a couple of times. I then removed the basket of flowers to the top of a filing cabinet and discovered several telegrams tucked under the edge of the desk blotter. One was from my parents, and the rest were from friends and relatives in the Far West.

I suddenly felt quite alone — and not a little scared. I had been advised that with the departure of the most recent editor, Bolton Mallory, his key staff of two had chosen to leave with him. Of course, the magazine had always relied on a large assortment of outside contributors. Fortunately, I knew many of these people, thanks to my two years with *College Humor*. But I realized that it was imperative that I find a good editorial helpmate to join me as soon as possible. I had had one man in mind from the moment I left Mr. Maxwell after the lunch at the Chatham. Gurney Williams had been a contributor to *College Humor*. He had also been editor of the *Gargoyle* during his undergraduate days at the University of Michigan. He had recently moved to New York to try his hand at free-lance writing. I found his phone number in my pocketbook and reached for one of the phones on my new desk to call him. I say one of the phones, because there were two phones, a black one and a blue one. As I reached for the blue one, someone entered my door and said, "Ah, ah, I wouldn't touch that one if I were you." The caller introduced himself as Bill Scott, and explained that he had written a regular column of paragraphs for *Life* over a period of several years — a feature called "Scott Shots."

He hardly gave me a chance to say a word, but instead launched into a speech that sounded as though he had been rehearsing it for some time. The theme of his diatribe was that he had at last decided he would never again work for a magazine headed by an advertising man. He loudly declared that Maxwell was a mean, no-good so-and-so. His speech ended with a table-banging pronunciamento that did little to contribute to my peace of mind for the next ninety days.

"That lousy bastard fired Bob Sherwood, he fired Norman Anthony, he just fired Bolton Mallory — and, by God, you can take my word for it, he will fire you within the next three months."

As Scott went out the door he paused and said: "By the way, that blue telephone is a direct wire to Mallory's girl friend, Nancy Carroll. You had better be sure she is permanently disconnected before you try to use it."

After Scott's departure I absentmindedly pulled the center drawer of my desk out a few inches. It appeared empty except for a few paperclips. I pulled it out some more and heard something rattle sharply. It was a large pair of scissors with a name scratched deep in the black enameled handle: R.E. SHERWOOD.

IV

Advent of Roosevelt and Hitler

I HAD BEEN ON the job only a week when Gurney Williams joined me. With the expert assistance of Mrs. Hughes, Gurney and I managed to put together an August, 1932, issue of the magazine, mostly from things on hand. We immediately, however, made a point of meeting all prospective contributors who called at the offices — and they came from far and wide, eager to test the sales resistance of the new editors. We also got in touch by phone and letter with *Life*'s better-known writers and artists.

Life had, since its founding in 1883, actively crusaded against all manner of real and fancied evils, great and small. Its editor-founder was the cartoonist John Ames Mitchell, who had edited the Harvard *Lampoon* in his college days. For years he aimed his darts against Tammany Hall, against check-reins for horses, and against the tendency of beautiful American heiresses to cross the sea and marry titled Englishmen. *Life* had campaigned so vigorously against American entry into the League of Nations that the man who first proposed the League wrote the following personal note to the editor, Charles Dana Gibson:

2340 S Street N.W.
Washington D.C.

19th November 1922

My dear Mr. Gibson,
I hope you will permit me to yield to the impulse to write and tell you how much pleasure I derived from your cartoon, "The Straphanger." It seems to me extraordinarily fine.

May I also venture very respectfully to hope that "Life" will return to its editorial policy of supporting the League of Nations. I have been deeply disappointed to see it reverse that policy, for it seems to me that all enlightened forces of the nation ought now to pull together and pull in the same direction. I am sure you will understand that this suggestion is made in the most sincerely friendly spirit and because I value highly the influence that "Life" can exert.

Mrs. Wilson joins me in warmest regards to Mrs. Gibson and you. With sincere regard,

Faithfully yours,

WOODROW WILSON

For many years the magazine had railed vociferously against prohibition. *Life* had only recently sponsored a page ad in a New York newspaper denouncing the Eighteenth Amendment and suggesting that readers send in contributions to pay for more advertising space. An avalanche of checks poured in and *Life's* crusade was carried in scores of newspapers coast to coast.

During the latter half of the year 1932 there was nothing very exciting to crusade about. New York's Governor Franklin D. Roosevelt had been elected to the Presidency in a landslide victory over Herbert Hoover. The repeal of the Eighteenth Amendment now loomed as a certainty. Mayor James J. Walker of New York City was forced to resign after a successful drive by Samuel Seabury to "turn the rascals out." Americans in all walks of life waited anxiously to see what the new U.S. President would do to get the slumping economy of the nation moving again.

At *Life* we found we had to scratch a little to find something to poke fun at. One source of relief from the excitement of the recent election was provided by Mrs. Roosevelt. While her husband had been engrossed in campaign oratory she chose to take on the editorship of a new magazine called, of all things, *Babies Just Babies*. I made a full-page cartoon depicting my imaginary impression of the new publication. The scene was the reception room outside the door of Editor Eleanor Roosevelt's office. In the foreground were infants in the bath, the crib, and the playpen. Seated, waiting hat in hand, was FDR while a switchboard receptionist was announcing into her phone, "It's Mr. Roosevelt, just Mr. Roosevelt." The week the picture was published *Life* received a letter from the Executive Mansion, Albany, N.Y., stating that Mrs. Roosevelt was very much taken with the cartoon and would like to have it for her collection of memorabilia. The letter was signed by her secretary, Malvina Thompson. Clair Maxwell was so pleased by the request that he had the original cartoon framed and dispatched to Albany forthwith. A charming response soon followed:

Executive Mansion
Albany

Dear Mr. Eggleston:

I am very grateful to you for giving me the cartoon. We were all so amused by it that I was most anxious to have it. There has been a lot of teasing about the title of my magazine, but this seemed to me the most amusing.

With many, many thanks for your kindness, I am

Very sincerely yours,
ELEANOR ROOSEVELT
(Mrs. Franklin D. Roosevelt)

In the fall of 1932 I did another in *Life*'s series of "Impressions of Magazine Offices." This was of Time, Inc., an imaginary scene outside the office of its editor in chief, Henry Robinson Luce. I wondered if this one hadn't gone a step too far in kidding the self-consciously successful newsmagazine. Apparently not. The day *Life* appeared with the cartoon Bill Furth called me and said *Time*'s managing editor, John Martin, wanted to know if he could buy the original to hang in his office. This drawing was framed and sent to Martin with *Life*'s compliments.

Toward the end of 1932 we attempted a short-lived crusade. We had noted with curiosity that New York's buses and subways carried quite a number of advertising placards for undertaking establishments. "A Complete Funeral for $100.00," said the ads. We had an able legman working for us at the time, Cal Tinney, who was later to become a well-known radio personality. Cal embraced with enthusiasm the assignment to look into the complete funeral business. He made several calls around New York, then went to Philadelphia, Jersey City, and Boston. In each funeral parlor he introduced himself as the suddenly bereaved nephew of a deceased uncle of modest means. He said he wanted to see what was included in the complete $100.00 funeral. The net of his reporting on the story was that the $100.00 figure was merely bait. He ran into so much high-powered salesmanship for fancy coffins with bronze handles and special upholstery that he had to confess that any truly bereaved person would have felt like a guilty cheapskate spending only $100.00 for a "complete funeral."

This little crusade was short-lived because there was no reason to carry it for more than one issue. We received irate mail from undertakers all over the U.S. and a few threats of lawsuits. But nothing ever came of it.

In the spring of 1933 I received a request from *Delineator* magazine saying they were putting together a feature article containing the favorite humorous stories of a group of magazine editors — would I send in my selection to be included in the lot?

The *Delineator*'s bold effort to produce a feature of fun, during the grim post-Crash era, resulted in as curious a collection of trivia and profundity as had seen the light of print in some time. The feature ran under the bold headline: "THEY KNOW THEIR JOKES — By FIVE EDITORS." A subhead stated : "The editors of five of the wittiest magazines in the country select for *Delineator* their favorite jokes or anecdotes."

The "jokes or anecdotes" were printed in this order:

From George Eggleston
Editor of *Life*

Favorite stories come and go, but a current favorite of mine concerns a class in Freshman English at Princeton. The professor, hoping to start his charges off with a few important don'ts, concluded his first lecture as follows: "And now, young gentlemen, there are two words we shall never use in this class: one is 'swell' and the other is 'lousy.' "

There was a moment of silence. Then one lad in the rear of the room scrambled to his feet and asked, "What are the words?"

From Henry R. Luce
Editor of *Time*

The London *Daily Express,* enterprising stunter, invited its readers to state what people they liked to read about most (and least). Public Bore No. 1 was George Bernard Shaw. After him in order of boredom: Amy Johnson Mollison, Sir Oswald Mosley, James Ramsay MacDonald, Greta Garbo, Adolf Hitler, Leslie Hore-Belisha, Lady Astor, Douglas Fairbanks, Max Baer, the Mdivanis.

No. 1 Public Favorite was David Lloyd George; No. 2, Winston Churchill; No. 3, William Maxwell Aitken, Baron Beaverbrook, the tireless master of the *Express*.

From Frank Crowninshield
Editor of *Vanity Fair*

Oscar Wilde's "Ballad of Reading Gaol" was published in 1898 shortly after he had finished his prison sentence there. The next two years of his life were passed on the continent, where, in poverty, illness, and distress, he died on November 30, 1900.

As his illness progressed his friend Robert Ross came from London in order to be with him when he died.

On seeing Wilde's condition Ross suggested that a distinguished London surgeon be sent for, thinking that if an operation were performed he might save Wilde's life.

The poet inquired as to the surgeon's probable charge for such a commission. On hearing that the cost would approximate a hundred pounds, he turned on his bed and said, a little sadly: "No, no, don't send for him; I should hate to die beyond my means."

From Jack Shuttleworth
Editor of *Judge*

I don't believe that I have a favorite joke. But if one must choose a favorite I think I'd select the one about the hillbilly who left his cabin home for an Eastern city, where he learned, among other things, the rudiments of hygiene. So with the first money he earned he bought a bathtub, had it crated up and sent home to his parents. Not long after, he received a letter from his father thanking him profusely, but asking, "Where are the oars?"

From Arnold Gingrich
Editor of *Esquire*

My favorite anecdote is a Whistler story, hence so old that it is barely possible that there may be some to whom it is new. One day Whistler was stopped on the street by Charles Condor, who slapped him on the back and wrung his hand. Whistler blinked at him blankly.

"But surely you know me — I'm Condor. We met the other night at the home of Lady Such-and-so."

"Oh, yes, to be sure. Goodbye, Condor."

It was not surprising that the *Delineator* feature included no contribution from the *New Yorker*'s Harold Ross. He probably threw the request to send in his "favorite joke" into the wastebasket. In James Thurber's biographical notes on Ross he quotes the *New Yorker* editor as lamenting the dwindling supply of humorous contributions reaching his desk. "You find a guy that can write humor," said Ross, "and the first thing you know he turns in a piece about a man stumbling over the body of his wife on the floor, or something like that."

As *Life* began to gather a little momentum we introduced a series of three-dimensional covers, a new technique in the use of color photography later widely used by several magazines. One of these modeled designs brought us some attention from overseas. Our central cover figure was a beautifully carved and gowned Miss France by sculptor Lesta Gaba. The lady stood on a pile of simulated gold coins. Its title, "I can't give you anything but love," sparked an irate reaction in the French Chamber of Deputies. The French were oversensitive at the time because several U.S. congressmen were harping on France's reluctance to repay old war debts despite a large gold reserve.

The year 1933 was definitely a Roosevelt year — a year in which, in the eyes of the citizens of the U.S.A., the man in the White House could do no wrong. In March FDR delivered his first fireside chat, and signed the act to legalize 3.2 per cent beer. In June the President signed the National Recovery Act, which was supposed to remedy the nation's economic ills. In December the Eighteenth Amendment was repealed and Prohibition abolished while thousands cheered.

One sunny September day of 1933 New York's Fifth Avenue was the scene of the biggest parade in U.S. peacetime history. Clair Maxwell stopped by my office and asked me to walk with him the two blocks from the Lincoln Building to Fifth Avenue and see the spectacle. With difficulty we worked our way through the great crowds blocking all traffic in the side streets. We watched for half an hour as a segment of the 250,000 marchers filed by. When we left Clair made the prophetic remark, "This thing is phony." In a hundred cities across the country similar parades were held that day to proclaim that under the new banner of the Blue Eagle U.S. business would voluntarily raise wages, reduce hours, and promise to end cut-throat competition. Some months later the Supreme Court was to concur with Maxwell and declare the NRA void.

By the spring of 1934 the public and the press were so bedazzled by the many facets of the Roosevelt program that no one took time out to be critical. There were new agencies springing up every minute to join the alphabetical parade led off by the NRA, AAA, PWA, CCC, and TVA. The New Dealers were in their seventh heaven, with unchecked billions to spend in literally every direction. The shock of the crash was wearing off. People hearkened to the words of FDR's ringing declaration, "This generation has a rendezvous with destiny." People were even starting to have some fun again. Will Rogers, Rudy Vallee, Ed Wynn, Fred Allen, and Jack Benny were riding high on the airwaves. On Broadway Cole Porter's *Anything Goes* was packing them in. In fact people in the U.S. were so preoccupied that almost no one noticed that a new figure had risen to absolute power on the European scene — one Adolf Hitler had become President and Chancellor of Germany. His rise to power had coincided with the rise to power of Franklin D. Roosevelt in the U.S.

When, in March, 1935, Reichsfuehrer Hitler tore up the Versailles Treaty and ordered all-out conscription of German manpower, we promptly denounced him in our pages. And our magazine was as promptly banned in Germany. We were the first U.S. publication to brand Hitler for what he was. We anticipated by three years the anti-Nazi, anti-Fascist posture of the Lucepress — *Time, Fortune,* and the future photo-weekly *Life.*

In our editorials and cartoons we also denounced Mussolini for his bloody invasion of Ethiopia. And *Life* was officially banned from Italy.

The feeling in Washington was that if indeed Hitler and Mussolini were sowing the seeds for a new war in Europe, this time America would stay out. To insure America's noninvolvement, the Congress voted the Neutrality Acts of 1935. By joint resolutions of both Houses the law henceforth "forbade the export of arms, ammunition or any implement of war to any belligerent either direct or by transshipment." This was compatible with the Johnson Act of 1934, which prohibited loans to any nation that had not paid its old war debts, an act of Congress also aimed at keeping us out of European wars.

We on the staff of *Life* strongly supported the position taken by the Congress and thought that America's true destiny called for a strongly armed U.S. and the observance of a strict neurality so that we might be peacemakers to the world.

We were anything but pacifists in our thinking. Our publisher, Clair Maxwell, had rushed to the colors in World War I. As a Boy Scout during that war I had won a citation for selling Liberty Bonds. I later did several years of ROTC in high school and college, and earned a lieutenant's commission in the U.S. Army Air Force

Reserve before graduating from the University of California. Our attitude was typical of most Americans in 1935: We believed we could trust our Government to keep a well-armed, neutral U.S. at peace.

There was, however, one prominent American who had some doubts about our leadership. The November, 1935, issue of *Esquire* carried an essay by Ernest Hemingway, "The Malady of Power," which will stand forever as a most incredible venture into prophecy. Here is a key paragraph from that article:

> Your correspondent believes that the fate of our country for the next hundred years or so depends on the extent of Franklin D. Roosevelt's ambition. If he is ambitious only to serve this country as Cleveland was, we and our children and their children will be fortunate. If he is ambitious personally to leave a great name to eclipse the name he bears, which was made famous by another man, we will be out of luck, because the sensational improvements that can be made legally in the country in time of peace are being rapidly exhausted.

The future Nobel Prize-winner went on to declare that Europe was headed for war, and if the U.S. hoped to *stay out,* the decision to *stay out* would have to be taken immediately and irrevocably — "now, before the propaganda starts." He predicted that the U.S. would again be asked to fight a war to "save civilization." He further predicted that if FDR chose the road to war, he would be a famous world figure for a short time, but "when the excitement was over, we the people would be left holding the sack." It was his opinion that during the years ahead we needed a president who would put aside any personal thirst for fame and instead keep the nation at peace. All candidates for the 1936 elections should be examined against this criteria, he added.

By late 1935 we had reason to point with pride to the progress of our magazine. Although our editorial budget was tight, we had managed, thanks to the good name of *Life,* to attract some excellent talent to our aegis. Regular contributors were George Jean Nathan, theatre, Don Herold, movies, Kyle Crichton, books, and Paul Gallico, sports. Ogden Nash, Arthur Lippman, and S.J. Perelman were also regulars. We were the first U.S. publication to recognize the artistic talents of Ludwig Bemelmans and Boris Artsybascheff. We ran the first cartoons of Chon Day, Richard Decker, and many others whose names would become well known. It is fair to say there was not a writer, illustrator, or cartoonist alive who did not want to be represented in *Life*. The signing of George Jean Nathan to conduct *Life*'s theatre department was definitely a contributing factor in getting the magazine moving again. *Life* was simply not *Life* without an authoritative drama critic. Robert Benchley and Dorothy Parker had in years past been *Life*'s stalwarts in this area.

In more recent years Nathan had reigned as New York's undisputed dean of drama critics. George Bernard Shaw called him the only drama critic worth reading. At fifty-two Nathan was in his literary prime. Despite our very limited editorial budget, I brashly put in a telephone call for Mr. Nathan at the Royalton Hotel, where he lived, introduced myself, and asked if I might talk to him about writing for us. He suggested I meet him the following Friday at the Ritz Men's Bar. "I'll be at the far corner table at five o'clock," he said. This meeting became the first of many at the same place, same table. Almost every Friday for two years I had the pleasure of Nathan's company and enjoyed the sparkle of his conversation on every subject under the sun. On certain pet dislikes, such as doctors and exercise, he could be as caustic as in past years when he and H.L. Mencken edited the *American Mercury*. But he could be very amusing also. "The other day an idiot doctor told me that if I wanted to enjoy perfect health and long life I must go in for vigorous exercise at least two hours every day. Look at the animals, he said, look at all wild life — exercise is the key to health, vigor, and longevity. Hokum, I replied. Look at the tortoise, the laziest living thing on earth and with a life-span of two hundred years. And look at the beaver, the most active of all animals. The busy little beaver kicks the bucket at ten years, half the age of the indolent donkey. And as for the bee, the active little bastard dies in six weeks, while the queen bee, snoozing while the other damn fools hustle, lives from four to five years."

A highlight of the year 1935 was my election to membership in the Players. A sad event of that year was the passing of the club's most widely quoted wit, Oliver Herford. Herford had in his youth been a valued contributor of illustrations and verse to *Life*. In retirement he spent most of his time around the club — ever ready with a quotable riposte. Best known was the anecdote about the odd-looking gray derby he turned up wearing one day. He explained it as just a whim of his wife's. When a fellow member advised him to throw the thing away, he said, "Oh, but you don't know my wife — she has a whim of iron." Of the many curiosities to be pointed out to a visitor at the Players — the Booth Room, the Hamlet props, the tiny elevator that Sarah Bernhardt was once trapped in, the table for nontalkers — Herford was a standout attraction. He was a small elfish man with thinning, uncombed gray hair. Gray was his color. Besides the derby, he always wore badly fitting gray suits and gray shoes topped by pearl-gray spats. Around his neck was a long gray ribbon from which dangled a monocle. My introduction to him took place in front of the club bulletin board, where he was squinting through his monocle studying the black-bordered cards announcing the deaths of several members. After reading the names on each, he shook his head slowly and muttered, "Always the wrong one." A repeated target for Herford's barbs was the portrait painter E.E. Simmons, who had a habit of cornering a fellow Player in the bar and reciting an endless tale about his latest commission. To cope with this Herford hung a sign over the door, EXIT IN CASE OF SIMMONS . When a member announced one day that he was going to offer Simmons a thousand dollars to resign from the club, Herford remarked, "I'd advise him to hold out for a better offer." Herford's wit was not necessarily confined to the premises of the Players. Once, when riding a crowded bus up Fifth Avenue with a young nephew on his lap, he was suddenly confronted by a beautiful model. "Get up, sonny," said Herford, "and give the lady your seat."

At the time of my admission to the club there was something of a controversy going on whether or not to do some redecorating and modernizing of the building. The conservatives finally won, and nothing was changed. But the "radical" group still insisted that air-conditioning should be installed in the downstairs bar, where the atmosphere always hung heavy with cigar smoke and alcoholic fumes. To counter this group, Herford led the opposition with the slogan, "This air was good enough for Booth — it should be good enough for us."

When Hazel Nicolay and I first met in the New York home of mutual friends in the fall of 1935, it was a case (at least on my part) of love at first sight. By January, 1936, we were talking seriously of setting a date for the wedding. When Hazel said, "I hope it can be in a small church in the country," I immediately replied, "I know just the one." This was the Congregational Church of Windsor, Connecticut, which had been established in 1632, with my forebear Bagot Eggleston as one of its founding fathers.

At the time of our marriage Hazel was keenly interested in golf, a sport that does not mix too well with the hobby of sailing. But after I took her to the Armstrongs for a couple of breezy Sundays on *Amourette,* she decided to put her golf clubs on the shelf. Then, when Rolf and Louise moved to California, we rented their Bayside house and purchased *Amourette.* Hazel thereupon devoured H.A. Calahan's *Learning to Sail* and was soon a confirmed salt.

In February, as *Life*'s circulation figures showed a climb over 1932 from a low of 87,000 to 129,000, and advertising figures conclusively proved that we had moved from deficits to profits, our little group of management and editorial people sat down together and decided it was time to consider going from monthly to weekly publication. We did not underestimate the challenge of this decision. In order to produce a weekly magazine of more pages, more use of color, and long overdue raises in rates of payments to contributors, we would have to raise what to us was a considerable sum of money — a round figure of a million dollars. Clair Maxwell was certain that a block of new stock issue would be purchased by Fred and Louise Francis. He also felt certain his friends the Bristol brothers, of Bristol-Myers, would be interested in making an investment.

For my part I had an uncle by marriage who was a very wealthy man. William Chamberlain, a young struggling lawyer at the turn of the century, had married my father's sister, Ethel Eggleston, upon her graduation from the University of California at Berkeley. Uncle Will had worked his way up through the corporate structures of a number of Middle West utilities operations and by the early 1930's was president of United Light and Power Company. He was also on the boards of a number of large corporations. My aunt had confided in me on more that one occasion that her husband liked me especially because I was the only one in a vast army of relatives who had never touched him for a loan. I went to him with a prospectus of our situation that had been prepared by Henry Richter, which he checked over very carefully. His verdict was that he would help us in every way he could. He promised to write to a list of people he thought we should see, starting with Paul Mellon.

A New York friend whom Hazel and I dined with occasionally was Douglas MacCollum Stewart, Harvard '16, who owned a market analysis service. We had been introduced to Stewart by Jim and Frances Bradley of San Francisco. Douglas Stewart liked our magazine and especially some of the jibes we had been printing as we became disillusioned with the New Deal. When I told him of our future plans for the weekly, he showed keen interest in helping. He took Henry Richter down to Wall Street to meet his cousin and close confidant Jeremiah Milbank. Milbank had been a treasurer of the Republican Party.

At about this moment in *Life*'s editorial reorientation we received an unexpected visitor. Around noon one day a secretary came to my office and said there was "a Mr. Wallace of *Reader's Digest*" in the reception room. He had asked to see the publisher, and when told that Maxwell was out of town, he had asked to see the editor. I immediately went out, introduced myself, and brought Mr. Wallace into my office. Years later, when the *Digest* had acquired worldwide prestige, investigative reporters were to describe De-Witt Wallace as a shy person, rather difficult to know. On this first meeting I felt he was as warm and easy to know as anyone I had ever encountered. He was a tall man, erect in bearing, handsome, well tailored, and altogether impressive looking. He was about forty years old at the time. I believe that what was taken to be shyness was in fact a gentleness — the gentleness of a person at peace with himself and sure of his objectives.

Nothing was known about *Digest* circulation figures at the time. Since no advertising was carried, no figures were quoted by the Audit Bureau of Circulations. Copies of the *Digest* that I had read I found stimulating. But I had wondered how a magazine that carried no advertising could make ends meet. I took Mr. Wallace to lunch, and without his saying so in so many words, I soon had an indication that his magazine was doing fairly well. He said he was prepared to offer *Life* a contract for exclusive reprint rights and would work out terms of payment agreeable to publisher Maxwell.

The budding friendship at this luncheon was to blossom into a continuing relationship that would endure into future decades.

At another lunch with Mr. Wallace some time later he told me he was looking for a couple of editorial people to add to his staff and wondered if I had any suggestions as to possible candidates. (In retrospect I suppose that this was one of those moments in one's lifetime when a new door is opened and one should step right in. Had I at that moment offered myself as a candidate, and been accepted, I might have saved myself many an editorial heartache.) At any rate, in reply to the Wallace query, I immediately suggested Bill Furth of Time, Inc. as a qualified prospect.

A couple of days later I had lunch with Furth and told him of my proposal. Furth was suitably impressed and grateful for the suggestion, but had just been promoted to a top editorial post on *Fortune* and explained that he could not very well let Henry Luce down by negotiating for another job. But Furth, with his keen reportorial brain, was at once curious to learn more about what had been going on with "the little magazine in Pleasantville," which had so far been an unknown quantity in the publishing world. He immediately put some *Time* researchers to work, and out of their efforts came a lengthy *Fortune* article revealing for the first time that the *Reader's Digest* was a publishing phenomenon. The *Digest*'s list of paid subscribers was already pushing 1,500,000, a larger circulation than any other nonfiction magazine in the United States. The Wallaces had recently approved architects' plans to build a multimillion-dollar complex of offices to house the burgeoning operation.

The appearance of the *Fortune* story brought about two predictable repercussions. The very fact that the *Fortune* story revealed the *Digest*'s unprecedented success caused a host of short-lived imitators to spring up. Also from here on Wallace was to be pestered by ad agency men eager to have him open the pages of the magazine to advertising.

V

Henry Luce's "Time-Bomb"

THE DATE WAS MAY 5, 1936. The place was "21." The occasion was a small luncheon party to celebrate the fact that our magazine, after a short dip in its fifty-year record of earnings, had recovered its equilibrium and was again a profitable operation. In attendance were Maxwell, Richter, Gurney Williams, and myself.

The famous bistro called "21," located at 21 West 52nd Street, was also known to old-timers in its speakeasy days as Jack and Charlie's. Clair Maxwell had known the partners, Jack Kriendler and Charlie Berns, on a first-name basis through all the Prohibition period. Thanks to Clair our party received VIP treatment. In a pre-lunch tour we were shown the vast cellars where 10,000 cases of wine and whiskey had been concealed behind concrete paneling that could be swung open only by pressing a hidden button that set a high-powered motor to work. We were told that one night in 1930 six federal agents armed with search warrants spent hours futilely combing the premises without finding a single bottle of the illicit booze. In those days the bar area was also engineered to fool the feds. A turn of a lever would drop all displayed evidence down a hidden brick-lined chute leading to a sewer drain.

Our lunch began with a brief toast to the past year, after which Maxwell outlined his hopes for the coming year. Thanks to the 50 per cent rise in *Life*'s circulation, future advertising commitments were the most promising in several years. The efforts in progress to raise capital to convert to weekly publication had so far been most encouraging. At the end of Maxwell's speech he added a gossipy bit that was an eye-opener. "The latest returns on our friendly rival *Vanity Fair* show that that noble publication has taken a nose dive in circulation over the past four years — down to a low of 86,000 copies per month. *Vanity Fair* is going to close down very shortly. And if I may be forgiven for making a rather unchivalrous comment, that magazine's decline from 1932 to 1934 took place under its managing editor, the glamorous Clare Boothe Brokaw, the new bride of Henry Luce."

With the 1936 Presidential election coming up, we had some fun lampooning both FDR and Alf Landon in our August, September, and October issues. We were quite sure that Roosevelt would win a second term, but we hoped Landon would rally enough votes to give the New Dealers the message that the country was getting fed up with the deficit spending programs and burgeoning bureaucracy sponsored by the incumbent.

We did, however, find reason to cheer FDR loudly for his Chautauqua, New York, speech opening his campaign. In it he won votes and acclaim by declaring his dedication to world peace. He underlined his desire to maintain "neutrality regardless." He warned against "Americans who would be tempted for fool's gold to break down or evade our neutrality." He also personally wrote the plank into the Democratic platform: "We shall continue to observe a true neutrality in the disputes of others . . . to work for peace, to guard against being drawn into any war which may develop anywhere."

In early October the rosy dreams for the future of our magazine were to be proved short-lived. The new advertising pages had come in as hoped for, the circulation department reported gains in newsstand sales and subscription renewals, but all the while, unbeknownst to us, a Time-bomb had been ticking just a couple of short blocks from our Lincoln Building offices.

On an upper floor of the Chrysler Building Henry Luce had been seeking for months the perfect name for the photo-news weekly he was about to launch. Time, Inc.'s official historian, R.T. Elson, has described in detail what was taking place in the Luce office during that period.

In response to a Luce memo asking that *Time's* experimental department come up with a list of suggestions, some hundred names had been submitted to the boss. Some of the better ones were: *Candid, Sight, Show, Witness, Pageant, Picture,* and *Dime.* Of these the only title that had so far appealed to Luce was *Dime.* Of course *"Dime"* would have proved a disastrous title to live with, as inflation gradually moved the per-copy price up to fifty cents. But

Luce had a sentimental, and almost a superstitious feeling, that he must find a four-letter word like T-I-M-E and L-U-C-E. In another memo to the staff Luce wrote, *"Dime* will reveal more of the contemporary life of the world than has hitherto been revealed in pictures." To Luce's chagrin the name *Dime* was unanimously vetoed by his associates. One editor brashly spoke up, "Why not call the new magazine *Tent;* it covers everything."

Of course, the most obvious four-letter name for a photo weekly that planned to reveal the contemporary life of the world was *Life.* This title had been suggested to Luce by several people, including his new bride. But Luce had been advised that *Life* was very definitely not for sale. Luce finally took heed of a letter from James A. Linen, Jr., the father of a future president of Time, Inc. and an old family friend. Linen wrote: "The name *Life*, if it were to be preempted, would appear to me to best typify the proposed publication." Luce reacted to Linen's letter by directing his advertising manager, Howard Black, to see Clair Maxwell at once and find out if *Life* could be purchased. Money would be no object; Luce had put aside a kitty of five million dollars to absorb the costs and losses of the new venture.

Black and Maxwell had known each other for years, and a luncheon date was quickly arranged. The Black-Maxwell meeting was on a Friday. That day and weekend I was in Baltimore conferring with *Baltimore Sun* columnist Frank R. Kent, who was doing a series of anti-New Deal editorials for us. The Monday morning I arrived back in New York one of the gossip columns — Walter Winchell's — carried this item: "Is it true that magazine tycoon Henry R. Luce is ogling *Life* mag. . .to buy the name?"

When Clair Maxwell arrived at the office, he immediately took Henry Richter and me down to the coffee shop. "Yes, it's true," said Clair. Looking rather sheepish, he confided that Black had relayed to him an offer of a hundred thousand dollars to close us down and take over our name. "And," added Clair, "they will take our entire personnel into Time, Inc. — with some appropriate raises in salary." Henry and I were for a moment so flabbergasted we could scarcely talk.

"But Clair," Henry spoke for both of us, "you surely wouldn't consider such a thing. You wouldn't want to kill the magazine just as we have gotten it on its feet again? Of course you will tell Black the answer is No at any price."

But it was quickly apparent to us that Clair had already thought the matter over and was eager to do business with Time, Inc. He made a feeble attempt to explain to us what a wonderful feeling one could experience working for a large, well-financed company. Clair was, after all, an advertising man right down to the soles of his shoes. Henry and I realized suddenly and with sadness that Clair would have sold out to anyone from *Popular Mechanics* to *National Geographic Magazine* if he thought the price was right. In talking the offer over with us Clair knew we had no real say in the matter. He and Fred Francis held the controlling stock in the company. After a phone call to Francis, Clair called Black and said the deal was on. The announcement that *Time* had bought *Life* was in all the afternoon newspapers.

The irony of the situation was that Maxwell, the super-salesman, never for a moment realized how much Henry Luce wanted our good name. When Luce later described the situation to his biographer, he said: "I practically whispered the name *Life* to Howard Black when I asked him if he thought we could buy it. I never spent such a long, nervous weekend. It was Monday before Black reported back. The answer was Yes."

When Clair, Henry, and I returned to the twelfth floor, one could easily sense by the look on every face in the office that the gossip column had been passed round and round and left them all wondering if there was any truth in it. The first thing I did was pop into Gurney Williams's office and tell him the bad news. Gurney was one of the least money-minded persons I had ever encountered. He had long enjoyed an independent income from a trust fund and had never given much thought to his economic future. He loved the work he had been doing and was a real pro in the world of humor, as was proven in his subsequent career. To my announcement that there would be a desk waiting for him on the fifty-first floor of the Chrysler Building, he said in his best Timese, "As it must to all men, death came today to balding, flap-eared G. (for Gurney) Williams."

The flurry of excitement for the rank and file of the office soon died down as Maxwell passed the word that everyone was assured of a job at *Time* and that some raises were in the offing. Gurney and I were immediately busy getting in touch with all our loyal contributors and attempting to offer our consolation. In our embarrassment we could only say that the blow was totally unexpected — it was not our idea.

Also immediately Time, Inc. sent a six-page release to the wire services, which began with the paragraph: "This month, as it must to all men (even to many national institutions), death came to *Life*, first and oldest of U.S. humorous magazines."

In the wire release and in a lengthy story in *Time* lavish praise was poured upon the magazine that was undergoing the knife. "*Life*, the magazine of ripe years and reputation, will pass into the realm of great things gone forever . . .To most literate U.S. citizens with memories measuring a decade or more the loss of this magazine that had received decorations from three allied governments and was called by Woodrow Wilson one of the most influential magazines in America will bring real sorrow." *Time*'s obituary ended with a nodding reference to *Life*'s recent past. "Publisher Maxwell and Editor Eggleston went manfully to work revamping its editorial style to meet the times, winning new readers. *Life* breathed again, made a profit in its dying days."

Time's story made the overall observation that *Life* had been in a state of steady decline since World War I. Oddly enough, this observation does not agree with the audited statistics. *Life* showed a profit in 1917 of $157,061 — in 1929, $178,847. In fact, *Life* never showed a year of loss from 1890 to 1930.

The old *Life*, under the original management of Mitchell, later Gibson, and more recently Maxwell, never nursed any ambitions to be a magazine of large circulation. In 1935 the *New Yorker* was making money with a circulation of 125,000. The old *Life* circulation had averaged around that figure for decades.

From here on almost every day brought its share of surprises. The first emissary from Time, Inc. to call on us and commence working out details of our dissolution was Ralph McAllister Ingersoll. Ingersoll at the time had reached the apogee of his career in the publishing business. He was second only to Henry Luce in the editorial high command at Time, Inc. In appearance he fitted well the description a *Time* colleague had written of him — "a tall, stooping man, bald except for an encircling fringe and a compensating mustache, fleshy nose, full lips, protuberant and mournful eyes."

Ingersoll had graduated from Yale's Sheffield Scientific School intending to be a mining engineer. Then, after a short stint as a newspaper reporter, he applied for a job with Harold Ross, who in 1925 was just beginning to get his infant *New Yorker* magazine past the toddling stage. Ingersoll worked for Ross from 1925 to 1930, and there are many anecdotes about the relationship between the two. One person who knew both men intimately in this period was the late James Thurber. According to Thurber, Ross hired Ingersoll because he was impressed that Ingersoll was a grand nephew of Ward McAllister and "had social connections with a lot of Park Avenue and Long Island blue bloods." Added Ross: "He knows all about New York society — who owns the private Pullman cars, who belongs to the right clubs — it's damned important for a magazine called the *New Yorker* to have such a man around." Some time before Ingersoll quit the *New Yorker* to work for *Time* his relationship with Ross had soured. After Ingersoll resigned, Ross said: "He knew too goddam many people. He was always on the phone with his brokers or Cornelius Vanderbilt, Jr. If I gave him a thousand dollars a week to sit in an office and do nothing, in twenty-four hours he would have six assistants helping him."

Ingersoll's first visit with us was rather strained. With the exception of Maxwell, we of the about-to-be-dissolved magazine felt pretty much the way a group of manacled slaves must have felt as their new owner came by on an inspection trip prior to sending them down the river. Our erstwhile president was, on the other hand, feeling pretty chipper because he had recently been promised a vice-presidency at *Time* and a doubling of his present salary. As our small group sat around in our front office discussing with Ingersoll the procedure of putting out a farewell issue announcing the new photo-weekly *Life*, Clair sought to break the ice with a story. The story had something to do with a man who miraculously escaped uninjured when his ancient but smooth-running Rolls-Royce was smashed to bits in a collision with a locomotive. The man consoled himself that he had managed to salvage the unscratched nameplate from the wreckage as a souvenir. Clair managed a chuckle at the end of his story, Ingersoll managed a faint smile. The rest of us were too absorbed in our thoughts to react at all.

To change the subject I suggested that I get in touch with E.S. Martin, who wrote the first editorial for *Life* in 1883, and ask the old gentleman to write the farewell address for the final issue. Ingersoll nodded to this idea and also to my suggestion that we run a two-page spread of a famous Charles Dana Gibson drawing to accompany the valedictory message.

A couple of days later, around five in the afternoon, Ralph Ingersoll called on us again to discuss some final details. On this occasion he brought with him Dan Longwell, who had been appointed by Luce to serve as the new magazine's executive editor. Longwell was as unlike Ingersoll physically as a man could possibly be. He was of medium build, had some dark hair on top of his head with a wisp of gray combed to cover the bald spot above his forehead. His rugged regular features made me think he looked as General Ulysses S. Grant might have looked in his clean-shaven youth.

Longwell was as outgoing and gregarious as Ingersoll was tight-lipped and silent. I immediately took a liking to the new executive editor, and as I walked with them back to the Chrysler Building, Longwell seemed to go out of his way to be agreeable. He said he had noted some of the color pages we had been running in *Life*, especially the series on great American painters such as John Sloan, Grant Wood, Reginald Marsh, John Steuart Curry, Edward Hopper, and Thomas Hart Benton. He said that although they had a great many editors and staff photographers interested in black-and-white pictures, they hadn't as yet lined up anyone to deal with color pages, of which they were hoping to run a great many.

As we entered the Chrysler Building's express elevator to the Cloud Club floor, Ingersoll vouchsafed the only observation he made during our walk. "You guys have really been damned lucky that *Life* lived past the half-century mark. Many magazines have had to fold up after thirty years or so." (He didn't know how prophetic this remark was to prove. Just thirty-six years later came the surprise announcement that *Life* was to cease publication following losses of $30,000,000.)

No sooner had we taken a table in the bar lounge than we were joined by Charles Stillman, treasurer of Time, Inc. I was introduced to Stillman and asked what I would like to drink. A drink at this point was certainly a welcome suggestion, but as I politely hesitated, Longwell grinned and said, "How about a very dry Martini, that's what I would like." Stillman ordered the same. Ingersoll ordered a ginger ale. As the drinks were served Stillman made the observation that Time, Inc. was presently moving from the status of a big small company to that of a small big company. I learned later that this statement had been made recently in a Luce memo to his executive staff.

Our gathering reminded me of the sort of looking-over one experienced when as a college freshman several seniors decided whether or not to proffer a bid to the fraternity. After a half-hour's chat about nothing at all Ingersoll rose, and we all went down in the elevator to the ground floor, shook hands, and parted.

Next morning Longwell phoned and asked if it was convenient for me to drop by and see him at ten. He sounded as cheery as before, and I assumed from his voice that so far I had not been blackballed. At ten on the dot Longwell received me with a smile and said, "Come on upstairs now, and meet Harry." I noted the ease with which he referred to the great Henry Robinson Luce as Harry.

Luce was standing by a window when we entered his office talking to Roy E. Larsen, who had been a top lieutenant in the organization since *Time*'s founding and had just accepted the new title of publisher of *Life*. Mr. Luce shook my hand cordially, introduced me to Mr. Larsen, then asked us all to be seated as he perched on the edge of his desk and fitted a cigarette into a long holder. I was agreeably surprised to note that Henry Luce did not look as fierce as he was sometimes described. William J. Miller, a veteran *Time* editor, once wrote, "His beetling brows, powerful jaw, and cold blue eyes gave him the visage of a timber wolf."

My audience lasted only a few minutes. Mr. Luce said that he understood from Longwell that I was to set up a department with emphasis on color features, a field in which he had a great personal interest. He remarked that color features could cover a wide range of subjects from fine art to new issues of postage stamps. "We are glad to have you with us," he added. "Things are in a pretty chaotic state at present, but we have found from past experience that problems have a way of getting solved around here."

Dan Longwell had come to Time, Inc. in the early 1930's from Doubleday, Doran Publishing Company, where he had edited a number of successful picture books. Luce had long been interested in the power of pictures to implement text, and as the candid camera and fast film techniques were perfected, he was one of the first to see the possibilities they opened. Longwell was soon appointed special assistant to *Time*'s managing editor, with sole responsibility to produce more and better photography for each issue.

During the first six months of 1936 Longwell and his staff had produced, under Luce supervision, two experimental issues of the photo-magazine, which were circulated among the advertising fraternity, and received with varying degrees of enthusiasm.

In the hectic early weeks of the photo-news weekly I sometimes took a few minutes of my napping time on the late and early commuting trains to and from Bayside, Long Island, to wonder whether or not I had been catapulted into some sort of a dream sequence. I often searched my thoughts trying to discover a few glints of humor in all that had happened since our little world at the "Old *Life*" had been atomized.

Although all was mostly hustle and bustle in the Chrysler Building *Life* offices, there were a few light interludes. One was often supplied by Thomas Wood, a former *Time* staffer who had been transferred to *Life* to write captions. Tom was a huge, roly-poly figure in his late twenties. He had been a tackle on the Harvard football team and had written some humor for the *Lampoon* in his undergraduate days. A penchant for wearing black shirts was one of his ways of manifesting his generally irreverent attitude. Another was an amusing habit of talking in mock *Time* style. A Monday morning exchange with him, for example, might go like this:

G.T.E.: "Good Morning Tom, how are things?"
TOM: "As it must on occasion afflict most men, the lot at week's end of beetle-browed, bandy-legged newshawk Thomas A. (for Adolphus) Wood was to suffer an early morning hangover."

The greatest relief from office pressure came during the famous controversy over the profile of Luce that Wolcott Gibbs was preparing for the *New Yorker*. With tongue in cheek *New Yorker*'s Harold Ross sent a first draft of Gibbs's piece to Luce asking that it be checked for accuracy. The piece was full of inaccuracies — purposely planted to irritate Luce. (Ross was till peeved about several uncomplimentary things the Lucepress had written about him in *Fortune* in 1934.)

And Luce was definitely irritated by the tone of the article. He understandably resented Gibbs's reference to him as an "ambitious, gimlet-eyed Baby Tycoon." Also resented was the Gibbs jibe at Luce journalese: "Backward ran the sentences until reeled the mind."

A conference with Ross was soon arranged, and Luce took his lieutenant Ingersoll along for moral support. In tackling Ross,

Ingersoll did most of the talking. He complained that there was not a single favorable reference to Luce in the entire piece. He objected to a Gibbs paragraph that quoted from a prospectus issued by "Apollo-faced C.D. Jackson" of Time, Inc. *"Life*, wrote he, will show us the Man of the Week . . . his body clothed and, if possible, nude. It will expose the loves, scandals, and personal affairs of the plain and fancy citizen." He also complained about the way Gibbs described the Time, Inc. system for getting material. Time, Inc. staffers, according to Gibbs, followed a procedure of writing into the first draft of an article any wild gossip or figures that occurred to them. This was then sent to the victim, who angrily corrected the errors and thus inadvertently gave the writer a lot of facts that were none of his business. Luce and Ingersoll pleaded with Ross to cut this paragraph out of the piece.

They also pleaded that the references to Clare Boothe Luce's first play, *Abide With Me*, be deleted. Gibbs noted that the play had been unfavorably reviewed by all critics and that Richard Watts of the *Tribune* had chided the playwright for taking a bow despite the fact that there had been no audience cry for "author, author." The play had opened at the Ritz Theatre on November 21, 1935, just two days before Clare Boothe Brokaw's marriage to Henry Luce.

It was also suggested to Ross that a reference to Ingersoll's hypochondria be deleted, as well as a comment that Luce was devoid of a sense of humor. There were all sorts of other changes suggested, but only a few were allowed by Ross, who proceeded to print the piece almost exactly as originally written.

In the meantime some pixie in either the *New Yorker*'s office or *Time*'s managed to smuggle out a copy of Ross's final letter to Luce, which was passed around the Chrysler Building offices for all of us to read, although it was specifically marked "Personal."

November 23, 1936

Dear Luce:

I assume it is up to me to make certain explanations; at any rate I do so, to clear my conscience, with which I always struggle to keep current. I enclose a rough copy of the next issue with the parody. I have just been over this, reading the piece for what I pray to God is the last time and making notes of a few points I want to explain.

The staff here wanted to be fair, and McKelway and I put all of the important "matters of opinion" (as Ingersoll called a great many of the points raised in the *Fortune* piece on the *New Yorker*) which you raised to a sort of committee, consisting of Mr. and Mrs. White "(founders of a dynasty" — *Fortune*, August, 1934), Gibbs, McKelway, and myself. We considered these matters with a full sense of our responsibility, rather solemnly. Our office differs from yours in that our contents are signed and the writer of an article has the final say on changes, if it comes right down to it. In this instance, however, Gibbs abided by the group decision in every instance. To the special points:

You complained that there wasn't a single favourable word in the piece about you. It was generally felt that the total effect of the article and its being in existence at all were enormously favourable, and that in our listing of your remarkable growth, the figures themselves were complimentary in the highest degree, presenting you, in fact, as practically heroic. As Gibbs pointed out subsequently in a memo written to me: " Having chosen this (parody) form (and I think it's the only way we could possibly write about another magazine) the piece was bound to sound like *Time*, and you will go through a hell of a lot of copies of *Time* without finding anybody described in a way that would please his mother." I was astonished to realize the other night that you are apparently unconscious of the notorious reputation *Time* and *Fortune* have for crassness in description, for cruelty and scandalmongering and insult. I say frankly, but really in a not unfriendly spirit, that you are in a hell of a position to ask anything.

Your objection to the paragraph on the issuance of the prospectus was taken up next. This was allowed to stand, on the ground that it *was* issued, and *did* bear Jackson's name. I didn't seem to have any argument about this; we didn't have space for the full explanation, which was a behind-the-scenes one, and too detailed for a brief parody anyway.

We decided that our estimates as to some of the figures were as good for our purpose as yours would have been, since the article was a parody and some errors would only contribute to the general effect; the *New Yorker* figures in the *Fortune* piece were amusingly wide of the fact in certain instances. (Your passion for accuracy is in no wise doubted; your ability to attain it in many instances is questioned, naturally, by practical journalists.) We felt that the figure on average pay could not possibly be taken as anything other than a parody figure, since it went to five decimal points. (The figures are just out of Gibbs's head as he happened to hit the typewriter keys.)

I was confronted with an ample mass of evidence to substantiate the statements that the writers put "jokers," or "slithering insults," in their copy. Remember that there has been a considerable duplication of writing talent by *Fortune* and the *New Yorker* and that writers talk much. Quite a number of anecdotes about this.

The paragraph on *Fortune*'s methods of getting facts was allowed to stand as being justified, beyond doubt. Not only did we have the *New Yorker* piece as evidence on this point, but ample reports on several others. For instance, we were informed that your original piece on the Astor Estate contained one hundred and thirty-eight misstatements, or errors, which had to be painstakingly worked out.

Your unavailability for lunch for three weeks was based on a statement made by one of your own men to one of ours in the course of preparing our article.

The quote from Richard Watts was taken out of the text and run as a footnote. This was given solemn consideration, I assure you. It was unanimously felt that it should be retained in the parody, as being exactly the kind of item *Time* would pick up and use itself. I was definitely satisfied of this by much evidence offered. I quote from Gibbs's memo on the taste in the matter, naturally deferring to him on such a subject:

"I have no misgivings about using the Watts quote on Mrs. Brokaw. In the first place, it was the logical clip to choose, not because it was the most vicious, but because it had an additional anecdotal value, giving something of the atmosphere of the opening. It was news, in *Time*'s own sense, that Mrs. Brokaw took a bow not strictly in response to demand. I am convinced that it was exactly the sort of thing that Luce or Ingersoll themselves would have jumped on; and I think that it is a little bit innocent of a publication which regularly accuses people of harlotry, bastardy, physical deformity, etc., to complain about it. Nor do I think that Mrs. Brokaw was dragged into the piece. It is certainly part of any Profile to tell whom a man married, and if she is a public figure in her own right that is part of the story. Public figures, as somebody said yesterday, must expect to get kicked in the teeth."

Ingersoll's hypochondria was adjudged to be still existent. Not only did we have the advice of one of the greatest psychiatrists in the city on this (he told us, once a hypochondriac always a hypochondriac; on occasion it may be latent or nearly so, but such periods are only temporary and the patient should be watched carefully during them), but from direct testimony. Besides, it's no slur to call a man a hypochondriac. Most New Yorkers are.

You were adjudged to be by tradition a Tory, and no doubt whatever. Ministers of the Gospel are the very spearheads of Toryism; then Hotchkiss and Yale, both conventional, Tory.

Retention of the paragraph on presidential ambitions was also a unanimous decision. It was regarded as exactly the kind of thing *Time* is doing constantly; denying the weird and, as we called it, "fantastic" rumor after stating it, thereby getting the full news value of it. Moreover, *Time* enterprises are always speculating on peoples' ambitions. This seemed the perfect item for parody purposes.

That finishes my itemization of special points in the story. I would like to quote a couple of paragraphs from Gibbs's note to me, and do:

"Any criticism of the policy, style, etc. is as Ingersoll said of certain statements in the *Fortune* piece about us, purely a matter of opinion. I think *Time* has gratuitously invaded the privacy of a great many people; I think it draws conclusions unwarranted by the facts, distorts quotes, reprints rumors it knows have little foundation, uses a form of selective editing in getting together a story from the newspaper that throws it altogether out of focus, and that *Time*'s style is an offense to the ear. I said that Mr. Luce was humorless because I could find nothing in the source or in the reports of people who have talked to him that indicated anything else. Also I doubt very much if a humorist would last a week as president of Time, Inc. I'm not even sure that ' humorless ' is a disparaging term. In any case all statements and editorial conclusions in the piece are matters of honest opinion with me, usually made after reading the evidence of a great many people. Don't know if Ingersoll and Luce realize just how much source material went into this thing, and from what widely divergent people it came. In almost every case I've tried to follow the most temperate estimate, throwing out a lot of stuff that would have made the boys' hair stand up.

"From the point of view of the writer, or Forgotten Man, in this whole thing, I'd like to say also that the tone is dictated to a great extent by the parody form. That is, it is almost impossible to bring a note of admiration or appreciation into a kind of writing that is mocking by definition."

A little more, from me. After our talk the other night I asked at least ten people about *Time* and, to my amazement, found them bitter, in varying degrees, in their attitude. You are generally regarded as being mean as hell and frequently scurrilous. Two Jewish gentlemen were at dinner with me last night and, upon mention of *Time*, one of them charged that you are anti-Semitic, and asked the other if he didn't think so too. The other fellow said he'd read *Time* a lot and he didn't think you were anti-Semitic especially; you were just anti-everything, he said—anti-Semitic, anti-Italian, anti-Scandinavian, anti-black widow spider. "It is just their pose," he said.

There was telephoning about these proofs last week, but we didn't send them over to Ingersoll because I wanted to send some explanation with them when they went, and the whole thing seemed to get to a childish stage. Perhaps it still is in one, for I feel rather childish writing all this. It's all over now, anyhow.

Sincerely yours,

HAROLD WALLACE ROSS

Small man . . . furious . . . mad . . . no taste

VI

Inside Time, Inc.

WHEN, IN MY FIRST meeting with Henry Luce, he referred to the chaotic state of affairs at *Life*, he was thinking of a number of problems that bedeviled him at the moment. Problems that were only to be revealed in detail years later when the official history of Time, Inc. was published.

The editor in chief had just suffered a most embarrassing confrontation with Ralph Ingersoll concerning the part Clare Boothe Luce was to play on the new publication. The Luces were newlyweds of only a few months in the spring of 1936 when final plans were in the works to launch the new magazine. During the honeymoon Clare had shown so much interest in the photo-weekly venture that Henry had encouraged her in the thought that she would be drafted by the editors to fill a top spot on the masthead. Instead, Ingersoll called on the Luces one evening at their River House apartment and delivered a very blunt challenge. He said: "Harry, you have got to make up your mind whether you are going to continue to be a great editor or whether you are going to be on a perpetual honeymoon. Before you met Clare you used to work at your office until ten or eleven o'clock every night. Now you clear out every afternoon at five. If Clare really loves you, she won't get in the way of the success of this magazine." According to Clare's later account of the incident, she was so humiliated she went off to her room and had a good cry. Henceforth she resolved never to set foot in the offices of Time, Inc. again. The working partnership of Luce and his top executive understandably cooled after this, resulting in Ingersoll's eventual resignation from *Time* to found the left-wing New York tabloid *PM*.

Another painful matter confronting Luce was the problem of *Life's* managing editor. He had brought John S. Martin over from *Time* to handle the job, and just when the new publication was within weeks of going to press Martin showed every sign of having a nervous breakdown.

John Martin, a cousin of the co-founder of *Time* Briton Hadden, had come to the magazine in 1922 directly upon graduation from Princeton, where he had edited the *Daily Princetonian*. Martin had also made a name for himself on campus as a phenomenal athlete. Although he had lost his left arm in a hunting accident, such was his prowess with his right that he continued to be a crack shot. He not only played par golf, but earned his letter in varsity soccer as well. He had performed brilliantly as managing editor of *Time* — it was understood that he was the only Timeman who could write any part of the magazine more skillfully than Luce.

But at about the hour Martin's talent was most needed at *Life* he suddenly had a personality flip. He took to shouting down Luce at story conferences — calling Luce's ideas "buckeye" — bawling out Longwell before everyone at staff meetings, and becoming generally obnoxious all around. When it was discovered that he was drinking heavily, Luce sent him off on a year's sabbatical and brought *Time's* managing editor, John Billings, in to fill the *Life* job. Martin suffered no loss financially from the demotion; he had long since become a millionaire thanks to his Time, Inc. stock.

A still further vexatious interoffice situation developed when the Spanish Civil War exploded in full fury in the fall of 1936. *Time's* conservative foreign news editor, Laird Goldsborough, promptly slanted all news stories in his department in favor of General Franco's rebel insurgents. Liberal New Dealer Archibald Mac-Leish, on *Fortune,* promptly bombarded Luce with memos denouncing Franco's coalition of landowners, the Church, and the army, as "tools of fascism." In defining his position to Luce at the time, Goldsborough wrote: "On the side of Franco are men of property, men of God, and men of the sword. What positions do you suppose these sorts of men occupy in the minds of 700,000 readers of *Time*? I am convinced that our readers do not recoil at the sight of a U.S. Marine, a clergyman, or a prosperous householder. They resent communists, anarchists, and political gangsters — those so-called Spanish Republicans."

Luce tended to allow Goldsborough to continue with a free rein. But the early issues of *Life* reflect that the editor in chief had no firm convictions on international affairs in the mid-1930's.

The wife of the editor in chief had, however, some very firm opinions on international matters. Clare was violently anti-Franco and promptly contributed a thousand dollars to the pro-Communist Abraham Lincoln Brigade, which was gathering volunteers in New York City to fight against Franco in Spain.

According to Clare's friend and biographer, Stephen Shadegg, this 1936 phase of her life was but a brief interlude. To Shadegg, Clare explained that after she was rejected for any meaningful participation in her husband's new magazine, she decided that her marriage lacked the personal fulfillment she was seeking. This is why she indulged in a flirtation with Communism. She said she had been "primarily attracted to Communism because she was disturbed by the poverty and misery of the depression and felt a sense of guilt because of her own affluence." After several weeks of toying with her new ideology, she decided that it was not the answer. She forthwith wrote the enormously successful play *The Women*, which earned for her a quarter of a million dollars and gave her the feeling of identity she craved.

It was soon evident that Clare's submersion in the theatre gave her new husband the freedom he needed to pay proper attention to his job. John Billings recorded in his diary that the boss was at last looking into everything concerning the new magazine. "Now everything had to go to Harry for final Yes or No. When he wasn't squinting critically at layouts or editing captions, he was filling me full of *Life*'s principles and purposes. '*Life* would have unity, flow, change of pace, charm and shock!'"

John Billings was described by Time, Inc. historian Robert Elson as "steady, predictable, quiet, restrained, reticent. A genius for getting the best out of everyone. A stalwart who gave the organization a sense of balance."

Born in 1896 on a South Carolina plantation that had been in his family for generations, Billings came naturally by his polite and courtly manners. His years on *Time*, after Harvard and World War I service, had hardened him not at all. For John Shaw Billings *Life* began at forty. And office chaos noticeably diminished the day he took charge under Luce and over Longwell.

When Longwell gave me the two trial issues of the magazine to look over, he frankly stated that they contained quite a mass of trivia, of which he was not too proud. But he said he thought many of the feature picture essays were strong enough to run in future numbers of the magazine. The leading six-page feature in dummy one was a curious selection, in view of coming events. The overall title was "Edward VIII: War Lord," with the subtitle, "Faced by the ghastly challenge of the skies Britain is spending herself into possession of the most deadly forces the world's greatest Empire has ever had." This declaration could stand as the most inaccurate statement of the decade.

Of all the feature stories in the two dummies, most spectacular was one titled "Hitler Speaks," with several pages devoted to the glorification of the dictator during the massive 1936 Nazi Party meeting at Nuremberg.

> HITLER SPEAKS — never with such significance and authority as when he brings 1,000,000 Nazi zealots from all over Germany to the world's biggest annual camp meeting. The most stirring of his messages this year was a threat to seize Russian territory. He declared: "If I had the Ural Mountains, if we possessed Siberia, if we had the Ukraine, then Nazi Germany would be swimming in prosperity."

Besides the dozens of color projects on my desk, there were also black-and-white ideas to be produced. Here is an example of how the two were combined in a single trip: High on my must list was a call on the great Swedish sculptor, Carl Milles, in his studio at the Cranbrook Foundation in Michigan. Also high on my list was to reproduce the Thomas Benton murals in the State Capitol in Jefferson City, Missouri. These two assignments were managed on a trip of less than a week. And this was in the era of travel by train. My task force consisted of Alfred Eisenstaedt, to take care of the candid photography, and Fernand Bourges with three assistants to do the color work.

Eisenstaedt, a famous European candid-camera photographer, had recently been brought over from Germany to join *Life*'s embryonic photographic staff. Despite, or perhaps because of, his sketchy English vocabulary and limited knowledge of things American, he was a pleasant and amusing companion. Eventually he was to cover some 2,500 picture assignments for *Life*.

The shooting of the Benton murals was a formidable challenge. The painting covered over 45,000 square feet of wall space. I was fortunate that I could put my finger on Bourges to tackle the project. He had long been Condé Nast's ace color photographer and had helped me produce the three-dimensional covers on the old *Life*.

While Bourges was coping with complicated scaffolding problems in Jefferson City's Capitol Building, Eisenstaedt and I visited Benton in his studio. I had met Benton in New York in 1935 when we had done a piece about him in the old *Life*. At that time he was vehement in his disdain for what he called the "intellectually confused colony of studio painters" in Manhattan. The Eastern art establishment had been just as vehement in criticizing his "lusty, earthy, realistic style," as well as his careless dress and personal appearance. He was pleased when I told him that Henry Luce considered him "the most abused and most dynamic painter of the American scene today."

While Eisenstaedt capered about taking dozens of pictures with his Leica I made some notes about the mural. Benton considered that the Missouri Legislature had gotten quite a bargain for the $16,000 they had voted for the work. He had labored a year on it. (At the time of his death in 1975 his easel paintings were to fetch up to $90,000.) He chuckled as he told me that he had been getting some criticism locally from touchy Missourians, who objected to seeing Boss Pendergast, Jesse James, and Frankie and Johnny immortalized on his canvas. As we departed we were treated to a lively tune on the Benton harmonica.

When Eisenstaedt and I left the Capitol to entrain for our appointment with Carl Milles, Bourges assured us that his very trying assignment was under control.

Our visit with Mr. and Mrs. Milles in their lovely Cranbrook home was a welcome, restful interlude after the intense activity of Jefferson City. Milles, sixty-one, and his wife, a couple of years younger, exuded peace of mind and soul. The Cranbrook Academy of Art had brought Milles over from his native Sweden eight years earlier to be Sculptor in Residence, with a large studio facility at his disposal and freedom to do as much work on commission as he chose. Copies of his most notable works were on display at Cranbrook as well as some originals. The most famous of his originals was the Orpheus Fountain, which stands in front of Stockholm's Concert Hall.

Our visit came as he was putting the finishing touches on a new masterpiece called *The Wedding of the Rivers* to decorate the St. Louis Aloe Plaza. As we walked among the giant clay figures of tritons and naiads that were to be transformed into bronze for the

St. Louis fountain, he mentioned that he loved to listen to classical music as he worked, especially Beethoven. Beethoven's Fifth Symphony was playing from his recorder as we reentered his living room. The Milles visit resulted in a *Life* cover story as striking as any that Eisenstaedt's cameras would ever produce.

About half an hour before we left Cranbrook, and while Eisenstaedt was snapping some final photos around the grounds, I was invited into the Milles study, and, reversing our roles, he addressed a query to me. He said that he sensed I had some dreams and aspirations out and beyond a magazine job in New York. What would I like most to do if I might have a wish fulfilled? When I told him that my wife and I loved the sea, loved sailing, and hoped some time to spend a long holiday sailing in faraway places, he said that he too loved the sea and faraway places. He predicted that we would one day find our wish fulfilled, and suggested that in the meantime we correspond. An anecdote I liked best about this sensitive man was one I had found in the *Time* file before we left New York. In 1932 the City of St. Paul had offered him $65,000 to create a war memorial for their City Hall Plaza. The offer was summarily turned down. He told the City fathers that it was repugnant to him ever to do a *war* memorial *anywhere*. He would consent only to create a *peace* memorial. This resulted in the 36-foot-tall statue of an American Indian God of Peace, carved from fifty-five tons of cream-white onyx.

The projects that came to my desk in a six-weeks' period and were published in the magazine fell into no particular pattern, and were not meant to do so. A partial list of the things in color indicates how wide was the sweep of Luce's okays. These included full-stage, full-cast theatre spreads of Helen Hayes's *Victoria Regina* and Clare Luce's *The Women*. There were sequences of John Steuart Curry's Kansas, Muirhead Bone's Spain, Peter Scott's Wild Fowl, Charles Burchfield's America, and Winslow Homer's seascapes. To check personally on a number of things I had selected from a surrealistic show at the Museum of Modern Art, Henry Luce accompanied me thither in a taxi. From this exhibition *Life* reproduced the famed *Fur Lined Teacup* and Dali's early rendering of flannel timepieces called *The Persistence of Memory*. A tremendous challenge for Fernand Bourges and his color team was the task of reproducing the WPA murals painted by Henry Varnum Poor, George Biddle, and Reginald Marsh in the Justice

Department and Post Office buildings in Washington, D.C. This required several times the amount of scaffolding the Bourges team had to cope with in Missouri.

One surprising color feature that was passed along to me for scheduling was a collection of several watercolors painted by Adolf Hitler in his youth. I never did learn how they found their way from Berlin to New York. The caption, bearing the okay of H.R.L. and describing the work as having "remarkable flow and feeling," was printed with the pictures in the issue of November 30, 1936.

Oddly enough, in all the thousands of pictures in the news pages of *Life* during its early months of publication, Hitler and his Nazis were pretty well ignored. The only picture story about him, a seven-page sequence of his life and works, carried the caption: "More than any man alive he is the fulcrum on which peace or war in Europe teeters."

The Hitler essay contained a two-page spread of German naval strength. Also a series of close-ups of Der Fuehrer as "Thinker, Rabble Rouser, Charmer, Music lover and Dog lover." There was nothing in the piece that might have cause Time's *Life* to be banned from Nazi Germany.

When one searches the early issues of *Life* for some indication that the editor in chief was concerned with sorting out the good guys from the bad guys on the international scene, one finds that the focus was on the other side of the world. For China-born Henry Luce the real villains of the mid-1930's were the two young Communists, Mao Tse-tung and Chou En-lai, whose "communist armies of China have for 10 years fought a losing will-o-the-wisp fight against the nationalist government of Generalissimo Chiang Kai-shek."

In the issue of *Life* for December 28, 1936, under a large portrait of Chiang the Luce caption read:

His face is less well known than the faces of Hitler, Mussolini or Stalin. Yet he is overlord of more people than the Big Three rule together. In 13 years and twice as many wars he licked China's warlords, put down communists, brought his country to a greater degree of unity than it has known since the Manchu Empire collapsed in 1911.

Incidentally, Benito Mussolini received no play at all in the early issues of *Life*. Il Duce had appeared on several covers of *Time* in the 1920's. Henry Luce was on record as describing the dictator as "the outstanding moral leader in the world." In the pages of *Time* Mussolini had been "wise, courageous, brilliant, daring, and adored by the people of Italy."

Life's earliest issues set the pace for continuing editorial interest in sensational U.S. news. In a "Speaking of Pictures" section in the issue of December 14, 1936, under a photo of two University of California students dismantling a Berkeley street light, was the letter:

> Sirs — After the Cal-Stanford game November 21st, five thousand U.C. students ran berserk through the streets of Berkeley disabling street cars, blocking traffic and building fires at intersections from materials gathered from restaurants, nearby fences and stores. The Berkeley fire department couldn't keep pace with the fires.
>
> *MAURICE J. CURTIS*
> Richmond, California

> Editorial note — This is the kind of photography *Life* welcomes. If contributor Curtis had taken the whole university riot in narrative sequence *Life* would have gladly printed it in full.

During the weeks immediately preceding the publication of the first issue there had been much speculation among the working staff as to who might be listed on the masthead of Vol. I, No. 1. In such a situation a tension builds up not too different from the feeling in Britain as various government servants hold their breaths awaiting the announcement of the Queen's Honours List. Those of us who found our names officially in print as "Associates" under top editors Luce, Billings, and Longwell regarded ourselves as fortunate indeed. The casualty list of those who fell by the wayside was a long one.

My close friend and collaborator on the old *Life*, Gurney Williams, was not one of those who fell along the way. After only a few weeks in the Chrysler Building, Gurney left to become humor editor of *Collier's*. Time, Inc. had a payroll of some 650 persons when our small group was taken into the fold. Of our minuscule editorial staff only Gurney and I had chosen to move along with the name. Henry Richter soon adapted himself to the new environment as business manager of *Architectural Forum*. Our ad manager, Joe MacDonough, and two of his salesmen had been quickly absorbed into *Time*'s selling staff. Clair Maxwell was later to resign his vice-presidency to take on a liquor distributorship in Florida.

After several features that had originated on my desk found their way into print, I was invited to attend the holy of holies, a luncheon meeting in a Cloud Club private room with Messrs. Luce,

Billings, and Longwell. Luce's disinterest in food and partiality for beans and hot dogs had been described to me beforehand by my friend Bill Furth. Sure enough, the editor in chief ordered "franks and beans." The managing editor ordered the same; the executive editor ordered the same; and I did likewise. The boss ate only a part of his lunch and asked me to run over the line-up of future things that were already plated and ready for press. This done, he nodded his okay on a dozen other ideas that were waiting to be produced, which I noticed relaxed Billings and Longwell considerably. There was a brief period of staccato talk as Luce smoked a couple of cigarettes and made a few terse observations. The magazine continued to be a sellout, coast to coast. The newsstand sales would soon hit the million mark, might later reach several million, who knows? The question on everyone's mind was, should the circulation be controlled in the interest of quality or should it be allowed to run into the multimillions to compete with the *Saturday Evening Post* and *Collier's*? Only Henry Luce could eventually make that major decision. Longwell made the observation: "*Life* is certainly the biggest ten cents worth ever offered by any magazine in history." Billings replied: "*Life* is certainly the largest, most complex editorial operation in magazine history."

The decision was eventually made to fight a circulation war with *Collier's, Saturday Evening Post,* and *Look.* In the 1950's, when *Life* led the field with a circulation of 6,000,000, Luce declared "we believe in a competitive economy and we propose to compete the hell out of everybody on every front." In succession, *Collier's,* the *Post,* and *Look* were forced out of business prior to the demise of *Life* itself.

Among my souvenirs is a teletype I received at the printers in Chicago during another typical foray into the Middle West with Alfred Eisenstaedt and the Fernand Bourges color crew. The message well illustrates the close watch the editor in chief kept on day-to-day operations.

GEORGE EGGLESTON (IF EGGLESTON NOT THERE TRY HOTEL STEVENS) WILL LET YOU KNOW TOMORROW ON PACELLI OR LIVING AMERICAN ART. TRYING TO GET RELEASE ON PACELLI. LUCE IS RED HOT FOR GRANT WOOD'S MAIN STREET BUT COLD ON EISENSTAEDT'S GOING TO SAUK CENTER. PLEASE LET ME KNOW AT ONCE IF WE CAN HAVE WOOD COLOR FOR FEB 8 ISSUE.

JOHN BILLINGS

(I had had a portrait in color of Cardinal Pacelli plated in anticipation that he was to become the new Pope — a correct guess. The

Sauk Center reference was about a picture essay on the Minnesota birthplace of Sinclair Lewis.)

Life was only a few issues old when Luce was invited to address the American Association of Advertising Agencies. In his speech he made an unabashed appeal for an enormous appropriation of advertising dollars. He also frankly boasted: "*Life* is evidently what the public wants more than it has ever wanted any product of ink and paper." Then, in a curious digression in the speech, evidently thinking of the collapse of John Martin, he said: "Just as every floor of a skyscraper is said to cost one life, so every important magazine costs nervous indigestion for at least ten people."

I was fortunate that I was able to survive those hectic days in good health, thanks to a rugged constitution. But there were a dozen cases of nervous indigestion on the fiftieth floor of the Chrysler Building in 1936, including a few staffers who had been in the *Time* organization for years. Gurney Williams told me he had suffered several bouts of vomiting during the few weeks he had been on the job, but his stomach trouble ceased as soon as he quit.

I was busily working on advance issues, six months away on the calendar, when I decided that the hour had come for me to make my departure. The immediate thrust for my parting with Time, Inc. was thanks to Henry Richter. It was he who settled up the stock affairs of the old *Life* and handed me a check for $5,000. (In 1935, when the old *Life* showed a 40 per cent gain in circulation, I had been presented with some stock in the company.) When I returned home to Bayside that night and showed the check to Hazel, we both said at once, "Tahiti."

When I called on the editor in chief the next day and told him that I was resigning because I and my wife wanted to fulfill a longtime dream of spending a year in the South Sea Islands, he graciously said it could be a leave-of-absence. John Billings was more talkative. When I told him of my plans, he said: "Dammit, Eggleston, as an ex-editor of a defunct magazine, you should stick around. Things are just beginning to get under way around here." Billings was in truth the kindliest of men under his no-nonsense exterior. He hadn't meant to sound tough. He quickly added: "You've done a good job! I hope you come back."

VII

Sailing the South Seas

ALMOST EVERYONE who has ever sailed a boat has dreamed of sometime cruising in the South Seas. Our collection of books recounting the adventures of Herman Melville, Captain Bligh, and Nordhoff and Hall had thoroughly whetted our thirst to visit the islands of the Society Group and beyond. More recent books by small-boat sailors who crossed the Pacific gave us an idea of how we might make our dream come true.

We discovered in our reading that nearly every westbound yacht that put in at Tahiti had crew troubles that stalled the skipper and his boat in Papeete harbor for months until a new crew was signed on. Just as Captain Bligh's mutineers succumbed to the charms of the island's sirens, so did the many ocean-weary yacht crewmen.

With this in mind we felt that we were sure to find just the proper yacht for charter awaiting us upon our arrival in Papeete. Our overall plan was to spend six months or more leisurely visiting a dozen of the lesser-known islands.

When I outlined to publisher Pascal Covici what we had in mind, he responded by giving me a book contract. The firm of Covici-Friede was feeling quite flush at the time, having successfully launched John Steinbeck's *Tortilla Flat*.

In those days before transocean air travel, transportation to Tahiti was necessarily a very irregular procedure. We took a freight-er from San Francisco to Panama and there boarded a small battered French steamer, *Ville de Strasbourg,* for the slow crawl westward.

In Papeete Harbor we found the collection of yachts we had hoped for. The one we chose, *Viator*, was schooner-rigged, 32 feet overall, and in immaculate condition. Her skipper-owner, Harry Close, was a San Franciscan and a recent graduate of Stanford University. We felt mutually compatible at once. *Viator* had suffered the usual fate—Harry's crew of two had disappeared into the woods, accompanied by island belles, within minutes after the yacht's arrival.

Several days were required to run over and over our check lists while scouring the town for the supplies we would need for the months ahead. Also, knowing we would be out of touch with everyone for an unpredictable period, we had several duty letters to write. Impetus to write lengthy letters home was spurred by the arrival of a ship from San Francisco bearing a quantity of mail for us from well-wishing friends and relatives.

Anyone who has ever signed a book contract knows that one of the most vital ingredients needed by the writer to inspire the production of copy is the enthusiasm of the publisher. Bless Pascal Covici's heart. Word arrived from him perfectly timed for our sailaway.

COVICI-FRIEDE INC. PUBLISHERS
432 Fourth Avenue, New York City
February 25, 1937

Dear George,
    Your cruise to the islands to the west should be exciting and thrilling. How I envy you the trip, and I know there are thousands that feel the same way. Things should happen to you fast and furious now, and your book should almost write itself.
    With kindest regards to you and yours, and best of luck.

Yours,
PAT
Pascal Covici

Before we sailed away there was a certain call to be made. I had a letter of introduction to James Norman Hall that had been given to me in New York by Clayton Knight, one of his World War I comrades. Hazel and I had been wary about making the contact because we guessed that since the current brilliant success of *Mutiny on The Bounty* far too many visitors to the island had invaded the privacy of both James Hall and Charles Nordhoff.

Hall and Nordhoff, each fifty years of age, had but recently achieved literary fame. The two had become friends while serving in the French air force during the First World War. They had come to Tahiti in 1920 "to escape the blessings of civilization" and to collaborate as a writing team. But aside from a few magazine articles and one travel book about the islands, they had experienced many lean years before the inspiration came to do the tale of Bligh's mutiny.

After graduation from Iowa's Grinnell College James Hall worked for a time for a Boston welfare society. Then in 1914 he had gone to England. He was touring Wales by bicycle when the war commenced. Idealist Hall immediately enlisted in the Royal Fusilliers, and from that moment forward he was to experience more of that war at first hand than probably any other American. He was a machine-gunner in France during the first two years of the bloodiest trench warfare. In 1916 he was granted permission to join the American volunteers who made up the Lafayette Escadrille. As a pursuit pilot, in French uniform, he soon became an ace, receiving the Croix de Guerre and five Palms, the Medaille Militaire, and the Légion d' honneur. He managed to survive three crash landings with only a few broken bones— and finally, just before the armistice, he was shot down behind the German lines and made a prisoner of war.

A few days before we sailed off in *Viator* we were guests of the Halls for dinner at their home overlooking Matavai Bay. We had been surprised upon meeting the attractive Sarah Hall. She was quite unlike the description of her that had appeared in *Time* some months earlier. The *Time* story had described her as "a fat-lipped, dusky Tahitian." Mrs. Hall was definitely neither fat-lipped nor dusky. She was part Tahitian on her mother's side. Her father, Captain Joseph Winchester, was a white American who had settled in Tahiti. He had been a trading schooner skipper, well known throughout the islands.

During dinner the *Time* story was mentioned, and Mrs. Hall good-naturedly said she had almost lost her husband to several beautiful Tahitian damsels because of it. The other guests present at dinner were Mr. and Mrs. Carl Curtis. The Curtises were also expatriates, he an American, she English. Carl Curtis was yet another romantic who had read Melville and Frederick O'Brien in his youth. After he left Harvard in the early 1920's, he turned his back on the family law firm and headed for Tahiti. With an unexpected early inheritance he had purchased La Mahina plantation, the largest copra and cattle estate on Tahiti. Margaret Curtis had been an opera singer in her youth and was most outgoing and loquacious compared to the rather retiring Halls. She picked up the topic of Tahitian damsels where Sarah Hall had left it, and said: "Of course you have heard countless tales of Turia—already a legend in her young lifetime?" We said we hadn't. According to Mrs. Curtis, Turia had broken the hearts of at least four millionaire yachtsmen—a Dane, an Englishman, and two Americans. Each of these gentlemen had cast off a wife in the mad pursuit of Turia. Each had enjoyed a temporary affair with Turia and eventually been turned down by her when marriage was proposed. Turia liked variety, and she treasured her independence.

Turia was of the blood royal, an authentic princess, descended from the line of Tahitian rulers, the Pomares, I, II, III, IV, and V. She had been educated in Paris and London, spoke several languages, and although her travels had carried her to many exciting places, she preferred her native isles, Tahiti and Moorea, to anywhere else in the world.

When the dinner conversation got around to some mention of our proposed voyage on *Viator*, the comment from the Curtises was that we were going off on a rather rugged adventure—quite too uncomfortable to contemplate on such a small boat. Only Hall was encouraging and optimistic. He loved travel by sail and had made many interisland passages in native craft. He did not share with his friend Nordhoff an enthusiasm for motorboats. Nordhoff's hobby was fishing, and he spent much of his time at sea pursuing bonita in his small cruiser.

Hall in fact loathed most things mechanical. He wouldn't own an automobile, wouldn't have a radio or telephone in his house. He bicycled everywhere and loved to hike. He had made several attempts to climb Mt. Orohena, but never reached the top because he did not have proper climbing equipment. A professional mountain climber from France conquered the 7,334-foot peak in 1953.

Hall's personal philosophy was best expressed in a bit of verse he had once written for *Atlantic Monthly*.

> . . . News of highest consequence
> I miss; and feast of wit and flow of soul.
> I do not care. Mid-ocean solitudes
> Offer as of old, a recompense.

After dinner, as we sat on the Hall's veranda chatting over coffee and liqueurs, our host told us a fascinating tale about another

American couple, Eastham and Caroline Guild. The Guilds were ex-Bostonians who had followed up their reading of South Seas literature by becoming permanent residents of Tahiti. They had come to the island in 1923 and built a lovely house next to a waterfall about twenty miles north of Papeete. The Guilds were presently in French West Africa collecting rare birds to bring back to Tahiti. Tahiti, when first discovered by the early mariners, had an exotic population of birds. Over the years the rarest birds had been decimated, as in Hawaii, to make cloaks for the royal families, and also by the introduction of rats, cats, and firearms to the island.

Besides traveling to faraway places to bring back birds that might do well in Tahiti, the Guilds corresponded with bird dealers in many tropical areas of the world. They ordered hundreds from the bird market at Dakar, and, surprisingly, a high percentage lived through the long steamship passage from West Africa to Tahiti.

This was no small-time hobby. The Guilds actually imported and released over ten thousand birds of some sixty-three species. The newly arrived birds were first acclimatized and fed in large rat-proofed cages. Then a few were released at a time—and these at first hovered around the Guild grounds for further feeding. But gradually they circulated all over the island and multiplied. Some twenty-one species had bred successfully. The governor declared a closed season on bird shooting, and the Tahitian chiefs in the various districts persuaded the natives to cooperate in the conservation scheme. So, thanks to these American expatriates, where once there had been only the lowly grackle and some native pigeons nesting in the island's trees, there were now Painted Finches, Cordon Blues, Fire Finches, Orange Bishops, Long-tailed Wydahs, Scarlet Tanagers, African Weavers, Yellow Sugar Birds, Numean Parrots, Australian Waxbills, and scores of others.

Vincent Astor, after a visit to Tahiti on his yacht *Nourmahal*, arranged a shipment of Humming Birds and Western Bluebirds to the Guilds. It took sixteen months for the confused blue birds from north of the Equator to rearrange their seasonal breeding habits and successfully produce their young in the jungles of Tahiti. It would be interesting to check today to see how many of the species the Guilds introduced are still present.

As we relaxed in *Viator*'s cockpit the evening before we sailed, Hazel reminded us that almost a hundred years earlier a great American writer had described his emotions upon making the same landfall we were about to make. In the spring of 1843 the twenty-four-year-old Herman Melville sailed in a small boat across the channel from Tahiti to Moorea and wrote in his classic, *Omoo*:

> It was a pleasant trip. The moon was up—the air warm—the waves musical—and all above was the tropical night, one purple vault hung round with soft, trembling stars. The channel is some five leagues wide. On one hand you have the three great peaks of Tahiti lording it over the ranges of mountains and valleys; and on the other, the equally romantic elevations of Imeeo (Moorea), high above which a lone peak shot up its verdant spire.
>
> At last we heard the roar of the reef; and gliding through a break floated over the expanse within, which was smooth as a young girl's brow.

On our daylight crossing in *Viator* we had a twenty-knot beam wind, which put us off the northern tip of Moorea in two hours and a half. Then we had a full sail breeze that carried us down the lee shore, past Paopao Bay and Mount Rotui, to the pass in the reef off Papetoai Bay, clearly marked by the remains of a warship that had come to grief there. Our Pilot Book was helpful:

> Papetoai Bay. Directions: — The wreck of the French cruiser Kearsaint, on the west side of the entrance, is a good navigational mark for entering but should be given a berth of not less that 200 yards.

As we swung to enter, we took down the fisherman staysail and had a gentle beam wind that carried us along at about three knots. Hazel and I had the thrill of conning *Viator* from the cockpit while Harry climbed to the masthead to signal us past a succession of coral shoals. It was almost dusk as we glided to anchor inside the bay. We three were totally awed by the grandeur of the peaks around us—the virgin character of our surroundings — we seemed to be in the possession of an undiscovered mountain lake. As Melville's "purple vault of trembling stars" appeared overhead, we decided that we agreed with the many descriptions we had read. Papetoai Bay was surely the most beautiful anchorage in the world.

After a night's sleep — as deep a sleep of pure contentment as Hazel and I had ever experienced — we three were up at dawn for swims. After breakfast, as we sat in the cockpit still ohing and ahing at the fantastic setting, a small outrigger canoe put off from shore and came alongside. In it was a statuesque raven-haired figure dressed in a red-and-white patterned pareu. The raven hair that set off the handsome Polynesian countenance was adorned with several blooms of white frangipani. It was Turia.

Turia was by no means the willowy type beauty of the fashion magazines. Her figure was as described by Margaret Curtis, voluptuous and ample. She called, she said, to offer us the use of accommodations ashore. Hidden in foliage along the shore were the Moorea villas of three of her friends, the Wessels, the Philips, and the Kellums. The owners of the three houses were presently vacationing abroad. She explained that she was interim caretaker for the bay, and had just completed building a bungalow of her own that she wanted us to visit. Under her guidance we towed her canoe to the Philips's dock, and Hazel and I were assigned a large master bedroom full of antiques.

In designing her own island villa Turia had not followed the styling of the homes of her expatriate friends. Her tastes were pure Polynesian. Her house comprised three units: living room, bedrooms, and kitchen, completely walled with woven bamboo. The roofs were of pandanus fronds fastened by coconut-fibre thongs to the supporting purau-bough rafters. Matted bamboo blinds swinging outward sufficed as windows. Flooring throughout was of waxed, maroon-tinted cement. Turia and a brother had built much of the place themselves. The furniture, each piece fashioned from native woods, was also their handiwork. Hand-dyed cushion covers in pastel shades harmonized with the furniture and flooring.

When we admired a hundred pale hibiscus blossoms radiating from an end-table vase, Turia explained that the stems were twigs of the orange tree. Fresh flowers were carefully gathered each morning and stuck one by one upon the tiny orange thorns. This was typical of every detail of the decor. As we chatted, Turia leafed slowly through a copy of *Vogue* Hazel gave her and paused at a full-page portrait of Lady Mountbatten. "I guess the world is truly a small place," she said, smiling as she nodded toward an autographed picture in a silver frame. "Lady Mountbatten gave me that when I was in England two years ago."

Her laughter was contagious, and she greatly enjoyed Harry's tale of his recent encounter with George Vanderbilt, whose *Cressida* was tied up near *Viator*. Vanderbilt had come aboard *Viator* and jokingly offered to swap his palatial schooner outright for Harry's little pumpkin seed. Several seamen of the *Cressida* had taken to crawling into the yacht's refrigeration compartments and developing cases of acute frostbite so they could be temporarily hospitalized in Papeete and left behind to enjoy the island's charms. Under Admiralty Law Vanderbilt was obliged to leave funds with the U.S. Consul to pay the crews' bills, as well as steamer fares back to America. Since the hospital staff had never encountered frostbite before, there was quite a bit of confusion as to just how to treat it.

Turia contributed an amusing anecdote of her own latest visit to California. At a cocktail party at the Mark Hopkins Hotel a woman gossip columnist had cornered her for an interview and asked for her impression of San Francisco. To have a bit of fun Turia replied with wide-eyed wonder: "I am stunned at the size of your lagoon and frightened when I think of how strong the current must be that runs out of your pass in the reef." The columnist wrote a feature article on this remark, pointing out how naive and unspoiled was the royal visitor from Tahiti.

We spent most of 1937 visiting islands, sailing all told about a thousand miles. After Tahiti and Moorea we visited Huahine, Raiatea, Tahaa, Bora Bora, Tubai, Maupiti, Mopelia, and Rarotonga. Aside from Tahiti we found all the islands charmingly unspoiled. We were very conscious of the fact that we were enjoying a "last look" before the curse of tourism spread to the few remaining paradises of the world. During most of our days and nights at sea the weather was idyllic. Only on our run of 500 miles between Mopelia atoll and Rarotonga did we experience some very strong winds and heavy seas. Hazel had stood all her watches throughout our cruise without complaint. But during this blow she said that when in her bunk below she understood how the man must have felt when he went over Niagara Falls in a barrel.

After a month in Rarotonga we were lucky enough to arrange a passage to San Francisco on a Union Steamship freighter out of Australia. Before we left Harry hired an eager Rarotongan as crewman, and following a farewell lunch party at our boarding-house we waved *Viator* goodbye as the little schooner headed west for Samoa. A long letter received by us months later in New York told how Harry had picked up a second crewman in Samoa, made a stop in Hawaii, and was blessed with good sailing all the way home to San Francisco. And to celebrate his homecoming he had married his fiancée Ruth, to whom he had been addressing letters from every port.

VIII

Lloyd George, Lindbergh, and FDR

WHEN WE ARRIVED in New York armed with several bulging folders of South Seas notes and some completed chapters of the chronicle of our voyage, we were rather nonplussed to learn that the firm of Covici-Friede was about to go out of business. Pat Covici was most apologetic. Despite the success of John Steinbeck's books, the company had been unable to offset some heavy losses. He hoped eventually to connect with another publishing house and perhaps my book could be taken on at some future date.

Obviously the thing to do was put the manuscript aside for awhile and think about the immediate future. I realized that if I took up my leave of absence at *Time-Life* I would suddenly be back in the high-pressure, competitive world from which we had escaped—the peace of mind that had come to us through our months of cruising would be pretty well shattered. A call on my old friend Fred Dayton resolved the situation. He invited me to come into the Nast organization and contribute what I could to a department experimenting with new magazine ideas. I worked two years in this operation, notably on a publishing scheme that had been brought to Nast by the American Society of Historians. Pulitzer Prize-winning biographer Allan Nevins was the guiding spirit behind this experiment, and considerable time and money were expended in putting together dummies and trial formats. Upon making the Nast connection, I wrote to Henry Luce thanking him for his consideration and telling him I was accepting a new assignment. His reply was most gracious, not at all the insensitive Luce often described by his critics:

All of us who were here will remember you as a valiant member of a very hectic team in those first months of *Life*. I hope you will always derive some pleasure from the recollection of the new *Life's* beginnings. Thank you for your letter and I hope our paths will cross again sometime soon.

The magazine of American History didn't get past the dummy stage, mainly because the fast-moving news of the day tended to make ancient history seem very ancient indeed. During the fall months of 1939 a number of events took place that suddenly awakened the world to the fact that a new European war was at hand. On August 24 Nazi Germany and Soviet Russia signed their ten-year treaty of nonaggression.

On the first day of September, as the news broke that Germany had declared war on Poland, Mr. Roosevelt called a press conference, and to a reporter's question, "Can we stay out?" he answered, "I sincerely believe we can, and every effort will be made by this Administration to do so."

On September 3, when Britain and France declared war on Germany, the President reassured the public of his peace-loving intentions over a national radio hook-up. Those "intentions" included:

Let no man or woman thoughtlessly or falsely talk of sending armies to European fields . . . . This nation will remain a neutral nation . . . . I want you to know that your Government has no information which it has any thought of withholding from you . . . . You are, I believe, the most enlightened and best-informed people in all the world.

And the "best-informed people in all the world" were 83 per cent for keeping the United States out of the new war.

On September 15 Col. Charles Lindbergh made the first of a series of radio addresses cautioning America not to be drawn into the conflict. What neither Lindbergh nor anyone else knew at the time was that soon after FDR delivered his ringing neutrality speech he sent a secret message to Winston Churchill indicating his desire to become involved.

Mr. Churchill was First Lord of the Admiralty in the Chamberlain government. In his memoirs he recalls that on September 11 "I was delighted to receive a personal letter from President Roosevelt. I had only met him once in the previous war. It was at a dinner at Gray's Inn. There had been no opportunity for anything but salutations."

Two sentences in the Roosevelt message were to change the whole course of world history: "I shall at all times welcome it if you will keep me in touch personally with anything you want me to know about. You can always send sealed letters through your pouch or my pouch." Thus began the exchange of hundreds of secret messages between the two.

The Roosevelt-Churchill secret correspondence soon propelled FDR into action. On September 21 he asked a special session of Congress to repeal all neutrality legislation. He declared that only by making the United States "the arsenal of Democracy" could he make good his promise to keep America out of the war. Leading the forces opposing FDR was Sen. Arthur Vandenberg, who declared: "I frankly question whether we can become an arsenal for one belligerent without being a target for the other."

FDR did not get all he asked for, but he managed to get the original Neutrality Act amended to permit Britain and France to purchase guns, planes, and tanks, cash and carry, to be transported across the ocean in their own ships. All war zones continued to be off limits for Americans.

On October 6, following the occupation of Poland by German and Russian troops, Hitler, in a speech to the Reichstag, proposed that Britain and France sit down with Germany and discuss terms for a general peace agreement, including disarmament and the establishment of a new Polish state. This proposal was immediately derided with scorn by Winston Churchill. "It never occurred to Hitler for a moment," he declared, "that Mr. Chamberlain and the rest of the British Empire and Commonwealth of Nations meant to have his blood, or perish in the attempt."

Mr. Churchill neglected to mention that there were a great many men of wisdom in England and the English-speaking world who thought there might be other ways of getting rid of Hitler than by a worldwide shedding of blood. Millions of humble folk in England, France, Germany, Australia, Canada, and America remembered that the First World War proved nothing, and resulted in millions of innocent dead.

Foremost among the British opponents of Churchill's war policy was Britain's famed prime minister of the 1914-18 war. The reaction of Lloyd George to Hitler's peace proposals is on record in several speeches in the House of Commons and in several newspaper articles. His feelings were also revealed in the diaries of A.J. Sylvester,[1] who served for many years as confidant and secretary to Lloyd George.

On the afternoon of October 3, 1939, Sylvester accompanied Lloyd George to the House to hear him make "a most remarkable speech in which he asked that any peace proposals receive very careful consideration." To Sylvester he confided: "I want to stop this war, otherwise it will mean the breakup of the Empire."

The speech that the Welshman made that day was indeed a memorable one. Sylvester wrote of it: "The mail which Lloyd George is receiving as a result of his speech in the House is the greatest I have ever known. It comes in large batches by every post, and he has received thousands. They all cry for peace . . . . Lloyd George is jubilant about the number of letters and he talks of nothing else. He received a wire from Rothermere [Viscount Rothermere, owner of the *Daily Mail*]'saying 'warm congratulations. Go on. You will win hands down'. . . . Bags and bags of mail keep arriving."

In the House Churchill challenged his old friend and former boss by declaring that Hitler's offer was a "peace offensive designed to weaken Britain's resistance." Lloyd George answered Churchill: "That is why I would have a counter-peace offensive which would baffle Hitler and strengthen us . . . . I have received and am still receiving letters of support for my appeal to the Government, from every part of the country, from men and women of every party."

On October 12, when Mr. Chamberlain formally rejected the peace proposals, Lloyd George wrote in an article for the *Sunday Express* that he did not believe that Mr. Chamberlain meant to "finally slam the door" on the German proposals:

> I am still hopeful that this is not the last word. A devastating war suits neither of the two parties. Not one of the three belligerent Powers is anxious to plunge irretrievably into this ghastly trial of strength, which, if it is fought out to the end, will leave them torn and bleeding and at least one of them broken and prostrate. This seems to me the time to call a conference. Later, when war and passion have blinded the combatant nations to their sufferings and when the voice of reason is suppressed in all lands and treated as treason — then it will be too late.

On October 21, after the country had been officially at war for six weeks, Lloyd George spoke at a huge rally for peace in Caernarvon

Pavillion. He summed up his call for a peace conference with the words: "I am not begging for peace at any price. We are not a beaten nation. We can negotiate from strength." His audience rose and gave him a massive ovation at the conclusion of his speech. On the same day the kings of Denmark, Norway, and Sweden, and the president of Finland issued a joint statement affirming their neutrality and offering to mediate at a peace conference.

In his many speeches and in his newspaper articles Lloyd George several times suggested that the ideal person to call a peace parley was President Roosevelt. To these suggestions FDR made no response.

It is interesting that Lloyd George and Winston Churchill continued to maintain a friendly relationship and mutual respect despite their totally opposing views. They frequently conferred together and dined together. In fact, Churchill repeatedly urged Lloyd George to accept a post in the war cabinet, and Lloyd George repeatedly declined.

By contrast, during the two years prior to Pearl Harbor FDR denounced as pro-Nazi all the senators, congressmen, and leading citizens in every branch of American life who spoke out against involvement in the war and in favor of a negotiated peace settlement. Mr. Roosevelt was especially annoyed when someone of military stature spoke out against American involvement. A new name was added to the White House blacklist following an address by Gen. Charles P. Summerall in November, 1939. Speaking at an Armistice Day dinner in Chicago, the former Chief of Staff declared: "Not one cent, not one soldier. Let the American people resolve never again to engage in wars not made upon them. We cannot settle Europe's quarrels nor maintain the balance of power there."

The reason Mr. Roosevelt was antagonistic to U.S. anti-war advocates was because he was listening only to the insistent pleas of Mr. Churchill that America join his crusade to crush Germany.

In the fall of 1939 I was surprised to note that the slant of the news in both *Time* and *Life* had suddenly become interventionist. Had I returned to work for Henry Luce I would have found myself very much out of step with the new editorial policy. I say *new* policy because prior to 1939 Luce was anything but a war promoter. At the time of the Munich Pact the Luce press had praised Neville Chamberlain for his peace efforts and had run his picture on the cover of *Time*.

In W.A. Swanberg's searching biography of Luce he states that the editor, at the time of Munich, "regarded the Axis as a God-given weapon aimed straight at Bolshevism."[2] Luce had long been an admirer of Mussolini and uncritical of Hitler. In May, 1938, a few weeks after Hitler had annexed Austria, Henry and Clare Luce were in Berlin on a visit arranged by a Berlin-based U.S. business-man. In a six-thousand-word report to his New York editors Luce wrote:

> The great and first impression I got is that National Socialism is a socialism which works mightily for the masses, however distasteful it may be to them personally in many ways. [He noted fifteen busy theatres in Munich.] Any idea that the Nazis have put the kibosh on culture is ridiculous.
>
> The German people are on wheels by the millions — the *People*, yes, the *People*, the meek people who have inherited the earth. We read of Germany as if it were the private domain of Hitler. . . . But the *visual* impression of Germany is a *People*'s land. I never saw Hitler, I saw no army. I saw only the People, the People, the People. I do not know what they are but they did not seem to be slaves. Their chains were not visible.

In the Elson *History of Time, Inc.* Luce is portrayed as being all-out for intervention from early 1939 onward. Said Luce of his *Time-Life-Fortune* editors: "The younger men who graduated after the 1920's were roughly isolationists, but men in my class and generation — Larsen, Billings, Longwell — were interventionists." Luce told his colleagues that he considered *Life* to be the most effective of the three magazines to get the U.S. involved in the war.

Luce immediately labeled the war *World War II*, causing many readers to write in and ask, "Why call it a world war when it is not yet a European one?" The *New York Times* and most of the nation's press were not to call it World War II until America became totally involved. From 1939 on the official policy of the Luce Press was to grant not one line of favorable publicity to Lindbergh or anyone else in the ranks of the millions of Americans dedicated to keeping the country out of the war.

In an early 1940 confidential memo to senior executives Luce defined what he called "journalistic duty":

1. To continue to sound the danger signal in all aspects—Danger to the Sovereign U.S.A.

2. To Cultivate the Martial Spirit.
3. To show that America is worth fighting for.

To implement this theme military writer Major George Fielding Eliott was engaged to do a series of scare pieces for *Life*. In the issue for May 27, 1940, Eliot wrote: "If Germany wins, the United States would face grim realities. As the one remaining democracy, the U.S. would become the power the Nazis *must* destroy." Other Eliot pieces carried maps showing air distances from various bases in South America where German air raids on the U.S. could originate. Eliot declared: "The speed of German conquest has brought much closer the period of maximum danger to the United States. We must prevent the establishment of enemy bases in the Western Hemisphere."

Although the Luce Press introduced Major Eliot as a "military expert," his credentials as listed in *The Reader's Encyclopedia* were modest:

ELIOT, GEORGE FIELDING (1894-   ). Army officer serving with an Australian contingent in World War I, writer on military affairs and radio commentator. Author of *The Ramparts We Watch* (1938) and *Bombs Bursting in Air* (1939).

Oddly enough, across the ocean, Britain's most highly respected military analyst saw the war picture from an entirely different perspective. Capt. Basil Henry Liddell Hart,[3] a close friend and adviser to Lloyd George, thought as he did that Hitler's logical route of expansion was to the East, against Russia. Therefore, prior to America's entry into the war Hart was among the most vocal of influential Englishmen calling for peace negotiations with Germany. In late 1939 Hart noted that "a suspension of hostilities would at worst allow time for our strength to grow. Better still, it would give the necessary opportunity for Russia and Germany to rub against each other."[4]

In May, 1940, a magazine seriously in need of a fresh editorial formula came to the attention of the Nast experimental workshop. The magazine was the *Commentator*, a pocket-size publication that had been started some four years earlier as a medium to carry original articles by some of the more famous radio commentators. Founder and owner of *Commentator* was Charles S. Payson, financier and lawyer. A luncheon with Mr. Payson soon established that he and I had a great many ideas in common. We were both firmly Republican in our politics, and wary of Mr. Roosevelt's pledges of peace and neutrality. We were convinced that he was hoping to get the country irrevocably committed abroad, including sending an expeditionary force at the earliest convenient opportunity. Because of our own New England backgrounds and English ancestry we had great sympathy and admiration for England. And for this very reason we felt, as did many an influential Englishman, that Hitler should be allowed to march east against his onetime sworn natural enemy, Russia. We reasoned that since France was about to drop out of the war, England could negotiate an honorable peace with Germany and let Hitler and Stalin fight it out to a point of exhaustion that would eventually bring the downfall of both dictators.

Mr. Payson was a handsome man in his mid-forties of tall, slim, athletic build. He came from a Maine background and had graduated from Yale, where he rowed on the varsity crew. On our first meeting he confided that his wife Joan shared his views with enthusiasm. She was a Whitney, the sister of John Hay (Jock) Whitney, and together they had inherited the Whitney fortune. The brother and sister did not see eye to eye on foreign policy. John Hay Whitney was as pro-intervention as she was "anti."

My own political and foreign policy convictions were all clearly on the record in the pages of the old *Life*. When Mr. Payson mentioned that he had invested over three hundred thousand dollars in the *Commentator* and would welcome some help both in responsibility and investment, I told him of the encouragement I had had on the old *Life* from Douglas Stewart and Jeremiah Milbank.

Hazel and I had seen quite a lot of Doug Stewart since our return from the South Seas voyage. Stewart, descended from an old New York family, was a widower. He was about the same age as Payson. Of stocky build, mustachioed, bald, he dressed and looked like a successful banker. As his name would indicate, his forebears were Scottish. He had many interests besides stock analysis. Often after we dined with him in his 68th Street apartment, he enjoyed playing a few popular tunes on the piano. At Harvard he had worked on two successful "Hasty Pudding" shows with Robert Sherwood. He liked sailing, and occasionally came up to Connecticut and sailed with us out of Riverside Yacht Club. He continued to view FDR's New Deal programs with dismay, and held the firm conviction that the President was intent on maneuvering us into war to solve the enormous U.S. unemployment problem. On the subject of war he was anything but a pacifist, having served in the Navy in World War I.

A series of meetings were forthwith arranged between Payson, Stewart, and Milbank, and by mid-1940 a partnership was established, duly registered as the Payson-Stewart Publishing Company. I was invited to come in as editor of the revitalized and enlarged magazine, which was to be called *Scribner's Commentator*. Mr. Payson had purchased the name Scribner's a short time before the merger.

So that readers might know where we stood, we announced our editorial aims and program in type bold and clear:

> WE BELIEVE: That America should concentrate on defending America with all the might, skill, and resources that make the United States the greatest nation on earth. With sanity, unselfish efficiency, and concentration on our own preparedness *now* we can stop any nation that is foolish enough to think it can launch a 3,000-mile attack on us.
> WE BELIEVE: That America is our one hope and our first allegiance. We are against the introduction into this country of all foreign *isms* antagonistic to democracy, whether they be communism, nazism, fascism, or socialism.

Just as we were organizing our editorial crusade against what we believed to be Mr. Roosevelt's push for war, Gen. Hugh S. Johnson, by coincidence, took the words right out of our mouths. It will be recalled that he had been head of Roosevelt's NRA and was in the President's inner circle of advisers until he disassociated himself from the New Deal over the drift to war. General Johnson felt so strongly that U.S. neutrality was being breached that he broadcast his views on the air over the CBS network, which, of course, we printed with enthusiasm. These are a few of the highlights of that address:

> America is being rushed into a fateful choice between involvement with war by its own warlike acts, or keeping out of war as long as it can and taking every moment of that precious respite to get ready to defend its shores. . . .
> There is no disagreement as to permitting England to buy from our industries whatever war materiel those industries can make and sell. But it is now proposed to send the ships of our navy, the war planes of

our inadequately equipped air forces, the artillery and small arms of our army to England. . . .

In the whole development of international law it has always been recognized that any nation not at war may permit either of two belligerents to buy in its markets without committing itself to war. But it has been equally recognized that for any nation as such to furnish either belligerent with warcraft, ammunition, and guns is an act of war against the other belligerent. . . .

There is not the slightest doubt in the world that Mr. Roosevelt is committed to the hilt to this course of WAR NOW.

IX

America Chooses Neutrality

IT WAS DURING THE early summer months of 1940, while we were reorganizing the magazine, that I first became acquainted with Colonel Lindbergh. In four radio addresses to the nation Lindbergh had very clearly expressed the views we held—that America rearm for any eventuality and resist in every way the drift of the Administration toward involvement in the conflict. I had saved the Lindbergh radio addresses that had been printed in the *New York Times*. It seemed to me that *Scribner's Commentator* could render a valuable public service by collecting the material in pamphlet form and distributing it on a nonprofit basis to our readers.

A phone call from the Milbank office to Juan Trippe of Pan American World Airways speedily resulted in a visit with Charles A. Lindbergh. He came to lunch with Douglas Stewart and me at the Stewart apartment and told us right off that he approved our proposal to print and distribute the pamphlet.

It was a rare privilege to meet and talk leisurely with this man about whom so many millions of words had been written, and about whom so many malicious untruths were being published since he had chosen a collision course with the White House. Frank, amusing, informative, smiling, self-effacing—he was all those things. When we asked him about the response to his radio talks, he replied that so many sacks of mail and telegrams had been received that there had been a serious handling and storage problem. Thanks to a kind offer from the Ford organization, all the communications had been stored in New York City in a Ford building at 1710 Broadway. When asked about the type of response, he said a check on several of the bags of mail selected at random showed a 95 per cent favorable response. He said he regretted that all the letters and telegrams could not be answered.

I suggested that we have a competent writer do a careful analysis of the mail and produce an article for us that might in a way acknowledge the effort made by so many people to respond to the speeches. The Colonel agreed to this and also gave us permission to make a mailing list for our own use in subscription promotion mailing.

After lunch we were told something of the feeling on Capitol Hill regarding the controversy. The Colonel had recently made several trips to Washington and had conferred with a dozen key senators and congressmen of both parties and had met only one man, Sen. Edward Burke of Nebraska, who leaned toward intervention in the war. The Colonel had had frequent, encouraging visits with Sen. Harry Byrd of Virginia. The roster of prominent legislators standing firmly for a U.S. policy of nonintervention included such senators as Vandenberg, Taft, Lodge, Johnson, Wheeler, Borah, Shipstead, Bailey, George, Gerry, Lundeen, Walsh, Nye, Bennett Champ Clark, D. Worth Clark, Reynolds, and La Follette. Congressman James van Zandt of Pennsylvania had been especially outspoken. His credentials to disagree with the President were perfect. He had been National Commander of the American Legion.

Between visits to Washington Lindbergh had had many conferences in New York with ex-President Hoover, whom he found to be 100 per cent in agreement with his views.

During our first visit with Lindbergh, Stewart and I were curious to know something of the circumstances that had led him to make his radio addresses. The details on this were not to be revealed until the publication of the Lindbergh *Wartime Journals*[1] many years later. In his diary entry of September 7, 1939, Lindbergh wrote: "I do not intend to stand by and see this country pushed into war if it is not absolutely essential to the welfare of the nation. Much as I dislike taking part in politics and public life, I intend to do so if necessary to stop the trend which is going on in this country." Lindbergh at that moment in history was actively involved in research work and consultation with the War Department, reporting directly to Gen. H. H. Arnold, head of the U.S. Army Air Force. Before delivering his first radio address Lindbergh told General Arnold of his intention to speak out as a private citizen against American involvement in the war. He received the

General's assurance that he saw no reason to advise him not to do so. When, however, Arnold told Secretary of War Woodring of Lindbergh's intention, the Secretary said that such a speech would be very displeasing to the Administration. Then, just a few hours before Lindbergh was to broadcast, a verbal message from Secretary Woodring's office was delivered to General Arnold. The message was relayed to Lindbergh by his old friend, Lt. Col. Truman Smith: "If Lindbergh would cancel his speaking plans, he would be offered a newly created Cabinet post as Secretary of Air."

The night of the broadcast, September 15, 1939, Lindbergh wrote in his diary: "This offer on Roosevelt's part does not surprise me after what I have learned about his Administration. It does surprise me, though, that he thinks I might be influenced by such an offer."

From September, 1939, when German and Russian troops moved into Poland and Hitler offered peace terms to England and France, Lindbergh believed that the Fuehrer's alliance with Stalin would prove short-lived. Lindbergh, Hoover, Taft, Vandenberg, and hundreds of prominent Americans believed that Germany's logical ultimate enemy was Russia, and only in that direction would Germany find the additional "living space" it sought. Therefore, they reasoned, peace between Germany and the West was desirable and possible.

When men as divergent as Ambassador Joseph Kennedy and John L. Lewis, realizing that England was powerless to win a war against Hitler without total U.S. participation, suggested that a negotiated peace was in order, they were ridiculed and lambasted by the pro-war groups led by the White House clique, who claimed that Hitler was out to conquer the U.S. and "the world."

It is fascinating therefore to discover that no less a figure than Churchill's top war chief, Field Marshal Viscount Alanbrooke,[2] was later to assess German war aims as follows:

Hitler's ultimate objective never changed. He sought eastward expansion of the Reich at the expense first of the Versailles Treaty States and then of Soviet Russia.

Because he was a central European with little feeling for the sea, and because he had a certain admiration for England — born of her valour in the first war and her supposed Teutonic origin—he had wished to make an ally of her and leave her her naval power and Empire. Yet, though he had made a pact with Russia and freed his hands to attack the Western Powers, his goal remained the same—not the overseas empire and seaborne trade of Britain and France, but the continental spaces, the wheat and oil of Russia, the Ukraine and the Caucasus.

At the outset of the Polish campaign he had therefore ordered his troops in the West to stand strictly on the defensive and do nothing that might turn Britain's and France's nominal declaration of war into an active one.

In early May, 1940, as the British Expeditionary Army was retreating to Dunkirk and France was about to surrender, a spate of articles appeared in the pro-war press of New York and Washington to the effect that the U.S. was next on Hitler's list for conquest and that we were in mortal danger of invasion.

To answer this Colonel Lindbergh went on the air May 19 at 9:30 P.M. over the nationwide network of CBS. The gist of his address is contained in these paragraphs:

> Let us not be confused by this talk of invasion. The defense of America is as simple as the attack is difficult when the facts are known.
>
> A foreign power could not conquer us by dropping bombs on this country unless the bombers were accompanied by an invading army. Great armies must still cross oceans by ship. As long as we maintain reasonable defense forces there will be no invasion by foreign aircraft. No foreign navy will dare approach within bombing range of our coasts.
>
> Let us stop this hysterical chatter of calamity and invasion. If we desire peace we need only stop asking for war. No one wishes to attack us and no one is in a position to do so.

According to the diaries of Henry Morgenthau, Jr.[3] this particular Lindbergh speech infuriated FDR more than any of the others. To Morgenthau FDR declared, after reading the speech, "I am absolutely convinced that Lindbergh is a Nazi." The President was further enraged by the tens of thousands of letters praising the Lindbergh speech delivered to the White House and Capitol Hill urging neutrality and peace. The Associated Press reported that the Senate and House mailrooms received, in just one day, the staggering total of 200,000 letters, telegrams, and postcards — and 95 per cent carried the message "KEEP OUT OF THIS WAR."

The day after the Colonel's speech FDR ordered that all incoming letters and telegrams critical of White House policy be turned over to the FBI to be scanned for subversives and fifth columnists, and the following day, May 21, 1940, was the historic date that a President of the U.S. first authorized the Attorney General to commence the bugging of private phone lines.

In the same month Roosevelt received Duff Cooper, former First Lord of the Admiralty, at a luncheon for two in the President's study at the White House.[4] Mr. Cooper wrote of his host: "He was then evolving his theory of the Four Freedoms, about which he talked to me, and also the problem of unemployment." The latter remained a serious drawback to the country's economic recovery. In 1940 there were still 11,000,000 unemployed in the U.S. Some 16,000,000 Americans were destined to be in uniform in the crusade for FDR's Four Freedoms.

During June, while the Republicans were preoccupied with choosing their candidate for President, Roosevelt was in daily touch with Winston Churchill, now Prime Minister. Diplomatic pouches reaching the White House brought details of the British retreat to Dunkirk and the ferrying of some 300,000 troops across the Channel to England. With the British evacuated and remnants of the French army fleeing before the Germans, the French seat of government was moved from Paris to Tours. French Premier Reynaud had already cabled an urgent appeal to President Roosevelt begging for help. In his desperate desire to keep France in the war, Churchill flew to Tours and had a dramatic confrontation with Reynaud, Marshal Pétain, and General Weygand.

Before takeoff June 11 Churchill sent this cable to FDR:

> The French have sent for me again, which means that crisis has arrived. Am just off. Anything you can say or do to help them now may make the difference. We are also worried about Ireland. An American Squadron at Berehaven would do no end of good, I am sure.

Of his meeting with the French Churchill wrote:

> In effect the discussion ran on the following lines. I urged the French Government to defend Paris. I emphasized the enormous absorbing power of the house-to-house defense of a great city upon an invading army. I reminded Marshal Pétain how in 1918 Clemenceau had said, "I will fight in front of Paris, in Paris and behind Paris." The Marshal replied with dignity that in those days he had "a mass of maneuver of upwards of sixty divisions. Now there was none. Making a ruin of Paris would not effect the final event."

Three days later the Germans entered Paris, and Churchill sent the most strongly worded of several pleas to FDR:

I am personally convinced that America will in the end go to all lengths, but this moment is critical for France. A declaration that the United States will if necessary enter the war might save France.

Roosevelt found it difficult to answer this, since he knew he was due to be "drafted" within the month to run for a third term, and he would have to run on a "no war" slogan. The best he could do for France at the moment was to send a cheery cable of goodwill to Reynaud promising redoubled material aid and adding: "The magnificent resistance of the French and British Armies has profoundly impressed the American People. . . .I am personally particularly impressed by your declaration that France will continue to fight on behalf of Democracy even if it means slow withdrawal, even to North Africa and the Atlantic."

Back again at 10 Downing Street, Mr. Churchill sent a long cable to Reynaud urging him to fight on. In it he reported:

On returning here we received a copy of President Roosevelt's answer to your appeal of June 10th. Cabinet is united in considering this magnificent document as decisive in favour of the continued resistance of France. . . . If France on this message continues in the field and in the war, we feel that the United States is committed beyond recall to take the remaining step, namely, becoming a belligerent in form as she already has constituted herself in fact.

On June 22 Reynaud signed the armistice agreement with Germany that put France officially out of the war.

And so, as of July, 1940, with Britain's only fighting ally out of the war, Lloyd George once again urged the Prime Minister to consider peace feelers emanating from the German capital.

According to Liddell Hart: "It is one of the most extraordinary features of history that Hitler and the German Supreme Command had made no plans or preparations to carry the fight to England. So sure was Hitler that peace on generous terms would be acceptable to Britain, he informed his generals that the war was over. Leaves were granted, a part of the Luftwaffe was shifted to other potential fronts, and thirty-five divisions were ordered demobilized."

On July 22 Harold Nicolson, M.P., at his post in the Ministry of Information, wrote in his diary: "Philip Lothian telephones wildly from Washington begging Halifax not to say anything in his broadcast tonight which might close the door to peace. Lothian claims that he knows the German peace terms and that they are most satisfactory."

Halifax had already been told by Churchill that there could be no peace with Germany. The Prime Minister had turned a deaf ear to peace proposals advanced through the Vatican and to the British Embassy in Washington by the German Chargé d'Affaires there. He had cabled the embassy: "Lord Lothian should be told that on no account to make any reply to the Chargé d'Affaires' message."

While Churchill and Roosevelt had been busily occupied advising the French that they should never negotiate a peace with Germany, Hitler's ally, Stalin, seized the opportunity to annex the three Baltic states, Latvia, Lithuania, and Estonia, thus putting some six million more souls behind the iron curtain.

X

The Battle of Britain Won

TWO MONTHS WENT BY before we saw the Colonel again. The Lindberghs spent part of July, 1940, at North Haven, the Morrow family summer home in Maine. In August the Colonel went to Chicago to speak to an audience of some forty thousand at Soldiers' Field. There he stayed at the home of Col. Robert McCormick, publisher of the *Chicago Tribune*. He was introduced to the crowd by Avery Brundage, President of the American Olympic Association.

Shortly after returning from his Chicago appearance the Colonel invited Stewart and me to dinner at Lloyd Manor, which the Lindberghs were then renting at Lloyd Neck, Long Island. It was suggested we take the 5:39 train to Huntington and bring our swimming gear. The Colonel met us at the station and after a short drive pulled up at the entrance to the house, a well-preserved, prerevolutionary, two-story dwelling in a setting of large chestnut trees.

We were welcomed at the door by the Colonel's gracious wife and introduced to their young sons, Jon, aged eight, and Land, three. We were put further at ease by a friendly introduction to Thor, a large police dog that had been taught to salute with one paw and say "hello" with two quick barks.

Lindbergh, Stewart, and I then changed into swimming things and were soon immersed in the refreshingly cool waters opposite the lighthouse at the entrance to Oyster Bay. We had been swimming only a short while when we suddenly discovered that the Colonel had disappeared. A very long two minutes later he just as

Cover of a 1932 issue of the satirical *Life*, edited by the author, which riled the French Chamber of Deputies.

Imaginary scene in the Time, Inc. offices, drawn by the author and published in a 1932 issue of the satirical *Life*. This page was also reprinted later in the official *History of Time, Inc.*

Editorial cartoon by Gregor Duncan in the satirical *Life*, May , 1935, which caused the magazine to be banned in Germany.

Thirty-two-foot yacht *Viator* at anchor in Papetoai Bay, the island of Moorea.

Lindbergh at the rostrum in Manhattan Center, New York, April 23, 1941.

Lloyd George addressing a political rally, 1935.

The Bettmann Archive Inc.

September, 1939 — Senate mailroom (above) went on double shifts to handle the quarter million neutrality letters a day.

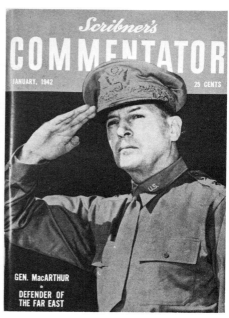

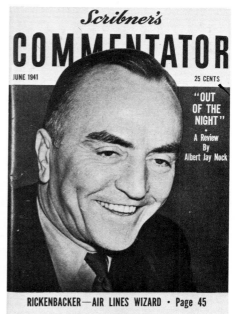

Typical *Scribner's Commentator* front covers, 1941-42.

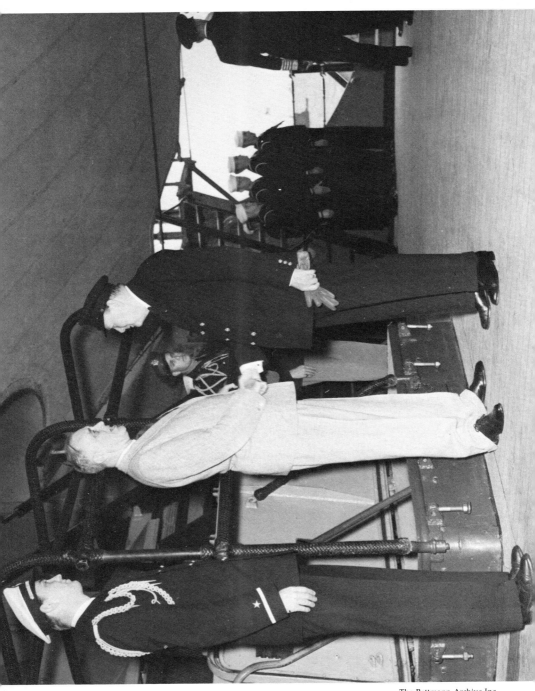

The battleship meeting of Roosevelt and Winston Churchill in August, 1941, with FDR's sons Franklin, Jr. and Elliott in attendance.

suddenly reappeared—and in each hand he held a large Oyster Bay oyster. "I just wanted to show you that there are still a few of these things left around here," he said, grinning.

During our swim a lovely blue-hulled yawl, with spinnaker flying, glided past the lighthouse, and the Colonel pointed to it with admiration. He said that he and Anne had always wanted to do some sailing, but knew little about the sport aside from a bit of small boat sailing they had done in Maine. When he asked if I had done any sailing, Doug Stewart kicked a cascade of water into the air and with a loud guffaw said, "Watch out, Colonel, you may be told more about sailing than you care to hear." I straight away explained that compared to many of our sailing friends Hazel and I considered ourselves rank amateurs. But I managed to admit that we had done some sailing in the Society Islands and that we had recently taken our small sloop *Mai Tai* on our annual cruise to Nantucket and back. The Colonel asked many questions and showed keen interest in my abbreviated replies. When we returned to the house he gave Anne a summary of my remarks. We learned that the Lindberghs were hoping that during the coming winter they might join an old family friend at Fort Myers, Florida, and sail among the tiny islands off the coast of the Everglades.

Dinner on the veranda was intimate and informal. We agreed that we were greatly disappointed Taft had not won the Republican nomination. We knew he could have been counted on to honor the plank in the party platform declaring for nonintervention in the war. All we knew about Wendell Willkie was what we had read in *Time* and *Life*, where he had been presented as nothing less than a genius. The Luce magazines had repeatedly referred to the other Republican contenders as "inept and bumbling." It was obvious to us that Willkie, as the Luce-endorsed candidate, could be expected to follow the Luce-endorsed foreign policy of FDR.

Another topic of interest we discussed was the newly formed Committee to Defend America by Aiding the Allies, under the chairmanship of William Allen White, venerable editor of the *Emporia* (Kansas) *Gazette*. This committee, sponsored by the White House, was already having trouble within its ranks. According to reports in the press, the board of directors of the CDAAA was split into two factions—one for all-out aid short of war, one for declaring war on Germany at once. Since the public opinion polls showed that almost no one in the U.S. favored entering the war, ever, the White Committee people were in a quandary as to how to resolve their differences.

On one subject the White Committee executives were in complete agreement. The press releases of the committee had since May repeatedly pressed the suggestion that the U.S. transfer forty or fifty destroyers to Britain. The Colonel said he guessed that such a warlike act would be too much for FDR to try to get away with.

Each of the Lindberghs contributed to the evening's conversation with animation and optimism. The polls had made it apparent that for every interventionist in the country there were tens of thousands of noninterventionists. Even Roosevelt himself claimed to be a noninterventionist!

We discussed the anti-war and pro-war press. In New York the *Times* and *Herald Tribune* were very vocal behind Roosevelt's moves to take more and more "steps short of war." The *New York Daily News* was just as vocal in supporting the Lindbergh thesis that steps short of war meant war. Loudly interventionist were the *New York Post*, and a newcomer to the scene, the daily tabloid, *PM*.

The Scripps-Howard papers were cautious in their criticism of U.S. foreign policy, but Roy Howard, president of the chain, had often privately expressed to Lindbergh a sympathetic interest in his views. Across the nation the Hearst papers were as staunchly noninterventionist as Colonel McCormick's *Chicago Tribune*. At Hearst's personal direction his editors gave front-page headlines to all Lindbergh's speeches, as well as unlimited columns of favorable publicity to the anti-war cause.

In the magazine field both the *Saturday Evening Post* and *Collier's* favored Lindbergh's point of view and ran pieces by him. The *Reader's Digest* had published several articles by both Charles and Anne Lindbergh. At the same time the Luce Press, *Time, Life,* and *Fortune,* were all out for more intervention and more involvement no matter what the risk. *Life* had gone so far as to run a nightmarish sequence of drawings showing how the U.S. could be invaded by hostile armies from abroad. The portrayal of the destruction of the U.S. fleet off Brazil was startling. Even more startling was the march through our coastal cities by jackbooted hordes of conquerors, and the ultimate scene of U.S. envoys suing for peace in Philadelphia's Independence Hall before a dictator's tribunal. This wild pictorial flight of fancy was supposed to answer the calm conclusions of a host of our generals and top military experts that this nation could not possibly be invaded if we maintained an adequate air force.

Overwhelming proof that the U.S. generals and Lindbergh were right in their faith in air power was the fact that even as we talked England was winning the Battle of Britain. Churchill was to declare in a speech to the House of Commons, on August 20, 1940:

In what may be deemed one of the decisive battles of the world the Royal Air Force, far from being destroyed, is triumphant — our fighter pilots remain unconquerable and supreme. Thus Britain has been saved. The Fuehrer must now decide to postpone any ideas of invasion indefinitely. . . .We have rearmed and rebuilt our armies and have ferried across the Atlantic in the month of July, thanks to our friends over there, an immense mass of munitions of all kinds: cannon, rifles, machine guns, cartridges and shell, all safely landed without the loss of a gun or a round. The whole British Army is at home. More than 2,000,000 determined men have rifles and bayonets in their hands tonight. We have never had armies like this in our island in time of war. The whole island bristles against invasion from the sea or from the air.

Our Navy is far stronger than it was at the beginning of the war. The seas and oceans are open. The U-boats are contained. The merchant tonnage under the British flag after a year of unlimited U-boat war, after eight months of mining attack, is larger than when we began. We have in addition under our control at least 4,000,000 tons of shipping from captive countries which has taken refuge here or in the harbours of the Empire. Our stocks of food of all kinds are far more abundant than in the days of peace, and a growing program of food production is on foot.

We have overflowing reserves of every type of aircraft and an ever mounting stream of production both in quantity and quality. Our new production already largely exceeds the enemy, and American production is only just beginning to flow in. Our bomber and fighter strengths now, after all this fighting, are larger than they have ever been. We believe we can continue the air struggle indefinitely.

We are now able to verify the results of bombing military targets in Germany. I have no hesitation in saying that this process of bombing the military industries and communications of Germany, and the air bases and storage depots from which we are attacked, may in another year attain dimensions hitherto undreamed of and affording the most certain if not the shortest road to victory.

Even if the Nazi legions stood triumphant on the Black Sea, or indeed upon the Caspian, even if Hitler was at the gates of India, it would profit him nothing if at the same time the entire economic and scientific apparatus of German war power lay shattered and pulverized at home.

The Lindberghs seemed pleased with my report that I had located the proper person to do the article on the Colonel's mail. At a recent luncheon with my friend Paul Palmer I had explained what we had in mind and asked his advice. Palmer, then a roving editor for the *Reader's Digest*, said he was presently between assignments and would very much like to do the article for us. Paul was a former editor of the *American Mercury*, a skilled journalist, and an ardent noninterventionist.

During the following month Palmer, with some clerical help furnished by our office, spent many time-consuming hours studying the contents of the crates of mail in the Ford storerooms. It was a tremendous job, but we thought the results fully justified the effort. The article, in part, follows:

COL. LINDBERGH'S MAIL —
AN AMERICAN PHENOMENON

by Paul Palmer

Is the Lindbergh mailbag, bursting with tens of thousands of listener-letters, the real answer to our warmongering press?

What do we Americans *really* think about Col. Charles A. Lindbergh? If an investigator from Mars, hunting the answer to that question, were to devote himself entirely to reading our metropolitan newspapers, he might conclude: "Not much." The most generous comment he could find in the *New York Times*, for instance, would be the deftly supercilious admonition that an aviator is not as competent to express an opinion on international affairs as, say, an editorial writer. And the worst he could read would be the blunt statement that the former hero of millions of Americans must now be openly denounced as a Fifth Columnist and a traitor to his country.

But the man from Mars, if he knew our extraordinary nation well enough, might have some reasonable doubt as to whether New York City newspapers truly reflect American opinion. What other source of information, leading to a competent answer to the question, would there be? Just one. The private, uncensored, unpublished opinion of tens of thousands of American citizens as they have voluntarily expressed themselves.

I have been granted access to this source. Col. Lindbergh has allowed me to spend hours going through the bales, boxes, and heaps of letters and telegrams which have come to him following his recent radio addresses. And the story that these essentially personal communications have to tell is a very different one from the sensational newspaper version. It is a straightforward American story that one does not soon forget.

The sheer number of the unsolicited letters and telegrams is little short of astounding. Just how many thousands there are no one yet knows because the end is not in sight. Lindbergh regrets that he cannot answer every individual letter: He could not do it were he to spend the rest of his life at the job.

In attempting to get an estimate of the extent of this nationwide response, I talked with several broadcasting officials. They told me that more Lindbergh mail was received at the radio stations than has ever before been received following an address by any other person in this country.

But this striking evidence of the young man's immense popularity among his fellow-citizens is not the extraordinary part of the story. The amazing fact is that over ninety-four per cent of these thousands of letters and telegrams express ardent approval of the Colonel's anti-war position.

In almost a score of years of newspaper and magazine work I have read many thousands of letters from angry and pleased subscribers; in the offices of Representatives and Senators in Washington I have often examined huge stacks of mail from aroused constituents; and in the headquarters of various polling organizations I have run through bales of ballots. But, in all that experience, I have never seen a mail so obviously honest, sensible, and genuine as that in Col. Lindbergh's boxes. The experienced reader of such missives learns to spot the vaporings of the lunatic fringe at a glance, easily detects organized letter-writing, and knows the genuine expression of honest opinion when he sees it. I can truthfully report that I have never before been so completely convinced that I was reading the unadorned, heartfelt opinion of a people. To study those letters, realizing they were from a nation struggling with the grim problem of war or peace, was a lesson in Americanism.

Of the batch of letters which I opened, the very first was in many ways typical. It came from California:

> I just listened to your splendid radio speech, and I want to commend you from the bottom of my heart. Of a family in which some member has fought for this country in every war in which it has been engaged, I yield to no one in devotion to my country and to the ideals on which it was founded. I believe, as you do, that we should plan and execute an adequate defense, but I am unalterably opposed to going into the current European war either openly or by the present drift which, if unchecked, will certainly take us there. I want

to do my little part to help, so if you will air-mail me a copy of your speech I will have it printed at my own expense and send it out to at least a thousand people.

In going through the letters I paid careful attention to the matter of nationality, because I was naturally curious to know how many of the letters had been written by Germans, or those of German descent. I was somewhat surprised to find German names in a very small minority, between eight and nine percent. A recitation of the letter-writers' names would sound like an average roll call in the A.E.F., or the list of members of the House of Representatives.

The Palmer article quoted from dozens of letters and telegrams of approval of the Colonel's position. Nowhere in the great mass of congratulatory mail did he find any indication of pro-Nazism or pro-Hitlerism, only a repetitive and constantly emphasized pro-Americanism. In the 6 per cent of the mail opposed to Lindbergh a great many of the communications were illiterate and incoherent. A number of extremists expressed themselves in language so abusive and obscene as to be unfit for print. Most of this hate mail was unsigned.

In September President Roosevelt, without consulting Congress, announced his transfer of "fifty overage destroyers to Britain" in exchange for ninety-nine-year leases of air base sites in Newfoundland, Bermuda, and the West Indies.

The post-war papers of Winston Churchill were to offer an interesting appraisal of this transaction:

There was of course no comparison between the intrinsic value of these antiquated and inefficient craft and the immense strategic security afforded to the United States by the enjoyment of the island bases. . . .There was another reason, wider and more powerful than either our need for the destroyers or the American need for the bases. The transfer to Great Britain of fifty American warships was a decidedly unneutral act by the United States. It would, according to all standards of history, have justified the German Government in declaring war upon them. The transfer of these destroyers to Britain in August 1940 was an event which brought the United States definitely nearer to us and to the war, and was the first of a long succession of increasingly unneutral acts in the Atlantic which were of the utmost service to us.

In a series of private messages to Roosevelt from mid-May onward Churchill had been asking for the fifty destroyers. The President managed to bypass Congress on the matter because the deal was a trade, not a sale. An Administration spokesman explained that since no money was involved, Congress was powerless to block the transaction.

The *St. Louis Post Dispatch* assessed the Destroyers-for-Bases deal as follows:

> Mr. Roosevelt today committed an act of war. . . . Under our Constitution treaties with foreign Powers are not legal without the advice and consent of the Senate. This treaty, which history may define as the most momentous one ever made in our history, was put over without asking the Senate for either its advice or consent. . . . The fact is that the transfer of the destroyers is not only a violation of American law but is also a violation of the Hague Covenant solemnly ratified by the United States Senate in 1908. . . . It is an outright act of war.

In a House of Commons speech September 5, 1940, announcing confirmation of the Destroyer deal, Mr. Churchill had this contradiction to offer, undoubtedly with tongue in cheek:

> Only very ignorant persons would suggest that the transfer of American destroyers to the British flag constitutes the slightest violation of international law or affects in the smallest degree the non-belligerency of the United States.

XI

An Era of Total Deceit Begins

FOLLOWING PUBLICATION of our article on Colonel Lindbergh's mail scores of favorable letters came in to the office daily, many of them accompanied by subscription checks. Charles Payson was especially pleased with a note from his friend Stuart Symington (who was later to serve as Secretary for Air under President Truman, and as the senior senator from Missouri for many years). It was typical of our growing acceptance:

W. S. SYMINGTON
1824 Washington Ave.
St. Louis, Mo.

October 18, 1940

Dear Chas:

Kindly send R.W. Herrick, President, Tecumseh Products Company, Tecumseh, Michigan, an annual subscription to *Scribner's Commentator* and send the bill to me here. Mr. Herrick is a comparatively unknown but very successful Middle Western businessman; a former associate of Henry Ford.

No doubt you know of General Wood's splendid talk in Chicago against this false war fever. If you would like to, by all means send him a subscription also.

Willkie made a wonderful talk here last night. He finally said what most of us think; this in an extemporaneous addendum to the speech, namely, that Roosevelt is only waiting for his re-election to put an American Army abroad if he can get away with it.

Regards,

STUART

The main highlight of the 1940 campaign was without doubt the speech Roosevelt delivered in the Boston Arena, when, over a national radio hookup, he spoke these famous words:

> And while I am talking to you mothers and fathers, I give you one more assurance. I have said this before, but I shall say it again and again and again: Your boys are not going to be sent into any foreign war.

Robert E. Sherwood was the ghostwriter who wrote those lines into the President's speech. In Sherwood's later book on Hopkins he said he did it because there was a tremendous anti-war sentiment in Boston and it was vital that FDR appear as the super-champion of peace. Sherwood shamefacedly admitted later: "I burn inwardly whenever I think of those words 'again — and again — and again.' But unfortunately for my own conscience I urged him to go the limit in this, feeling as I did that any risk of future embarrassment was negligible as compared with the risk of losing the election."

Following the Boston speech there were some skeptical editorials in the *Christian Science Monitor* and elsewhere to the effect that perhaps the President left a loophole for himself, in that *any* war in which the U.S. became involved would be a U.S. war, not a foreign war. To this challenge FDR replied in a speech broadcast on October 26: "No person in this government has ever suggested in any shape, manner, or form the remotest possibility of sending the boys of American mothers to fight on the battlefields of Europe."

But the President continued to be plagued by skepticism in the press, H. L. Mencken being its most articulate spokesman. He wrote:

> Roosevelt himself has promised categorically, on at least a dozen occasions, to keep us out of war, and with the most pious and eyeball-rolling solemnity, but no one in fact believes him. His foreign policy has been unbrokenly devious, dishonest, and dishonorable. Claiming all the immunities of a neutral, he has misled the country into countless acts of war, and there is scarcely an article of international law that he has not violated.

Because every move of the President toward deeper involvement was accompanied by another solemn pledge that his sole aim was to keep America out of the war, it became increasingly difficult for his adversaries in the Congress to challenge him. To most Americans a President's word of honor had always been considered inviolate.

The paradoxical situation was analyzed in a *Saturday Evening Post* editorial:

> The strategists who controlled the war propaganda knew better than to name their objectives. Therefore they advanced under such hypnotic phrases as "measures short of war" and "defend America by aiding the Allies." On the ground they occupied they could not be attacked, precisely for the reason that it was false ground. Anyone who challenged their slogan had to prove a meaning that was not literally there and one which they plausibly disclaimed. Measures short of war were to keep the country out of war. If you doubted it you were a fascist, a fifth columnist, or an appeaser.

Among the pro-war intellectuals were many who admired Roosevelt's political technique and excused his program of deception on the grounds that the end result would prove he knew what was best for Amerca. An old Russian proverb has it that "Even virtue needs guile to triumph over evil in this world." Harvard history professor Samuel Eliot Morison admitted that FDR was anything but forthright in his policy, but forgave him on the ground that he was "compelled to do good by stealth." Morison was certain that the end would justify the means.

Sir Liddell Hart, in his massive *History of the Second World War*, was to assess the final "good" the Roosevelt program brought to mankind, in a single sentence: "This catastrophic conflict, which ended by opening Russia's path into the heart of Europe, merely produced the looming fear of another war."

The reaction to our "Lindbergh Mail" piece, while overwhelmingly favorable, also produced a few pieces of unsigned crank mail. Several notes were given to name-calling. Two were death threats; these we turned over to the FBI.

Aside from the hate-mail, we received an occasional letter of criticism from a person of some standing. To these critics we always sent a polite reply. Here are letters from two well-known New York editors, both fellow members of the Players and the Dutch Treat Club.

FARRAR and RINEHART
Publishers
232 Madison Avenue
New York

My dear George:

Surely you haven't my name on any of your lists. I was shocked to get a solicitation to subscribe to *Scribner's Commentator*. It has been difficult for me to understand your position and your attitude, and my patience is strained to breaking point when I find in my morning mail your circular.

Sincerely yours,
JOHN
John Farrar

JOHN O'HARA COSGRAVE
39 East 79th Street
New York

George T. Eggleston
Editor, *Scribner's Commentator*

Dear Sir:

Sometime ago I made up my mind that persons who did not realize that Nazism is a direct threat to the kind of civilization we enjoy were morons or Fifth Columnists. If not either, then lamentably short-sighted. Don't you realize that if Hitler wins it will mean no more freedom of the seas, free enterprise, free speech, press or worship. There will be bombers over New York and our economic system in ruins.

Yours,

JOHN O'HARA COSGRAVE

In the case of John Farrar, the poor fellow received yet another of our subscription promotion circulars, despite my telling the promotion department to take his name off our lists. He was especially indignant because we had quoted George Washington's advice to his countrymen to avoid foreign entanglements.

Mr. George T. Eggleston
Scribner's Commentator

Dear Sir:
   Look, George Washington lived a long time ago. I don't wear the same kind of hair-do he did. If you want to that's your business. America is going ahead to assume her full responsibility in the world of nations and perhaps out of all this will come a decent stable order where our children will have learned to expect peace and freedom, and I'm darn sure that is what George Washington and Thomas Jefferson would have wanted America to help build.

Yours,

JOHN FARRAR

   Neither Farrar nor Cosgrave lived to see how FDR's foreign policy eventually extinguished liberty in a dozen countries around the world and created a Russia strong enough in nuclear weapons power to threaten every city in the U.S. with instant destruction.
   A surprising blast came from a person I had quite lost track of after the demise of the old *Life*. It was a telegram from Ralph McAllister Ingersoll, editor and publisher of the new Manhattan daily tabloid, *PM*.

CHARLES PAYSON, SCRIBNERS COMMENTATOR
654 MADISON AVENUE, N.Y.

WE ARE PUBLISHING AN ARTICLE DESCRIBING HOW WRITERS OF "FAN" MAIL TO LINDBERGH, THROUGH A LINK BETWEEN YOU AND HENRY FORD, WERE INCORPORATED INTO A MASTER LIST OF APPEASERS AND PRO-NAZIS AT FORD'S EXPENSE. IN FAIRNESS TO YOU, *PM* WOULD LIKE YOUR VERSION OF CIRCUMSTANCES UNDER WHICH THESE LETTERS WERE RECEIVED BY YOU AND TURNED OVER TO A GROUP OF SECRET FORD EMPLOYEES IN A SECRET ROOM IN THE FORD BUILDING AT 1710 BROADWAY, NEW YORK CITY.
   1. DO YOU SAY THAT FORD HAS NOTHING TO DO WITH SCRIBNER'S COMMENTATOR?
   2. WHY WERE THESE LISTS OF PRO-NAZIS USED AS A BASIS OF YOUR MAILINGS?
   3. WHERE IS THIS MASTER LIST NOW?
   4. WHAT USE ARE YOU AND HENRY FORD MAKING OF THIS LIST?

EDITOR *PM*

   We sent this message down to Payson's office at 120 Wall Street. His reaction was that the thing sounded so silly it didn't merit a reply. This was not the end of the matter, however. *PM*'s editors expanded their pipe dream into a whodunit section of their paper with full pages devoted to drawings and diagrams and ominous arrows showing the path from our offices to the "secret rooms" in the Ford building. Of course there had never been any secret about our using the Lindbergh letters for our mailing list. The list comprised the sort of people who were naturally predisposed to favor our editorial policy; thus the mailing resulted in a healthy increase in our subscription list.

The story of Ralph Ingersoll's launching of *PM* with Marshall Field as the principal angel has been told in detail in Field's authorized biography, written by Stephen Becker.[1]

According to the biography, Marshall Field III, in his early forties, was an unhappy and frustrated man. He badly needed psychiatric help and found it in the person of Gregory Zilboorg, a noted New York psychiatrist. After seeing Zilboorg five days a week for a year and a half, Field emerged from his analysis with the feeling that mere philanthropy was not fulfilling enough for a man with a net worth of over $100,000,000. He felt he must channel his life into more definitive paths of service. "He became intrigued by the new breed of educated, imaginative, impassioned public servants that the New Deal nurtured." According to stories in *Time* and the *Saturday Evening Post,* it was at this point in Field's life that he met Ralph Ingersoll, also a patient of Gregory Zilboorg.

At the time of Ingersoll's fortuitous meeting with Marshall Field, the ex-*Time* executive was raising money to launch his newspaper, and had already tapped several "liberal interventionists" for $100,000 each. Among the investors were such well-known names as Huntington Hartford, Philip Wrigley, Lessing and William Rosenwald, Dorothy Thompson, Payson's brother-in-law Jock Whitney, Lincoln Schuster of Simon and Schuster, and Harry Scherman, president of the Book-of-the-Month Club. Mr. Field listened only a few minutes to Ingersoll's sales pitch and declared, "Put me down for two of the hundred-thousand-dollar units. Thank you very much."

Ingersoll's promotion brochure presented prospective investors with the following credo:

> We believe that any newspaper should crusade in the interest of truth.
> We are without political affiliation because we believe political affiliations circumscribe crusades for truth.
> We are against people who push other people around.
> We propose to crusade for those who seek constructively to improve the way men live together.

Ingersoll also carried in his briefcase a letter from Franklin Roosevelt:

THE WHITE HOUSE

May 2, 1940

Dear Ralph,

This is to welcome *PM* to the New York and American scene. Your interesting prospectus leads me to believe that you are about to add a notable chapter to the history of our free press.

It is more important than ever in these fast moving times that people be fully, reliably, and quickly informed of significant events. They should get all available facts and get them straight.

FRANKLIN D. ROOSEVELT

Vol. 1, No. 1 of *PM* appeared on the newsstands of New York June 18, 1940. By nightfall the press run of half a million copies had been sold out. But by mid-August sales were down to 30,000, and several of the stockholders were disturbed by the prodigious losses. The paper needed a daily circulation of 200,000 to break even. To quiet the disgruntled investors Field stepped forward and bought them all out at twenty cents on the dollar. Thenceforth Field cheerily absorbed all the losses, stating: "I respect the basic conception with which *PM* was started. I am proud of *PM*'s persistent crusade against isolationism, international appeasement, and internal Fascist forces in America."

Promptly with Field's announcement of unlimited financial backing Ingersoll sounded off with a signed front-page editorial: "I denounce Col. Charles A. Lindbergh as the spokesman of the Fascist fifth column in America."

Before and soon after Roosevelt won his third term Doug Stewart and I had several more conferences with Colonel Lindbergh. On our second invitation to Lloyd Neck the Colonel had just returned from Detroit, where he had been visiting the senior Fords. In a meeting at the Ford offices he and Mr. Ford had been joined by Gen. Robert A. Wood, president of Sears Roebuck, and young R.D. Stuart, Jr., who was to become chairman of the Board of Quaker Oats. Stuart was a recent graduate of Yale, where he had led a campus no-foreign-war crusade. He had sought out General Wood and Mr. Ford for backing in his plan to form a national organization to buck the White House drive to war. Following this meeting, and with a promise of financial help from Mr. Ford, young Stuart returned to Chicago and enlisted the interest of an impressive number of prominent citizens in forming the National Committee to Defend America First, out of which grew the America First Committee.

The Colonel told us he had been asked to speak under the auspices of the new group and had agreed to do so. As we were about to leave Lloyd Manor on the evening of this conference, Stewart and I were presented with parting gifts — first edition copies of Anne Morrow Lindbergh's *The Wave of The Future*,[2] autographed by the author and, on a separate page, by the Colonel. Ten of the first copies off the press had been delivered to Lloyd Manor that morning. The book was soon to become a coast-to-coast best seller despite some vitriolic criticism by the pro-war press of New York. Anne Lindbergh's summation of her thoughts in *The Wave of The Future* eloquently supported the subtitle of the book, "An Expression of Faith":

> The leaders of Germany, Italy, and Russia have discovered how to use new social and economic forces. . . .I oppose as deeply as any American the forms this revolution has taken: aggression, terror, race or class persecution. . . .The evils we deplore in these systems are not in themselves the future, they are the scum on the wave of the future.
>
> It seems to me that our task, instead of crusading against an inevitable "revolution" or change in Europe, is to work toward a peaceful "revolution" here—or rather a reformation—to reform at home rather than crusade abroad.

During the fall months the America First headquarters in Chicago gained considerable momentum and announced a steering council with Gen. Robert E. Wood, chairman, supported by Gen. Thomas Hammond, Gen. Hugh S. Johnson, Capt. Edward Rickenbacker, Henry Ford, Avery Brundage, Hanford MacNider (former National Commander of the American Legion), Alice Roosevelt Longworth, Janet Ayer Fairbank, Mrs. Burton K. Wheeler, and Mrs. Bennett Champ Clark. This nucleus was in turn supported by several well-known business figures, including Jay C. Hormel of Hormel Packing, Sterling Morton of Morton Salt,

Edward L. Ryerson, Jr. of Inland Steel, William H. Regnery, president of the Western Shade Cloth Company, and Robert Young, railway magnate. Others active in the early organizing of America First were Robert M. Hutchins and William Benton, president and vice-president of the University of Chicago, advertising executive Chester Bowles, former Under-Secretary of State William Castle, and writers John T. Flynn, Kathleen Norris, Oswald Garrison Villard, John P. Marquand, Clarence Budington Kelland, Irvin S. Cobb, and Carl W. Ackerman, dean of the Columbia University School of Journalism.

Also during the fall months there was a feeling among noninterventionists in the East that a totally new committee should be set up to compete directly with the William Allen White group. To oppose famous small-town newspaper editor White, Hanford MacNider suggested the name of the editor of the Pulitzer Prize-winning *Cedar Rapids Gazette,* Vern Marshall. Marshall was named chairman of the new group, called the No Foreign War Committee, with the strong backing of Jeremiah Milbank, Charles Payson, and the Richardson brothers, owners of the Vick Chemical Company. Marshall came to New York for a month's tour as head of the committee, and during that time he raised enough money to sponsor full-page newspaper ads in a coast-to-coast anti-war crusade. When he returned to his job in Iowa, his Manhattan staff was absorbed into the New York chapter of America First, headed by the writer John T. Flynn and the investment banker Edwin Webster.

Payson, Stewart, and I continued to see the Colonel at luncheons and an occasional dinner. From him we learned something of the remarkable growth of the America First Committee, which soon had chapters in several hundred cities across the country. One small audience the Colonel addressed was of particular interest to him and to us as revealing the current feeling in the colleges. The Colonel spoke at Yale on the invitation of Kingman Brewster, editor of the *Yale Daily News*, and later president of Yale. Preceding and following the talk Lindbergh was the guest of Professor and Mrs. Whitney Griswold[3] at their home.

The Yale gathering was in Woolsey Hall, which has a seating capacity of three thousand. Every seat was occupied, and the walls were lined with standees. It must be underlined that this was not a mass meeting of young pacifists. The message they cheered was a plea for an invulnerably strong America, manned by an army, a navy, and an air force ready to die in defense of the United States, ready to destroy any aggressor bent on invasion from overseas. The Lindbergh thesis was clear-cut, as usual, and not open to misunderstanding. He stood for an impregnable America and noninvolvement in the European conflict.

During the period we were frequently seeing the Colonel I was occasionally asked by friends if I thought he had a sense of humor. He had indeed, a wonderful sense of humor. In conversation he was anything but the stiff-necked man with the mechanical heart so often depicted by his detractors. His tale of an encounter with Marshal Hermann Goering was one of the most amusingly told anecdotes I have ever heard. On one of Lindbergh's pre-war missions to Germany, on orders from the U.S. State Department to find out all he could about Nazi air strength, a U.S. Embassy official took him to Goering's Berlin residence for a visit. The Marshal greeted his callers garbed in a powder-blue uniform covered with medals. The Colonel said the Marshal looked as though he had just stepped out of the cast of a comic opera. After being ushered into a drawing room, the Colonel and his friend were startled to see a large lion cub saunter in through an open doorway. Upon sight of the lion Goering at once sat down in a large easy chair, and the animal climbed onto his lap, putting both forepaws on his shoulders. Goering, all smiles, seemed greatly pleased with himself for a few moments — then suddenly the Marshal's face turned beet-red as he rose, rolling the heavy beast onto the floor with an oath. The house pet had urinated on his master, completely saturating the powder-blue uniform. Goering thereupon disappeared for half an hour, to reappear in an all white-and-gold outfit, again bemedaled, and smelling to high heaven of eau de Cologne. The miscreant pet was not seen again.

Often in our conversations with Lindbergh he spoke admiringly of Henry Ford. Friendship between the two had begun in 1927 when the Colonel had taken Mr. Ford for a flight in the *Spirit of St. Louis* — the first time the automotive genius had ever been up in an airplane. Lindbergh saw Ford as a very human person, a great American in no way dominated by the machine age he had helped create. Over the years the Lindberghs had often been guests at Fair Lane, the Ford home near Dearborn. Both Mr. and Mrs. Ford had shown a keen interest in, and support of, the America First program since its inception. When I suggested to the Colonel that perhaps Mr. Ford could be induced to write an article for *Scribner's Commentator*, he called Detroit and arranged for Stewart and me to go out to the River Rouge plant for an interview.

When we arrived at the main entrance to the Ford plant for our 11:30 A.M. appointment and identified ourselves, we were immediately shown into the nearby office of Harry Bennett, where, after a few minutes chat, we were joined by Mr. Ford. Bennett fitted the several descriptions we had read of him—"a small, quick-moving, energetic, self-assured man." He greeted us with bone-crunching handshakes, saying he was glad our magazine was firmly in opposition to the pro-war propaganda so loudly promoted by much of the Eastern press. Bennett had been closely associated with Henry Ford since 1918. He was presently chief of personnel, labor relations, and plant security for the entire automotive empire.

After Mr. Ford joined us, shook hands, and motioned us to chairs, he turned to Bennett and said, "What can we do to help these fellows?" Bennett nodded to us for reply, and Stewart said, "We must tell you at once, Mr. Ford, that we are not here seeking financial help." I joined in and explained that our magazine would very much like to run an article by him, stating his views on the current drift of the Administration toward involvement in the war. He replied that no one had ever paid very much attention to his views on keeping out of foreign wars. He had always considered that our participation in the 1914-18 European war, in which tens of thousands of American lives had been needlessly sacrificed, was a tragic mistake. In 1939, when FDR first agitated for repeal of the Neutrality Act, Mr. Ford had declared: "If we change our stand one iota we will take the first step toward getting into this war." To reporters at the American Legion Convention in Chicago that year he repeated this opinion, adding: "We should not meddle in the affairs of any people. A lot of pressure will be brought to push us into the war. . . but I am confident that we can keep out." At the same time Mr. Ford shared the Lindbergh view and the American Legion view that the U.S. should build an invincible air force, army, and navy as guarantors against attack from any source. In fact, at the very moment of our interview, Ford engineers were perfecting plans for a new aircraft engine factory to be erected on an immense area adjoining the Rouge plant, a forty-million-dollar operation.

We were impressed that at the age of seventy-eight Mr. Ford, in manner and speech, seemed a much younger man. As I noticed the well-tailored gray business suit he wore, I thought of a Ford aphorism: "Mere wealth is unimportant to a man's happiness — after all, he can wear only one suit of clothes at a time."

Mr. Ford chatted easily with us over a wide range of subjects. He mentioned with emphasis a favorite Ford theme, the hope expressed in Tennyson's *Locksley Hall* that some day there would be a "parliament of man," a worldwide spirit of brotherhood, and an end to armed conflict. He abhorred the diabolical Hitler persecution of the Jews and the Stalin purges of the peasant farmers. He had a total revulsion of both Nazism and Communism. "Anything that breeds hate is repulsive to me," he said.

With a genuine show of interest he asked how our magazine was faring. When we told him something of our encouraging gains in circulation, and added we were finding it rather uncomfortable to publish in New York City, he observed that the U.S. was a very large country west of Manhattan, an enormous country with a much more American point of view than might be found in the East. When we parted, he said: "Yes, I will write down some of my thoughts for you. Goodbye and good luck."

We felt so greatly refreshed by our reception at the Rouge plant that instead of returning at once to New York, at my suggestion we made a visit to Lake Geneva, Wisconsin. I had often recalled with nostalgia drives to the shores of this beautiful lake during my two years in Chicago. I wanted Doug Stewart to see it. And in line with Mr. Ford's remarks about the atmosphere in America west of the Hudson I thought it might be the perfect spot to consider as a new headquarters for *Scribner's Commentator*. En route from Detroit to Lake Geneva we had a long and serious talk about the idea of a move out of New York. Our mention to Mr. Ford that we found it rather uncomfortable to publish in New York City was an understatement, to say the least, of the situation. The incessant attacks by the Marshall Field-Ingersoll press, calling Lindbergh, the America First Committee, and *Scribner's Commentator* pro-Nazi and pro-Fascist, had caused a number of news dealers to sabotage sales of our magazine. Recently two sacks of incoming mail had been stolen out of our mailroom. The theft of our mail was a most serious federal offense, and when we reported it to the FBI, several agents pursued the matter with vigor, but did not locate the culprit or culprits, or the missing mail.

Doug Stewart was instantly charmed by the setting and wooded surroundings of the little resort town of Lake Geneva on the lake - front.The November weather was cool and bracing, the dark blue water of the lake an empty expanse compared to the lively yacht-racing scenes I remembered from summer visits there. When we called on a prominent local realtor and told him of our exploratory plans, we found that he was not only a reader of our magazine but an active supporter of America First. He promised to make a survey of possible office arrangements in the town and write us concerning his findings.

The publication of our article by Henry Ford created a good deal of favorable publicity for *Scribner's Commentator*. Excerpts from the piece were picked up by all the wire services. Feature stories appeared in papers across the U.S. stressing the Ford belief that America's rightful place in world affairs was to fill the role of peacemaker to the warring nations.

Our article by Mr. Ford was, of course, dutifully denounced by Ingersoll's *PM*. The New York tabloid more loudly than ever shouted that mailing lists of *Scribner's Commentator* were part of a Lindbergh-Ford conspiracy to promote pro-Nazi peace propaganda in the U.S.

XII

The "Civilization in Danger" Hoax

WITH ALMOST A YEAR to go until Pearl Harbor, the most unusual character ever to represent a President of the United States turned up at No. 10 Downing Street. Winston Churchill was to write:

> On January 10, 1941, a gentleman came to see me with the highest credentials. Telegrams had been received from Washington stating that he was the closest confidant and personal agent of the President. Thus I met Harry Hopkins, that extraordinary man who played and was to play a sometimes decisive part in the whole movement of the war. At our first meeting I soon comprehended the outstanding importance of his mission. With gleaming eye and constrained passion he said: "The President is determined that we shall win the war together. Make no mistake about it. He has sent me here to tell you that at all costs and by all means he will carry you through, no matter what happens to him—there is nothing that he will not do so far as he has human power."

Shortly after Hopkins arrived in England he spent a weekend with Mr. Churchill at Chequers, and told his host something of the overall war sentiment in the United States. He said that Navy Secretary Knox and War Secretary Stimson were spokesmen for a group representing the 10 to 15 per cent of the country in favor of an immediate declaration of war. A Joe Kennedy group was for helping Britain, but to "make damn sure not to get in the war." A third division (presumably the millions of Americans backing the America First movement) was described by Hopkins as "a small group of Nazis and Communists sheltering behind Lindbergh, who declared for a negotiated peace." Hopkins summed up: "A majority supported the President in his determination to send the maximum regardless of risk." This conversation was recalled by Churchill's wartime secretary, John Colville,[1] who also noted in his diary at the time: "After dinner Hopkins expressed the belief that if America came into the war the incident would be with Japan."

According to the Colville diaries, Harry Hopkins, Ambassador Gil Winant, and FDR's Roving Ambassador Averell Harriman were regular weekend guests at Chequers whenever they were not needed elsewhere. Colville recalled a memorable after-dinner conversation over the brandies when Winant received a message from the President saying he was ordering U.S. naval patrols to penetrate deeper into the war zones . Of this Colville wrote:

> I asked if that might mean war between the United States and Germany. "That's what I hope," said Harriman. Winant smiled his assent.

General Ismay, who was then Mr. Churchill's chief staff officer, wrote a rather more rounded-out description of Hopkins and his mission in his *Memoirs of Lord Ismay:*[2]

> Harry Hopkins was as unlike one's picture of a distinguished envoy as it was possible to be. He was deplorably untidy; his clothes looked as though he was in the habit of sleeping in them, and his hat as though he made a point of sitting on it. He seemed so ill and frail that a puff of wind would blow him away. But we were soon to learn that in that sickly frame there burned a fire which no flood could quench. Not even Churchill was more single-minded in his determination that Nazism should be remorselessly crushed.
>
> Churchill at once recognized the importance of this unusual type of envoy and decided to constitute himself Hopkins's personal guide, philosopher, and friend. He scarcely let him out of his sight. The first tour on which he took him was to Scapa Flow to inspect the Home Fleet.

After two days inspecting the fleet and naval establishments, Churchill, General Ismay, Charles Wilson (then Churchill's personal physician, later Lord Moran), and Hopkins went to Glasgow, where they attended a small dinner party hosted by the Secretary of State for Scotland.

Both Ismay in his memoirs and Wilson have described the highlight of this dinner in almost identical terms:[3]

Hopkins was persuaded to say a few words. Turning to the PM he said, "I suppose you wish to know what I am going to say to President Roosevelt on my return. Well, I am going to quote to you from the Book of Ruth: 'Whither thou goest I will go; and where thou lodgest, I will lodge: thy people *shall be* my people and thy God my God: where thou diest, will I die.'"

According to Ismay and Wilson this short flight of oratory stunned the dinner party. Ismay thought the statement indiscreet, but said: "It moved us all very deeply. It was a small party and the story never leaked." As Wilson recorded his reaction: "I was surprised to find the P.M. in tears. He knew what it meant."

This was secret diplomacy to the nth degree. From that moment in January, 1941, the British understood that it was only a question of time until the necessary divisions of American troops would arrive in England for an invasion of the Continent. But of course no one in the U.S. knew of this commitment.

Almost at the precise moment Harry Hopkins was delivering Mr. Roosevelt's pledge we editors of *Scribner's Commentator* were planning a piece for our February, 1941, issue based on Mr. Roosevelt's recent campaign pledge disavowing secret commitments. Four months earlier, in a preelection speech in Philadelphia, Roosevelt had stated categorically: "There is no secret treaty, no secret obligation, no secret commitment, no secret understanding in any shape or form direct or indirect with any other government or any other nation in any part of the world to involve this nation in any war."

Our proposed article was to be titled "WILL FDR KEEP THIS PLEDGE?" We were hoping to have the article written by Joseph W. Martin, House Minority Leader and Chairman of the Republican National Committee. Martin was on record as to why he distrusted the promises, pledges, and disavowals of the President. "Franklin Delano Roosevelt," said Martin, "has broken no less than fifty-seven major promises in eight years."

Immediately following the Hopkins mission of January, 1941, Churchill dispatched a secret British military mission to Washington. This group, comprising an air commodore, two rear admirals, and a major general, sat in continuing sessions with top U.S. military officials through all the months preceding Pearl Harbor. British war analyst Ronald Lewin wrote of this procedure:

Nothing illustrates better the fruitful but Alice-in-Wonderland relationship with the United States than these staff talks. The talks were conducted in the greatest possible secrecy. The British were supposed to be "technical advisors to the British Purchasing Commission" and always wore civilian clothes The dominating theme of these conferences was that should Britain and the United States become jointly involved in a war with Germany and Japan, their concentration of effort would be on *Germany First*. This plan was endorsed by the Chiefs of Staff of both countries.[4]

Our article on secret commitments never materialized because suddenly the Congress, the public, and the press were concerned with the controversy over a new White House proposal "to keep us out of war" labeled lend-lease. This program was embodied in a bill Roosevelt submitted to the Congress to nullify all existing neutrality legislation. To get the bill off to a dramatic start he had gone on the air in December, 1940, with a fireside chat in which he declared: "Never before since Jamestown and Plymouth Rock has our American civilization been in such danger." He stated that the Germans planned to conquer all of Europe and then invade America. He warned that "the distance between Africa and Brazil is less than from Washington to Denver . . . . If Great Britain goes down all of us would be living at the point of a gun."

In contrast to the Roosevelt message of disaster, Mr. Churchill hailed the close of the year 1940 with the observation: "We had beaten the German Air Force—there had been no invasion. The citadel of the Commonwealth and Empire could not be stormed."[5] Referring to September 15, 1940, as the date of the demise of Hitler's invasion plans, Churchill predicted that Hitler would now turn his attention East against Russia.

In a secret memo titled "Invasion"[6] Churchill prepared for the Commander in Chief Home forces, dated July 10, 1940, he said there was no evidence that the enemy had ever seriously contemplated invasion. He added: "It would be a most hazardous, and even suicidal operation to commit a large army to the accidents of the sea in the teeth of our numerous armed patrolling vessels, of which two or three hundred are always at sea. A surprise crossing should be impossible, the invaders would be easy prey."

Churchill also stated that some forty of His Majesty's destroyers were prowling Channel waters day and night to interfere with and break up any attempted landings: "It may be further added that at present there are no signs of any assemblies of enemy ships or small craft sufficient to cause anxiety."

British Intelligence knew all along that the Germans had not prepared the special landing craft or built the special armored vehicles required for an invasion. While Churchill was firm in his conviction that Britain was safe from invasion across the twenty-mile Channel, Roosevelt and the New York pro-war press kept up a barrage of scare propaganda warning Americans of a German invasion from across the Atlantic Ocean. In New York Mayor La Guardia had set up as early as November, 1939, a committee of air raid wardens, who thereafter scanned the heavens nightly on the watch for German bombers. In the issue of *Life* for June 3, 1940, Henry Luce declared in a full-page editorial: "America faces the greatest challenge to its survival since the Civil War."

Curiously enough, during the summer months of 1940 when Mr. Roosevelt and Mr. Luce were warning of the doom of Civilization, the British were carrying on business as usual. The *Times* of London for August 20, 1940, in an editorial praising the Churchill speech of that date, added: "It can now be officially stated that the British are actually shown to have dumped twice as much explosives on Germany to date as the Germans on Britain."

The entertainment column in the same issue of the *Times* announced that "*The Chocolate Soldier* is being revived at the Shaftesbury Theatre, and two revivals for next week are Priestley's *Cornelius* and Sutton Vane's *Outward Bound*. On Thursday Sadler's Wells Ballet *Baraban* will be revived."

During July, August, and September, 1940, as the Battle of Britain was being fought and won in the skies around London the columns of the *Times* sounded no hint of the fall of Western Civilization. In another entertainment note in August was the comment: "The crowded state of Queen's Hall last night showed that it can no longer be said that Haydn and Mozart are not popular. The London Symphony Orchestra was at its best." In the horse racing columns was the announcement that "Race schedules are to be resumed on all courses available and on days when there will be least interference with war work. National Hunt meetings may be also resumed as the flat racing season comes to an end."

On December 12, 1940, Britain's ambassador to Washington suddenly died. Churchill observed in his memoirs that this was at a very critical moment in U.S.-British relations and it was vital that Lord Lothian's post be immediately filled "by an outstanding national figure and a statesman versed in every aspect of world politics. I invited Mr. Lloyd George to take the post."

Churchill had first checked by cable with FDR and gotten approval of his choice. Both leaders realized that if Lloyd George were back in the government, he would be silenced once and for all as a proponent of peace negotiations. According to Churchill: "His outlook on the war and the events leading up to it was from a different angle from mine. There could be no doubt, however, that he was our foremost citizen and that his most incomparable gifts and experience would be devoted to the success of his mission."

Churchill had long talks with Lloyd George during the next two days urging him to take the assignment. After the seventy-seven year-old Welshman gracefully declined "for reasons of age," he told his friend Lord Hankey, then Secretary of the Committee of Imperial Defence and Chairman of the Scientific Advisory Committee, that he "could never come into a government that took the view expressed by Churchill that he would never listen to peace terms." In speaking of this afterward Hankey added: "My views and those of Lloyd George always coincided."[7]

Churchill next asked Lord Halifax to take the appointment. Halifax accepted, although he had formerly been among the group of peers who sought a peaceful settlement with Hitler.

The first response to the FDR announcement of the danger to American civilization came, oddly enough, from the high seat of interventionism. William Allen White promptly resigned his chairmanship of the Committee to Defend America by Aiding the Allies. Colonel Lindbergh was rather taken aback as he received the news of White's defection from the Roosevelt-sponsored group. In his diary the Colonel recorded:

Roy Howard called this afternoon and said William Allen White had just telegraphed a statement to him for release to the press. He read it to me over the phone. I was amazed as I listened. White says, among other things, that we should not carry contraband into war zones, that we should not repeal the Johnson Act (prohibiting loans to countries that had defaulted on World War I debts), or use our Navy to convoy. He says that if he were making a motto for use of his committee it would be "The Yanks Are Not Coming."

Publication of White's statement across the nation, with its implication that the Roosevelt Lend-Lease Act was in fact a pro-war bill, was a bitter blow to the President.

Finally, after weeks of prolonged debate, the Lend-Lease Act was passed by the House 260 to 165 and by the Senate 60 to 31.

Although Senators Taft, Vandenberg, Wheeler, and Byrd ably led the fight to defeat the bill, majorities in both the House and Senate chose to believe the President's positive assurance that passage of the Lend-Lease Act was the only sure way to keep America out of the war.

Thanks, however, to the efforts of Senators Taft, Vandenberg, and their colleagues, the essential clauses of the original Neutrality Act remained intact. Despite Roosevelt's desire to arm merchant ships and send them into the combat zones, the final provisions of the Lend-Lease Act specifically prevented this. Our position on the magazine was that the Roosevelt pro-war group should have been well satisfied with the way American goods had flowed and continued to flow to England. United States Maritime Commission figures showed that during the previous year 96 per cent of the cargoes leaving U.S. ports for England had reached their destination.

Preceding the Lend-Lease hearings Doug Stewart and I made several trips to Washington at the invitation of senators favorable to our editorial policy. In one memorable conference with Senators Vandenberg, Wheeler, Nye, and Bennett Champ Clark we were given a piece of advice by Senator Vandenberg with which we readily agreed: "Just remember one thing. The Administration can, by their maneuvers, put us into war suddenly and without warning—be prepared to reverse your editorial policy on a moment's notice." But we chose to balance the Vandenberg hint of defeatism with the statement of Senator Taft: "If in time of peace any citizen feels that the President's handling of foreign policy is wrong or likely to lead to a war which he thinks unnecessary, it is his right and duty to state that fact clearly and do whatever he can to change a policy which he thinks is likely to result in war."

During the height of the Lend -Lease debate we received many letters commending the stand of our magazine and containing an oft-repeated phrase: "Keep up the good work and don't let them intimidate you."

Efforts were definitely being made to intimidate us . The Colonel told us that friends of his in the FBI passed the word to him that the White House had ordered wire taps on the Lindbergh telephones and on all the America First phones. We learned that our lines at *Scribner's Commentator* had also been tapped. The Colonel's reaction was that he personally welcomed the "electronic surveillance," as he had nothing to hide. We felt the same way. In the same week the bugging began the Internal Revenue Service served notice on Lindbergh, Stewart, and me, and I suppose a long list of people on a White House spite list, to get together "all books, records and other data used by you in computing your income tax liability for the year 1940." Again we had nothing to hide and accepted the nuisance of several days of interrogation, which turned up nothing against us, as just another petty ploy of the White House of 1941.

We did, however, come up with an idea we hoped might clear the air somewhat. We suggested to Sen. Bennett Champ Clark that we would like to be investigated. This resulted in the following:

77th CONGRESS
1st Session

IN THE SENATE OF THE UNITED STATES

Mr. Clark of Missouri submitted the following resolution which was referred to the Committee on Foreign Relations.

RESOLUTION

Resolved, That a special Committee of seven Senators, to be appointed by the President of the Senate, is authorized and directed to make a full and complete study and investigation of the activities of any person, firm, committee, or corporation acting for or on behalf or in the interest of any foreign nation, by way of propaganda or otherwise, having as their ultimate goal or tending to cause, directly or indirectly, the influencing of the neutral position of the United States in the conflicts now being waged abroad . . . .

This proposed investigation sponsored by Senator Clark promised to be most interesting. It would give us and the America First Committee the opportunity to show for the record that we had neither sought nor received financial help from any foreign source. It would also serve to smoke out the mystery of where the millions of dollars came from that supported such publications as the *New Masses* and the *Daily Worker,* along with the dozens of Communist-front organizations endorsing every twist and turn of Moscow's foreign policy. It would have also exposed Britain's multimillion-dollar propaganda operation in the U.S.

About the same time the William Allen White committee was staggering from the resignation of its chairman, a new war-thirsty group sprang to prominence in NewYork, calling itself the Fight For Freedom Committee.There was no mincing of words about this committee's aims. Their literature boldly proclaimed that the U.S. should have sent troops to kill Germans immediately upon the heels of the German invasion of Poland. This literature took no note of the fact that Russia was an equally guilty party to the conquest of Poland.

One typical piece of FFF literature, "Why We Ought To Go To War," announced:

> We are the "all-out" people; we are the people who believe in war tomorrow, and think it is a mistake that we didn't go to war yesterday.

The Fight For Freedom literature harped on the theme that the Germans were barbarians and the fall of Western Civilization was at hand unless the German nation was crushed — and by U.S. troops. The familiar Administration theme, denouncing Lindbergh and all the senators and congressmen who favored peace as "Nazi-appeasers,"ran through all the FFF appeals for support.A most provocative statement in one of the FFF pamphlets flatly stated that the Germans had massacred some 1,500,000 men and women in Poland, with plans to massacre 1,500,000 more. Again there was no mention of the Russian role in Poland.

We were to puzzle in vain, wondering where this outfit obtained such startling misinformation — to puzzle for some thirty-six years until the publication of a book titled *A Man Called Intrepid*[8] appeared in England in 1976. This 500-page volume described the activities of a British Chief of Intelligence who operated in New York for almost two years prior to Pearl Harbor, and proudly took credit for having created and directed the Fight For Freedom Committee, "taking care to conceal the British connection," supplying them with money and false information. Intrepid's control and manipulation of the committee was only one of his many diversified interests.

"Intrepid" was the code name for one William Stephenson (not to be confused with the author of the book, William Stevenson), Winston Churchill's personal undercover representative in the U.S. Intrepid's title was "Chief of all British Intelligence Services, Worldwide." His base of operation was two floors of Rockefeller Center. He was boss of some thirty thousand intelligence personnel scattered around the globe, and he had two thousand specialists operating under his direct supervision from New York. The book revealed that "for the first time in four centuries of British espionage " here was His Majesty's central agency headed by one man, under the protection of the flag of a so-called neutral country.

Stephenson was given his code name in May, 1940, during a small supper party with Lord Beaverbrook and Winston Churchill, shortly following Churchill's elevation to Prime Minister. After Churchill told Stephenson he was to have a free hand setting up the top-secret New York operation, he explained that he was also to have access to Mr. Roosevelt at all times. He was to keep pounding in FDR's ear the message that Britain was in mortal danger of being conquered by Germany, and Germany would then cross the ocean and conquer the U.S. Churchill then said to Stephenson: "The man to bring the Americans into the war must be fearless." He paused. "Dauntless?" He searched for the right word while Stephenson waited. "You must be Intrepid."

Intrepid had his whole New York operation running smoothly by late June, 1940. He was personally registered with U.S. Immigration as a "Passport Control Officer." His heavily staffed office was registered with the U.S. State Department as having to do with a purchasing commission. No names of persons appeared in the document of registry. British Security Coordination, or BSC,was the official title. Intrepid noted that the arrangement "called for very close and friendly collaboration between the authorities of the two countries." By authorities he meant Churchill and Roosevelt. "I'm your biggest undercover agent," said FDR to Intrepid during one of their first secret White House meetings in 1940. Intrepid often carried tales to FDR to discredit Ambassador Joseph P. Kennedy, because Kennedy favored a negotiated peace and Churchill wanted him replaced by a pro-war type. Intrepid also promised FDR that ways would be found to discredit U.S. senators and congressmen who favored nonintervention. His book reveals that Churchill knew more about FDR's intentions than any American, with the possible exception of Harry Hopkins.

Intrepid records that the English King and Queen were invited to Washington and Hyde Park in 1939 because FDR "believed that we might all soon be engaged in a life-and-death struggle in which Britain would be America's first line of defense." The King made copious notes of his secret conversations with his host. He found the President confident that he could lead the United States to intervention if and when the expected war broke out. In his dispatch box the King brought back with him the personal Presidential pledge, "If London was bombed, the U.S. would come in." Intrepid informs us that "The King set such store by these (1939) statements from the President that British intelligence chiefs were advised to go on the assumption that Roosevelt was 'part of the family.'"

For many months the Intrepid set-up was known to only three Americans: Roosevelt, Robert Sherwood, and Harry Hopkins. Intrepid was on the receiving end of hundreds of top-secret communications from Churchill to be used to follow up the hundreds of secret communications that were passing by diplomatic pouch between W.C. and FDR. To FDR Intrepid dutifully dramatized the Churchill message that Hitler planned a "march of invasion across the earth with ten million soldiers and 30,000 planes." He also produced forged maps purportedly taken from German agents, showing a Nazified Latin America, with the Panama Canal captured and German bombers poised to strike U.S. cities. Intrepid told FDR further that the Germans had plans to send Focke-Wulf Condor planes on one-way bombing raids of New York and Washington. He repeatedly sounded the warning: "The destruction of Western Civilization is at hand." Intrepid often had long sessions alone with Roosevelt, going over speeches Churchill proposed to deliver to the House of Commons. On one occasion he passed the word from Churchill to Roosevelt that Hitler was about to release a poison gas attack on London to wipe out the population.

Intrepid was working twenty hours a day and had his personal hand in an incredible number of plots and counterplots. He arranged for his Fight For Freedom Committee agents to attend a CIO national convention in Detroit and falsify a poll to show that the delegates to the convention voted Colonel Lindbergh and Senator Wheeler "U.S. Fascists number one and number two, respectively."

The most incredible revelation in the book is the claim by Intrepid that his agents carried out the assassination of U.S. oil millionaire William Rhodes Davis. (Again, this is long before the U.S. got into the war.) Davis, who had extensive oil interests in the U.S. and Germany, was the man who brought the October, 1939, peace proposals from Goering to Roosevelt, at the instigation of CIO President John L. Lewis. For this gesture both Davis and Lewis were blacklisted by Intrepid and Mr. Roosevelt. In addition,

Intrepid declared Davis guilty of a plan to ship oil to the Germans by a devious arrangement with Mexican charter vessels. At any rate, Intrepid's files record that "Davis, a man in the prime of life at age fifty-two, experienced a sudden seizure of the heart" at his Scarsdale home. "Police inquiries were discouraged at the request of Intrepid, who noted that the swiftest way to put a stop to the Davis schemes was to remove Davis from the scene."

Following the reelection of FDR in 1940 Intrepid complained to him about the tens of thousands of copies of noninterventionist speeches going out of Washington under Congressional frank, traceable to some twenty-four members of Congress. He denounced this perfectly legal activity as "Axis propaganda," and told FDR he would work out a way to stop it. In other words, in peacetime America any American who spoke out for peace as Lloyd George did in England in wartime was a marked man.

Intrepid had the money and the connections to attract top professional agents into his spy network, but he preferred hiring what he called "enthusiastic amateurs. They were unlikely to be on enemy files and were free of careerist timidity." When he required an agent to pry secret information out of the Italian and Vichy French embassies in Washington, he managed to recruit a beautiful young American socialite, the wife of one Arthur Park, a commercial attaché in the British Embassy. Mrs. Park was American-born Amy Elizabeth Thorpe, the daughter of a career officer in the U.S. Marines. She had made her debut in Washington in the late 1920's. Mrs. Park's marriage was not a happy one, and following Arthur Park's contrived assignment to a post in Chile, his wife stayed on in Washington. She was well known to British Intelligence as a woman who carried on discreet love affairs in her husband's absence.

Intrepid approached Mrs. Park through a top lieutenant, code-named Johnny. After a couple of sessions with Johnny, Mrs. Park was code-named Cynthia and set up in a lovely house in Georgetown. Her general assignment was to use old friends and acquaintances and make as many new contacts with the diplomatic set as possible. She was directed to tell friends that she was presently engaged in writing articles for newspaper syndication.

Soon after she was settled in at her new home on 3327 O Street Johnny came down from New York and over martinis casually asked her if she knew anyone in the Italian Embassy.

When she recalled that some years earlier she had had an affair with one Alberto Lais, who had worked in the Naval Attaché's office, Johnny was electrified. "That's the very man we want," said Johnny. Lais had until recently been director of Naval Intelligence in the Ministry of Marine in Rome. He and his wife had just arrived in Washington after some years of absence.

Cynthia's first hurdle was to renew her acquaintance with Lais. This was easy. Following her phone call he was soon sharing the bedroom on O Street two or three evenings a week, as well as a stream of information to be relayed by Cynthia to her chief in New York. Next came a blunt request from headquarters. Could she get copies of the Italian Naval Cipher? She said she would try. She convinced Lais that she wanted the cipher for U.S. Intelligence, and that the still neutral U.S. was desirous of continued friendship with Italy. She procured the code on the eve of the recall of her "lover" to Rome.

Cynthia had so far never met, talked on the phone to, or corresponded directly with Intrepid. But so highly was Cynthia regarded by the chief, following her Italian conquest, that he called on her one day, in person, unrecognized until he revealed his identity to her after her maid announced him as a "Mr. Williams." He heartily congratulated her on her work and asked her if she might next penetrate the Vichy French Embassy and purloin copies of their code books—of vital importance to the British Admiralty. She said she would—and did. Using her reporter credentials she called on a Captain Charles Brousse, press officer at the Embassy. Brousse, a handsome man in his early forties, was a much decorated former naval fighter pilot. He and his fourth wife lived at the Wardman Park Hotel.

Upon Cynthia's very first visit to the Embassy Brousse fell head over heels in love with her and was soon a regular occupant of the bed so recently vacated by the Italian diplomat. In due course copies of the Vichy French code books were forwarded to London, and Intrepid was to describe Cynthia as "the war's greatest unsung heroine."[9]

Another enthusiastic amateur recruited by Intrepid was a twenty-nine-year-old legman in the employ of Dr. George Gallup. The young pollster was earning only forty dollars a week with Gallup, and to make ends meet in support of a wife and young child he was supplementing his pay by "moonlighting as adviser to the British Government on American public opinion."

Since knowledge of American public opinion was vital to the British propaganda network before Pearl Harbor, David Ogilvy's talents were eagerly purchased by Intrepid. The British-born Ogilvy had come to America to seek his fortune in 1938. He was a fanatic admirer of Roosevelt, and despite the overwhelming U.S. anti-war sentiment revealed in the Gallup polls, he was confident that British propaganda technique would, as in World War I, bring the millions of U.S. troops Churchill required for an invasion of Germany.

Several months before Pearl Harbor Ogilvy quit his Gallup job and went to work full time for Intrepid as an illegal, unregistered foreign agent. He wrote in a book recently published:[10]

> My first assignment was to attend a course for spies and saboteurs at a camp near Toronto. Here I was taught the tricks of the trade. I was taught to blow up bridges and power lines, to cripple police dogs by grabbing their front legs and tearing their chest apart, and to kill a man with my bare hands.

Ogilvy relates that he was eligible to be parachuted into occupied territory to "practice these skills," but his new boss instead put him in charge of collecting economic intelligence from Latin America.

> Our primary function was to ruin businessmen whom we knew to be working against the Allies . . . . I came to know more about these matters than anyone in Washington.

Ogilvy made so many contacts in high places in the U .S. that after the war he was able to parlay his knowledge into an advertising business that became one of the biggest agencies in the world. Ogilvy and Mather, with offices in twenty-nine countries and billings of $800,000,000 a year, and with such clients as the U.S. Government, the British Government, and the French Government as a base, was living proof that spy training under the patronage of the White House was an ideal way to get ahead in New Deal America.

One more choice tidbit in the Ogilvy book. He tells us that "A few days before Pearl Harbor Intrepid telegraphed to London that a Japanese attack was expected. No such report had come from the Embassy, so Stephenson was asked to identify his source. His reply, laconic as usual: 'The President of the United States.'"

Intrepid flew regularly to London for secret briefings with Churchill. On one of these visits he quoted the Prime Minister as saying: "Mr. Roosevelt has confided that he is seeking an incident to get America into the war openly. The President said he wants war with Germany but that he cannot declare it . . . . He would instead be more provocative."

It is no wonder that Robert Sherwood confided to Intrepid: "If the isolationists had known the full extent of the secret alliance between the U.S. and Britain in 1940, their demands for the President's impeachment would have rumbled through the land." Sherwood's remark accurately reflected the self-confident arrogance of the White House clique during the period of "steps short of war" deception.

In the opinion of Charles A. Beard, President Roosevelt had been guilty of committing impeachable offenses since 1939: "By arrogating unto himself complete control of foreign policy, including the power to make war, he had subverted the Constitution and the orderly process of government."[11] Beard, having served as president of both the American Historical Association and the American Political Science Association, and having been long regarded as dean of American historians, was well qualified to know what he was talking about.

Intrepid was to continue on as a top confidant and secret agent between Churchill and FDR until the President's death in April, 1945.

Having enjoyed instant access to FDR for so many years, Intrepid must have been thoroughly shaken when Harry Truman, upon moving into the Oval Office, ordered the entire Intrepid operation closed down and removed lock, stock, and barrel from U.S. soil.

Truman was a man of fierce loyalties, and he had been unaware of Intrepid's illegal vendetta against American legislators such as Senator Wheeler. (Intrepid is quoted in his biography as stating that one of his major objectives was to destroy the credibility of Senator Wheeler, and other prominent America Firsters.) Truman said of Wheeler:

When I first came to Washington he was the first senator who took the trouble to be kind to me — I never forget a thing like that . . . . Of course we disagreed on many things but he was honest as the day is long. I liked him.[12]

In the Truman book it is revealed that during his first week in the Oval Office, Presidential Assistant Gen. Harry Vaughn brought him a sheaf of wiretaps on prominent Washingtonians (an extensive practice during the FDR years). Truman glanced at a few paragraphs and was furious. "I authorize no such thing." he shouted. "This foolishness must be stopped." This incident no doubt sparked the President's sweeping edict on Intrepid.

XIII

Unlimited Aid for Stalin

IN EARLY MARCH, 1941, Colonel Lindbergh took Stewart and me to lunch at the Engineers Club and told us that he and Anne were about to leave for Florida and their long-planned sailing holiday off the Everglades. He also brought us up-to-date on his recent findings in Washington. He said there was a feeling in Congress that the will of the people was at last getting through to the President. During the Lend-Lease hearings letters by the hundreds of thousands had poured into Capitol Hill and the White House demanding that the country stay out of the conflict. Senator George of Georgia, Chairman of the Foreign Relations Committee, a staunch anti-interventionist, had told colleagues that in a long heart-to-heart talk the President had solemnly assured him that the only aim of the Administration was to keep America out of the war. The Colonel felt that regardless of whether or not FDR was telling the truth, there was a sufficient lull in the state of affairs to gain for himself and Anne a much-needed change, completely out of touch with New York and Washington for a few weeks. They were planning to sail out of Fort Myers, Florida, on a friend's yawl and spend some time in the Everglades, which, on a previous brief visit, had captivated them by its beauty and remoteness, and especially its wild and abundant bird life.

Lindbergh endorsed sympathetically our plans to move the *Scribner's Commentator* offices to Lake Geneva. Having been born and raised in the Middle West, he had never been entirely comfortable in the East. The ties that had bound the Lindberghs to residence near Manhattan were his consulting duties with Pan American World Airways and the necessity for frequent visits to Washington as an adviser to the War Department.

By early spring we were moved into our new quarters in Lake Geneva. The local real estate company had performed miracles remodeling the old Sawyer blacksmith shop on Main Street over-looking a trout stream flowing into the lake. Housing had been found for the dozen key employees who chose to go along with us. Moving vans had transported all our files and office equipment, as well as our personal belongings, without loss or breakage. We had transferred our printing arrangements from New York to the firm of Kable Brothers in nearby Mt. Morris, Illinois, without a hitch. And a trucking service had delivered my sloop *Mai Tai* to the launching ways of the Lake Geneva Yacht Club, where she was soon introduced to her first taste of fresh water. Actually the move represented an overall economy in the operation of *Scribner's Commentator* and was welcomed by the Payson-Milbank accountants. The bank building at 654 Madison Avenue in which our offices had occupied a generous spread of square footage was owned by Mr. Milbank. The future income from the space we vacated would more than balance the cost of the move. The cost of living in Lake Geneva, especially the moderate rentals for our dwellings, plus the priceless access to recreation facilities, was regarded by everyone on our staff as the equivalent of a raise. We were especially fortu-nate that a number of local housewives applied for, and ably filled, jobs as clerical and editorial assistants.

The Lake Geneva Lions Club officially welcomed *Scribner's Commentator* to the community with a dinner, at which Stewart and I expressed our gratitude for the cooperation we had enjoyed from all quarters in getting settled. The next day we responded in print in the *Lake Geneva Regional News*.[1]

Expressions of welcome came from many directions. A special bulletin from America First headquarters in Chicago announced:

> Our gallant ally, the monthly magazine *Scribner's Commentator*, has moved its editorial and executive offices from New York City to Lake Geneva, Wisconsin. The editors deserve a warm welcome to the Mid-dle West and all the encouragement that we can furnish them in their courageous fight to keep the United States out of war.

Upon receipt of a note inviting us to call at America First head-quarters, Doug Stewart and I drove in to Chicago and met young R.D. Stuart, the committee's organizing director, presently devot-ing his full time to the movement as an unpaid volunteer. Another full-time volunteer was Mrs. Janet Ayer Fairbank, a remarkable person, author of several successful novels, and Democratic Committeewoman for Illinois. Mrs. Fairbank was General Wood's vice chairman of the national group. After she had shown us through the offices and introduced us to some forty volunteer workers sorting enormous stacks of letters and telegrams, she told us something of the progress of the committee. During the Lend-Lease debate the Chicago chapter had distributed pamphlets to residents of Illinois urging persons who opposed the bill to write in or telephone. Chapter headquarters received over 700,000 signatures demanding defeat of the bill and 328,000 telephone calls voicing the same sentiment. Relays of extra volunteer workers on duty day and night could hardly keep up with the response. When we asked her what negative response had been received, she said one or two pieces of hate mail came in for every five thousand or so messages of endorsement. She said she realized there was a group in the White House that would stop at nothing to destroy the effectiveness of the America First movement. She had received a couple of letters from old Democratic acquaintances in Washington suggesting that anyone who spoke out in disagreement with the Administration's manipulations to involve the U.S. in the war was branded a traitor by the White House clique. Mrs. Fairbank smiled as she pointed to a placard on the wall lettered in bold type:

There are four essential human freedoms:
1. Freedom of speech and expression—everywhere in the world.
2. Freedom of worship—everywhere in the world.
3. Freedom from want—everywhere in the world.
4. Freedom from fear—everywhere in the world.
                                              FRANKLIN D. ROOSEVELT
                                              Jan. 6, 1941

Shortly after my visit to America First headquarters Hazel received a note from Mrs. Robert Wood inviting us to dinner with her and the General at their home on the Michigan lakefront north of Chicago. We had not met either of the Woods before, but Colonel Lindbergh had often spoken of their warm hospitality and his high regard for them both. Dinner with the Woods and their married daughter Anne was quite informal.

The evening was a pleasant one in which all sorts of subjects from gardening to sailing were discussed. On the war issue the General said that when he was in London in 1936 he was astounded, during a visit with Winston Churchill, to be frankly told, "Germany is getting too strong. We must smash her." Obviously, without U.S. help, England and France were no more capable of smashing Germany in 1936 than they were in 1917. Thus America was once again expected to supply an invasion force.

We agreed that Churchill's frankness was unique. No politician since Napoleon had ever dared speak out for war. All seekers for office in the U.S. had to promise peace to be elected. Years later Churchill, in his *The Second World War*, told how in March, 1936, he had risen before a House of Commons Foreign Affairs Committee and spelled out his "fight Germany" policy in detail:

> For four hundred years the foreign policy of England had been to oppose the strongest, most aggressive, most dominating power on the Continent. The question is not whether it is Spain or the French Monarchy, or the French Empire, or the German Empire, or the Hitler Regime. It has nothing to do with rulers or nations, it is concerned solely with whoever is the strongest or the potentially dominating tyrant. If the circumstances were reversed, we could be equally pro-German and anti-French. It is a law of public policy which we are following and not a mere expedient dictated by accidental circumstances, or likes or dislikes or any other sentiment.

The General said there was no doubt in his mind that Roosevelt was as eager for an invasion of Germany as Churchill, but for sentimental reasons rather than practical ones. He suspected Roosevelt would attempt to get us in via as devious a route as possible. If it was found to be too difficult to provoke a state of war directly with Germany, there was still a way to get America into the conflict by provoking Germany's Asiatic ally, Japan. Because of the U.S. embargo on shipments of fuel oil and metal to Japan, the Japanese armies were seriously bogged down in their military operations in China. There was presently an Administration trial balloon in the air suggesting that a freeze be put on all Japanese assets in the U.S., a move calculated further to frustrate Tokyo's ambitions in China. "Personally I believe the President will now try to get us into the war by the back door," said the General. Unlike Mr. Roosevelt, General Wood knew something of war at first hand. A West Point graduate, he had been a colonel in the famed Rainbow Division in the First World War, when General Pershing selected him to handle the job of quartermaster general in charge of all transport to the AEF. Among his decorations were the

U.S. Distinguished Service Medal and the Cross of St. Michael and St. George, awarded by the British.

In the mass of mail wishing us well in our new surroundings was a gratifying message from the *Reader's Digest*, offering a renewal of their contract to reprint material from *Scribner's Commentator*. Included in the message was a personal note from DeWitt and Lila Wallace inviting Hazel and me to visit them on any subsequent trips East.

A further voice of welcome came to our attention in a most. unusual way. A few days after Hazel and I had finished uncrating furniture and unpacking books in our lakefront cottage, we were roused from our early morning slumber by a rattling of pebbles thrown against our bedroom window. When we went to the front door in dressing robes and looked out, we were greeted by a smiling, distinguished-looking, white-maned, well-dressed figure doffing a porkpie hat. It was Frank Lloyd Wright.

"So sorry to wake you at this early hour. I was driving through to Chicago and wanted to say hello."

The renowned architect came in, had coffee with us, and told us that he was not only a reader of our magazine but had given away several gift subscriptions. Before saying goodbye and driving off he asked for a calendar and ticked off two possible dates ahead when he hoped we might come to "Taliesin" as weekend guests.

The summer months at Lake Geneva were all we had hoped for and more. We were soon included in the activities of several of the townsfolk, who invited us for afternoons of tennis and evenings of bridge. On weekends there were the summer homes of Chicagoans on the lakefront, where *Mai Tai* was welcomed to tie up while we were welcomed ashore. Mrs. Fairbank had a large rustic-style country place not far from our dock, and we enjoyed a number of Sunday parties there with her and her two sons and their wives, plus assorted friends.

When the first issue of *Scribner's Commentator* was produced in our new quarters, Charley Payson flew out to see us and compliment us on the operation. He said that the pro-war element of the New York press was plugging ever louder for total U.S. involvement in Europe.

Although my job as editor freed me of all responsibility concerning the business side of the operation, I was as pleased as Stewart when he reported that a series of subscription promotion mailing tests showed an enthusiastic response. On a test mailing to ten thousand names on the Lindbergh list and an America First list, the returns came back at over 20 per cent in paid subscriptions. Since direct mail appeals that yield as much as a 2 to 3 per cent return can be profitable, Stewart immediately got busy with plans to try a mailing of a million pieces of subscription promotion. With the results of his testing in hand, Stewart flew East to lay his plans before Payson and Milbank and recommend that he spend some twenty or thirty thousand dollars over the next six months to bring *Scribner's Commentator*'s circulation figures up to the point of making a profit. Stewart's reception in New York from Payson and Milbank was encouraging, but understandably the Payson-Milbank accountants asked to have some time to study the proposals.

Stewart had been back in Lake Geneva about a week when I received an unusual early evening call from him. He said over the phone: "Please come by the house as soon as you can. I found a very curious parcel in my front hall a few minutes ago—curious, to say the least." And he hung up. As Hazel and I discussed the call, we tried to imagine what the curious parcel might be. What with some of the death threats that had come in the mail, we guessed Stewart might have been the recipient of a small bomb, or something that looked like a bomb. We hoped he hadn't attempted to open anything that looked odd without calling in the local police or fire chief.

The parcel Stewart showed me was indeed curious, to say the least. In a loosely wrapped brown paper package were two stacks of greenbacks. He said they were all twenty-dollar bills, and he had counted them — a total of fifteen thousand dollars. He explained that his housekeeper had left the front door unlatched that afternoon after taking in a delivery of groceries. The unmarked package had evidently been delivered by a messenger driving through town. Stewart said that his immediate reaction was that the anonymous donation came from Ford. My first reaction was the same, but we could think of a score of wealthy anti-war friends of *Scribner's Commentator* who were becoming alarmed by recent speeches of Harold Ickes and other Administration spokesmen threatening and denouncing all critics of FDR's foreign policy. To these friends any such contribution as Stewart received would have been considered minuscule indeed. And we could quite understand the donor's desire for anonymity.

One might well ask in retrospect why we too hadn't as yet become frightened. For one thing, the continuing Gallup Polls showed a firm 83 per cent of the country still opposed to entry into the war. For another, almost daily new names of prominent citizens were added to the noninterventionist ranks — names such as former Vice President General Charles G. Dawes, Theodore Roosevelt, Jr., and former Presidential candidate Alf. M. Landon. But the primary reason we resolved to stand firm was the guarantee implicit in Article One of the First Amendment to the Constitution (December 15, 1791): "Congress shall make no law abridging the freedom of speech or of the press."

In June I flew to California for a visit with my family, and Stewart flew East to bank his gift parcel in New York, earmarked for the coming promotion campaign. In New York he found that Payson's reaction was the same as ours— the donation had most probably come from Henry Ford via a Bennett messenger.

In July Hazel and I drove to Spring Green, Wisconsin, to spend a weekend at "Taliesin" with the seventy-one-year-old Frank Lloyd Wright and his attractive brunette wife Olga. The thousand-acre estate of rolling hills and wooded valleys fanned out from a complex of Wright-designed buildings housing the Wrights in the central mansion and some sixty young apprentices in nearby units. In return for the privilege of learning how to use a drawing board in the Wright drafting room, the novices tended the fruit trees and vegetable gardens, cooked and waited on table, and did all the general chores. Several were skilled musicians; some forty good voices made up a choral group.

On Saturday evening everyone gathered on the lawn for a picnic barbecue followed afterward by a performance of the choir. A feature of this affair was the serving of iced watermelon freshly picked from the farm. On Sunday evening the entire fellowship joined the Wrights in their living room for a buffet meal accompanied by chamber music. In between all this activity we had some lively conversations with the Wrights. Of course, the all-absorbing subject of the moment was Hitler's sudden attack on his ally Stalin. On June 22 massed German armies had commenced the advance into Russia on a 1500-mile-wide front. Mr. Roosevelt had reacted to the attack by instantly embracing Russia as a long-lost friend, and offering Stalin unlimited lend-lease aid — without bothering to consult Congress. Harry Hopkins was sent to Moscow to give

Stalin FDR's personal pledge to supply Russia with billions of dollars worth of planes, tanks, and guns.The Wrights had difficulty understanding how Stalin could achieve sudden sainthood after so recently helping Hitler carve up Poland. And after so recently applauding Hitler's conquest of France and the British humiliation at Dunkirk.

Back on the job in Lake Geneva I found my desk stacked high with ideas for articles based on the ironies of the new situation. I also found quite an assortment of clippings from recent issues of the Communist *Daily Worker* and the Communist magazine, *The New Masses.*

These publications, which had been insisting loudly while Hitler and Stalin were allied that America remain neutral, now switched to an all-out demand that America declare war on Germany at once and send an army to France as soon as possible to relieve German pressure on Russia. The *Daily Worker* now took up Ralph Ingersoll's old refrain and denounced *Scribner's Commentator* as "The Organ of American Fascism." *The New Masses* put out a special issue with a full-page drawing depicting the America First Committee as a Nazi octopus. The tentacles of this monstrous creature were labeled Gen. Robert E. Wood, Charles Lindbergh, Henry Ford, Senator Wheeler, Senator Bennett Champ Clark, R.D. Stuart, Jr., Charles S. Payson, George T. Eggleston, Douglas M. Stewart, and *Scribner's Commentator.* In an accompanying editorial *The New Masses* demanded that the America First Committee and *Scribner's Commentator* be destroyed:

> Behind a heavy camouflage of "peace" talk these gentlemen and their assorted allies are the *political panzer divisions of Hitler's bestial war against mankind.* Our National health demands wiping out this *Hitler First* cesspool, into which pours everything foul and corrupt and treasonous in American life.

With the new White House propaganda drive on to sell Russia to the American people, it was refreshing to hear former President Hoover express himself on the subject:

> It has long been understood that Stalin's militant Communist conspiracy is a plot against the whole democratic world. It makes the argument of our joining Russia to bring the four freedoms to mankind a gargantuan jest.

And Senator Taft made this comment in a radio address broadcast nationwide:

> How can anyone swallow the idea that Russia is battling for democratic principles? Yet the President has announced that the United States will ship airplanes, tanks, and guns to Stalin to spread the four freedoms throughout the world. But no country was more responsible for the present war and Germany's aggression than Russia itself. Except for the Russian pact with Germany there would have been no invasion of Poland. In the name of Democracy are we to make an alliance with the most ruthless dictator in the world?

Hoover and Taft each vividly recalled the first tenet of Marxism so stated by Lenin:

> The capitalistic countries will supply us with the materials and technology we lack and will restore our military industry, which we need for our future victorious attacks upon our suppliers. In other words, they will work hard in order to prepare for their own suicide.

No detailed official accounting of the tremendous flow of U.S. material to Russia was ever made public. But thanks to the meticulous records of a dedicated U.S. Army officer an incredible picture of what went on was revealed following the war, with the publication of *Major Jordan's Diaries* by Harcourt Brace and Company. In it Major George Racey Jordan said:

> In the spring of 1942, when I was appointed Lend-Lease Expediter and Liaison Officer with the Russians, I was warned by my superiors that it would be a tough assignment, calling for "infinite tact." For my own protection I decided to keep a diary and make notes on everything that happened.

The staging field under Major Jordan's command was Great Falls, Montana, where hundreds of U.S. warplanes were flown off for delivery to Fairbanks, Alaska, to be turned over to Soviet pilots for ferrying to Russia. The major was not surprised by the prodigious number of aircraft that went through his checkpoint, but he was overwhelmed by what he discovered when, against vigorous Russian protest, he opened a sampling of the hundreds of suitcases assigned to the planes and addressed to "Director, Institute of Technical and Economic Information, 47 Chkalovskaya, Moscow 120, U.S.S.R."

In the suitcases Jordan opened were bulging folders of top-secret State Department documents, voluminous confidential reports filed by American attachés in Moscow, maps and diagrams charting American industrial plants, and dozens of folders stuffed with sensitive naval and shipping intelligence. In one suitcase he found a letter on White House stationery addressed to Commissar of Foreign Trade Mikoyan, and signed H.H.

> I remember removing the White House letter from a metal clip, which held two other exhibits. One was a large map bearing the legend: "Oak Ridge, Manhattan Engineering District." The other a copy of a report, two or three pages long, dated Oak Ridge. In the text of the report I encountered words so strange to me that I made a memo to look up their meaning. Among them were "cyclotron, proton, deuteron." For the first time in my life I met the word "uranium."

In a radio interview preceding publication of Major Jordan's book he told interrogator Bill Slater of "Americans Speak Up" that he had reported his findings to the U.S. Counter Intelligence Service at the time, but was ignored.

> I was promptly slapped down. Orders came direct to me by telephone from Harry Hopkins. They covered billions of dollars of things I felt had not been authorized by Congress. For example, we shipped 17 hydro-electric plants which cost American taxpayers $400,000,000 — plants that were not completed until after the war.

In Sterling North's review of Jordan's book in the *World Telegram and Sun,* he wrote:

> Here for the first time in full detail and with convincing documentation is the revelation of how America was duped and swindled by our Russian "allies" and their confederates in the American Government.

Mr. Roosevelt was fortunate, as he undertook to clothe Stalin in the robes of a saint, that most Americans were fuzzy on recent Russian history. Very much unreported had been the story of Stalin's blood-purges of the kulaks, which outmatched in horror even the fiendish atrocities of Hitler. Only a few U.S. newspaper editors had read the series of articles in the *Manchester Guardian* in 1933 describing the planned extermination of millions of Russian peasant farmers. Not until 1968 were the grim statistics of Stalin's handiwork brought to light by British historian Robert Conquest in his book *The Great Terror.*[2] To cite some his revelations:

In 1930 Stalin began his campaign to confiscate the lands of the peasant farmers and herd these men and their families into "collective" or state farms. To crush their spirit the regime created a man-made famine. Armed squads stripped vast areas of all grain, cattle and food. Starvation took at least 3.5 million lives. More than 3.5 million more peasants died in concentration camps. Prominent Bolshevik Nikolai Bukharin admitted "we were conducting a mass annihilation of defenseless men together with their wives and children." Between 1936 and 1938 at least a million "political offenders" were shot in the great purges which spread the terror within the Communist Party membership. At least 12 million men and women were to die in concentration camps from 1936 onward. For the Western mind, the contrived extermination of 20 million Soviet citizens is hard enough to grasp. But figures alone cannot encompass the full horror. The suffering and persecution of wives whose husbands disappeared, the desperation of children who were orphaned, the mental torment of lying in fear of unjust arrest and death night after night for years — these things are not subject to measure.

Our editorial policy at *Scribner's Commentator* was in hearty agreement with the utterances of Herbert Hoover and Robert Taft. And we planned to continue to publicize this point of view as long as America continued to be a nonbelligerent.

But Mr. Roosevelt paid no heed whatever to the strong criticism raised by his pro-Stalin policy. In August he arranged what he figured was the most dramatic meeting since the signing of the Magna Carta at Runnymede in 1215. The setting for FDR's meeting was Placentia Bay, Canada. He arrived on the U.S. cruiser *Augusta*. Mr. Churchill arrived on the British battleship *Prince of Wales*. Both leaders were accompanied by staff officers of all the services and also by an assortment of smaller warships.

Out of this naval extravaganza came the announcement the White House considered a world-shaking declaration of policy — the Atlantic Charter. Also out of this meeting came the Roosevelt-Churchill pledge of all-out aid to Russia. And also the Roosevelt promise to Churchill that the U.S. would get tougher with Japan. In a cable to Foreign Secretary Anthony Eden, Churchill said:

At the end of the note which the President will hand to the Japanese Ambassador when he returns from his cruise in about a week's time, he will add the following passage which is taken from my draft: "Any further encroachment by Japan in the Southwest Pacific would produce a situation in which the United States would be compelled to take countermeasures even though these might lead to war between the United States and Japan."

(One cannot blame Mr. Churchill for his concern for British interests in Southeast Asia. He always, quite understandably, put British interests first.)

But the two leaders found it very sticky going when they tried to state FDR's grandiose plans for a world charter guaranteeing "Four Freedoms Everywhere." In order not to embarrass Stalin they dutifully omitted from their declaration Freedom of Speech and Freedom of Religion. Thus the *Saturday Evening Post* was prompted to editorialize: "Mr. Roosevelt left Washington with his four freedoms and came back with only two." And of course the "two" he came back with were but empty words. As an expression of war aims of the so-called free world, the Atlantic Charter proved over the years not to be worth the paper it was written on.

Henry Luce must have sensed this, but he saw to it that the battleship meeting of FDR and Churchill received a glorious spread of pictures in the issue of *Life* for August 25, 1941. Luce, the ardent churchman, must have winced inwardly when he okayed *Life*'s dramatic view of the Sunday church service on the quarterdeck of the *Prince of Wales* with the great guns of the warship towering over the altar as the Anglican and Episcopal chaplains politely avoided mention of that most familiar of the Beatitudes: "Blessed are the peacemakers."

Peter Rowland's biography of Lloyd George[3] records that immediately prior to the great battleship summit meeting Mr. Churchill continued to press Lloyd George to join the War Cabinet. After a luncheon discussion at 10 Downing Street, Lloyd George repeated a bit of what took place to his friend Kingsley Martin, longtime editor of *The New Statesman.* He said that when he tackled once again the subject of peace negotiations, Winston became very excited and shouted, "Never never, never!" Martin noted that Lloyd George's voice was very sad as he declared, "Winston likes war."

Some eye witness observations of the Placentia Bay Summit were later recorded by FDR's son Elliott.[4] Elliott, a freshly commissioned captain in the Air Force, and Franklin, Jr., a newly commissioned Naval lieutenant, j.g., were on hand wearing aiguillettes as aides to the Commander in Chief. Shortly after Mr. Churchill was piped aboard the *Augusta* he was closeted with the President. Elliott describes their meeting:

> I joined the P.M. and Father in the Captain's cabin after lunch. The P.M. was clearly motivated by one governing thought, that we should declare war on Germany straightaway. [Later, during a formal dinner on the *Augusta,* Elliott noted that the P.M. dominated the conversation for hours.] While Father sat still and doodled on the tablecloth with a burnt match, and said only an occasional word, the P.M. hunched forward like a bull, hands slashing the air, eyes flashing: "You've got to come in beside us — it's your only chance. If you don't declare war — declare war, I say, without waiting for them to strike the first blow — they'll strike after we've gone under. The Americans must come in on our side. You must come in if you are to survive."

Churchill ignored the fact that in his secret cabinet memos he had repeatedly declared that England was safe from invasion. Also forgotten were his speeches of a year earlier announcing that Hitler, following the RAF triumph in the Battle of Britain, had turned his attention eastward to the USSR and that now, with Germany and Russia engaged in a death struggle, surely England, America, and Western Civilization were not about to go under.

In deference to Mr. Roosevelt most of the talks were held aboard the Presidential flagship. In deference to Mr. Churchill the official ban on alcohol aboard U.S. warships was waived to accommodate him. Of the midnight final session aboard the *Augusta* Elliott comments:

> The occasion was more intimate — the brass and braid had departed. It was Father and the P.M., their immediate aides, and Franklin, Jr., and I, and therefore it was much more of an opportunity to get to know Churchill. Once again he was in fine form. The cigars were burned to ashes, the brandy disappeared steadily.

The Prime Minister was in an especially jubilant mood. He was now more than ever convinced that the President could be counted on to supply the millions of U.S. troops needed to invade the Continent.

Back on the *Prince of Wales* Mr. Churchill cabled his War Cabinet:

> PRESIDENT OBVIOUSLY DETERMINED THAT THE AMERICANS SHOULD COME IN BUT CLEARLY HE SKATES ON VERY THIN ICE IN RELATIONS WITH CONGRESS WHICH HOWEVER HE DOES NOT REGARD AS TRULY REPRE-SENTATIVE OF THE COUNTRY.

In other words FDR regarded the opinions of Churchill as more truly representative of American opinion than the United States Congress. FDR also chose to ignore the fact that the public opinion polls continued to show 83 per cent of Americans opposed to entering the war, and he disregarded the statement of pollster George Gallup: "The judgment of the American people is extraordinarily sound. The public is almost always ahead of its leaders."

The eight points of the Atlantic Charter were announced to the press on August 12, 1941, under the title "Joint Declaration by the President and the Prime Minister." In lofty phrases the eight points covered such things as Freedom of the Seas, Integrity of Boundaries, Economic Collaboration, etc., while carefully omitting mankind's two most precious freedoms.

The Prime Minister was most elated by the wording of Point 6 of the Joint Declaration:

> After the final destruction of Nazi Tyranny they hope to see established a peace so that all men in all lands may live out their lives in freedom from fear and want.

Churchill was to write of Point 6 some years later in his memoirs:

> The fact alone of the United States, still technically neutral, joining with a belligerent Power in making such a declaration was astonishing. The inclusion in it of "the final destruction of the Nazi Tyranny" (this was based on a phrase appearing in my original draft) amounted to a challenge which in ordinary times would have implied warlike action.

During the summer and fall of 1941 the Luce press peppered away at the America First movement and its leaders with every device of scorn and ridicule. *Time* proclaimed that America First's chairman, General Robert Wood, "presided over a garden in which the weeds had gotten out of hand and threatened to choke it." *Time* and *Life* each ran a picture of Lindbergh and Senator Wheeler with right arms extended giving the familiar Pledge of Allegiance to the flag, and likened their gesture to the Nazi salute. *Life* never once pictured the fantastic overflow crowds—the hundreds of thousands of U.S. citizens who turned out to cheer Lindbergh in "standing room only" audiences at a score of America First rallies in major cities coast to coast.

A typical *Life* story in August, 1941, carried a full-page photo of Lindbergh checking his notes as he sat beside a vacant chair. The caption read: "Lindbergh sits alone on the platform of an America First rally. To his followers he is a remote, unreachable leader. He rarely relaxes."

Life did not identify the locale of this meeting, nor show the orderly crowd of seven thousand persons outside the meeting hall listening to the loudspeakers. This meeting took place in Philadelphia with every one of the eight thousand seats inside taken. Speakers, in addition to the Colonel, were the novelist Kathleen Norris and Senator David I. Walsh, chairman of the powerful Senate Naval Affairs Committee. The *Life* story also did not mention that the empty chair was soon filled by the chairman of Philadelphia's America First chapter, who introduced the three speakers. The article concluded: "Lindbergh has few contacts with America First leaders. When he retires to his home on Long Island's North Shore to write and rest he is as remote from the average member as Hitler in Berchtesgaden."

Now, it so happened that a week after this *Life* piece appeared there was a meeting of America First's board members at their Chicago headquarters, chaired by General Wood. Following the meeting a number of the national leaders drove to Lake Geneva for a luncheon given by Mrs. Janet Fairbank at her lakeside home. After Hazel, Doug Stewart, and I were greeted by our hostess, and by General and Mrs. Wood and Senator and Mrs. Wheeler, and introduced to General and Mrs. Hammond and an assortment of Mrs. Fairbank's volunteer helpers, we worked our way to the outer veranda and ran square into Charles Lindbergh. We hadn't seen the Colonel since March and found him just as warm and enthusiastic as ever. The party was fairly large, and soon Doug and I were tapped by our hostess to come and meet a couple of writers, leaving Hazel to an uninterrupted chat with Lindbergh. Hazel was to recall parts of this conversation vividly. When she told him she quite understood how much sacrifice was involved in keeping so many speaking engagements, since it left him so little time for his family, he replied: "Strangely enough, most people say something to me about this, but always from the angle that I must be harassed by the attacks on me, and the whole fight. The fight is fun. I like it — but not the fact that I have so little time for my personal life."

The Colonel said that he and Senator Wheeler had just flown in from Oklahoma City, where they had spoken to a capacity audience two nights before. This Oklahoma City engagement had involved some serious skirmishing, but nothing like a real fight.

Two days before the rally was scheduled to take place in Oklahoma City's municipal auditorium, the City Council, under pressure from some Fight for Freedom agents from New York, canceled permission to use the building. Immediately a dozen other Oklahoma cities announced that they would welcome such a meeting. Governor Leon Phillips denounced the Council for its decision and offered to find another gathering place for the rally. Finally, despite threats that local hoodlums would do their utmost to disrupt the meeting, it went off without incident, with 14,000 cheering people filling a local ball park. Colonel Lindbergh and Senator Wheeler were introduced to the crowd by former Governor "Alfalfa Bill" Murray, who drove from his hometown of Broken Bow, some 200 miles, to do the honors. The Colonel said he thought this was one of the best-run meetings he had attended.

I returned to the veranda just as the Colonel was saying that he thought we had made a wise move to come to this part of the Middle West. "You are in one of the loveliest states, here in Wisconsin. If it weren't for the war situation Anne and I wouldn't live in the East."

At about this moment in history there were a number of U.S. newspaper correspondents in England plugging for American entry into the war. Quentin Reynolds was being wined, dined, and toasted for his book, *The Wounded Don't Cry*. The best-selling author John Gunther (*Inside Europe, Inside Asia*), a staunch advocate of FDR's foreign policy, also found himself lionized at several literary teas, where he expressed his pro-war views. One of these gatherings honoring him is mentioned in the diary of Harold Nicolson, M.P.[5]

> 25th October 1941
> On to Grosvenor House for a party given by [publisher] Hamish Hamilton for John Gunther. The whole of the Press, Ministry and BBC are there. Gunther tells me that U.S. isolationism is dropping *slowly* like a pierced blimp.

During Gunther's London visit he asked for, and was granted, an interview with Lloyd George. Some highlights of this interview were noted by A.J. Sylvester, who was present:

> Gunther said that America could not seem to awaken to the realization of her own danger. L.G. interpolated that she was 3,000 miles

away. He said it was very difficult to realize the possibility of Stuka forces of Hitler crossing the Atlantic and attacking American cities.

Lloyd George added that he felt quite sure that the Germans would win the war against Russia — and also added, "I do not say Hitler will be able to invade this country. It is a very difficult channel to cross." Lloyd George said further that Hitler's invasion of Russia could only be stopped by all-out American intervention. "That means an army of millions. I cannot see the United States doing that."

A curious observation Gunther made in this interview was that Lindbergh's popularity was such that he feared the flyer might one day be elected President of the U.S.

XIV
The White House Attacks

We in the United States tolerate opposition unless it goes to the point of advocating violent overthrow of the Government.
—— ELEANOR ROOSEVELT

BY AN ODD COINCIDENCE, soon after Mr. Roosevelt's return to Washington following his dropping of "Freedom of Speech" from the Atlantic Charter we began to feel the long arm of censorship in Lake Geneva. In October, 1941, Stewart and I and several members of our staff were suddenly served with subpoenas summoning us to appear before a Federal grand jury in Washington.

We had thus far regarded it as rather a badge of honor that the Communist press demanded the destruction of *Scribner's Commentator* and the America First Committee. And we had not been surprised that Ingersoll's left-wing *PM* had followed the party line. Ingersoll himself had told biographer Stephen Becker that *PM's* editorial staff included six Communists and some thirty fellow-travelers. But since no reputable newspaper or magazine had ever questioned our editorial policy or our right to oppose the war drive of the Administration, we assumed that the Communist attacks upon us would be ignored by the White House. We should not have been so optimistic. John T. Flynn had repeatedly warned us that FDR, despite his tremendous responsibilities, somehow found the time to impose his personal brand of censorship on anyone offering even the slightest criticism of his policies. Flynn's critical study of FDR, the best-selling *Country Squire in the White House,* had not endeared him to the President. When in 1939 an article by Flynn appeared in the *Yale Review* critical of the power wielded by chief White House adviser Harry Hopkins, FDR immediately fired off a letter to the editor denouncing Flynn and stating:

> John T. Flynn should be barred hereafter from the columns of any presentable daily paper, monthly magazine or national quarterly such as the *Yale Review*.

Upon our arrival in Washington we immediately conferred with Senators Wheeler, Nye, and Bennett Champ Clark. It turned out that the Clark Resolution to investigate us and the Communist press, which we had originally requested, had been circumvented by the White House clique. Now that Stalin had been embraced by FDR, the Administration did not want the U.S. Communists investigated. The America First Committee, Lindbergh, and *Scribner's Commentator* were to be silenced piecemeal by a Federal grand jury.

Our friends on Capitol Hill told us that the President had become enraged almost to the point of hysterics by the recent sensational speech-making swing by Lindbergh across the nation. The Colonel had spoken to record crowds in Philadelphia, Chicago, St. Louis, Minneapolis, Los Angeles, San Francisco, and Cleveland. In every instance the attendance statistics were the same; in each hall, auditorium, or arena every seat was filled and thousands stood outside listening to loudspeakers. In June the Colonel had spoken in the Hollywood Bowl to the largest crowd in Bowl history — 80,000 in the stadium, plus thousands on the hillside above. To add to Roosevelt's fury, the Gallup Polls continued month after month to show 83 per cent of the American people opposed to the U.S. entering the war.

So, instead of a public hearing by a Congressional committee as planned by Senator Clark, we were to be interrogated in private by a New Deal prosecutor before a jury of twenty-three citizens of the District of Columbia. Even before we arrived in Washington a story had been leaked to the wire services and printed under the headline: "GRAND JURY INVESTIGATES SCRIBNER'S COMMENTATOR'S MAILING LIST." The story quoted the prosecutor, William Power Maloney, as stating that he "strongly suspected that *Scribner's Commentator*'s mailing list was used for a serious and sinister purpose." Maloney was described as a man dedicated to exposing Nazi propaganda in the U.S.

According to the *Encyclopaedia Britannica,* the institution of the grand jury, dating back a thousand years, was never meant to be used by the government to harass political opponents. Quite the contrary:"The importance of the Grand Jury derives from the great role it has played as a bulwark against royal aggression — against abuse by the Crown in instigating criminal prosecutions. This abuse by the Crown was the principal ground of the popular uprising against George III in America." William Power Maloney chose to use the grand jury for the exact opposite purpose for which the institution was originally intended.

The first "sinister figure" called into the private session was Bessie Feagin, our promotion director. Before coming to *Scribner's Commentator* Miss Feagin had been assistant to the promotion director of the National Broadcasting Company, Julian Street, Jr.. She was a seasoned pro in the business, and a quite unflappable young woman. But when Maloney finally gave up haranguing her after three days of testimony, she was ready for a rest home. Although the hearings were supposed to be secret, Maloney leaked so much each day to the press that even the little newspaper in Lake Geneva was carrying stories stating that Miss Feagin was threatened with contempt of court for not revealing the "sinister" use being made of *Scribner's Commentator's* mailing list. Maloney refused to believe her truthful statement that she knew of nothing sinister in our operation. Certainly every magazine in America collects mailing lists, which are used to promote new subscriptions.

On the morning of my appearance before the grand jury I spent a relaxed hour visiting with Senators Nye, Clark, and Wheeler in the latter's office. The senators were eloquent in praising the job we were doing with *Scribner's Commentator*. The grand jury witch hunt, they said, had been set up on direct orders of FDR, the idea being to try to harass us out of business. Senator Wheeler said: "Just remember that by actual vote count there are over three hundred members of the House and Senate who endorse your stand on keeping out of this war. And there are another hundred who believe in your right to express yourself."

Senator Wheeler had recently been denounced so violently by the President that a dozen senators had risen to speak in their colleague's defense. It must be recalled for the record that when FDR ran for his third term in 1940, his first choice for Vice-Presidential running mate had been Senator Wheeler. Senator

Wheeler had declined because he was totally opposed to Roosevelt's pro-war policy. Roosevelt never forgave this affront.

As I was leaving the Wheeler office to walk to the grand jury room, Senator Clark said he was pleased to see the article by his wife that had appeared in our September issue. Mrs. Bennett Champ Clark's article concerned a public opinion poll taken in Neosho, Missouri, by *Life*, which purported to show that a majority of people in that quiet little mid-Western town favored the Luce policy of intervention in the war. A lot of readers of *Life* were fooled by this "poll" conducted by a *Time* reporter. But when the newspapers of Springfield, Missouri, conducted a poll by ballot of the 3,500 citizens of Neosho—and the results showed an overwhelming majority opposed to U.S. entry into the war—the Luce magazines were strangely silent on the contradiction. I was happy to tell Senator Clark that his wife's piece had brought in a quantity of favorable mail. His parting remark to me was: "Remember that you have one hell of a lot of the American people on your side."

One of the strangest experiences in my life was to find myself in the witness chair facing a grand jury and a hostile prosecutor just a few minutes after leaving the group of friendly U.S. senators. It was like the sudden switch one experiences in a nightmare, a nightmare with surrealistic overtones. The fact that the twenty-three men and women on the jury looked so guileless and folksy in contrast to the intense Maloney seemed weird in itself.

Before entering the jury room I had imagined that I could make a simple statement to the effect that as editor of the old *Life* magazine I and that magazine had been banned from Germany because of our intense anti-Hitler and Mussolini stand. I had never printed or written a word in favor of any dictator. I agreed, however with former President Herbert Hoover, Colonel Lindbergh, and scores of U.S. senators, plus millions of Americans, that America should stay out of this war. To the Communist press in America, of course, I understood that the mere mention that the U.S. remain neutral branded one as pro-Nazi and pro-fascist.

But I was not allowed a split second to have my say. In the grand jury hearing the victim is not allowed a lawyer or a character witness. He is entirely at the mercy of the prosecutor, who in this case obviously expected to bully me into getting so tangled up in testimony as to make it possible for him to get the twenty-three citizens, tried and true, to vote an indictment. Maloney went after me hammer and tongs for three hours and asked hundreds of questions in a staccato that could not have been more intense if I had been suspected of planning to assassinate the President. When I went back to my hotel room, I wrote down some twenty-five pages of the questions and answers. Here is a sampling of the quizzing:

Q. How did Lindbergh get in touch with you?
A. I heard one of his broadcasts and suggested to Mr. Stewart we have a visit with him. Mr. Stewart arranged a luncheon at his apartment which was attended by Colonel Lindbergh and myself.

Q. What was discussed?
A. We said we admired his speeches and wished he would do an article for us. He said he was very busy writing speeches, but would do an article when he could find time. We asked him if we could do an article on his mail and copy names of the people who had written him, using the list for a promotion mailing. He was agreeable and said he had some 40,000 letters from a recent broadcast. Crates of Lindbergh mail had been stored in New York in a Ford Company storeroom as a courtesy to the Colonel, prior to having the mail shipped out to the Lindbergh museum in St. Louis.

Q. What lists do you have altogether and why?
A. Besides the Lindbergh names we have lists from Senators Nye, Wheeler, Holt, and America First. Obviously mail which came in to these people, in support of our editorial policy of a strong defense for America and nonintervention in the war, indicated that the writers of the letters were prospective subscribers to our magazine. On several test mailings of our promotion literature we found that we had a wonderful response in paid-up subscriptions to *Scribner's Commentator*.

At this point in the questioning Maloney abruptly switched direction and asked a number of questions about our personnel as listed on the masthead. "Where did treasurer B.D. Holt come from? And Managing Editor Edward Majesky? And Bookkeeper Mary Collins?" I answered that all of these people had been associated with Mr. Payson several years before I was hired as editor. B.D. Holt, for example, was Mr. Payson's brother-in-law and legal consultant. Charles Lind, our office manager, had been on the Stewart-Milbank payroll for fifteen years. Several local Lake Geneva housewives worked for the magazine, including Mrs. Batcheldor, wife of the Episcopal minister.

After this give-and-take had gone on for several minutes, Maloney suddenly had a glint in his eye that indicated he was about to fire off a blockbuster. He said: "And now about a man you recently hired named Ralph Townsend. Tell us about him."

I explained that Stewart had heard Townsend speak on a "Town Hall of the Air" radio broadcast. He had read two of Townsend's books urging a peaceful policy between the U.S. and Japan. Both these books had been published by Putnam's and widely distributed. Stewart had then written to Townsend asking him to submit article material to *Scribner's Commentator.* Townsend had contributed two articles critical of the propaganda techniques used by pro-war writers that Payson and Stewart and I found first-rate.

As for Townsend's background, he had been a career officer in the American Foreign Service. He had resigned to write books and to lecture, after an honorable record as a Vice Consul in Canada and China and a stint in the State Department in Washington. Stewart had invited Townsend to come out to Lake Geneva for the summer months and write more articles for the magazine. Townsend and his wife had rented a cottage in Lake Geneva in June.

After I had delivered this brief biographical sketch of Townsend, Maloney suddenly switched back to more questions about the mailing lists.

Q. How many names do you have on the America First list?
A. I think around 50,000.

Q. How many on the Holt, Nye, and Wheeler lists?
A. About 40,000 on each.

Q. How did you get the Nye list?
A. Stewart and I visited him in his office last spring and asked for it. Senator Nye and his staff said they would be grateful if we would list his mail, as their office had been so deluged with correspondence that thousands of letters had piled up unanswered and unrecorded.

Q. Where did you take Nye's mail to have it worked on?
A. I believe it went to a New York mailing house. Our promotion department would have the data on that.

Q. What part did *Scribner's Commentator* play in mailing out a pamphlet of Lindbergh's testimony in Washington?
A. As I recall, that originated in a phone call from Stanley Burke to me, which I turned over to Douglas Stewart.

(Here the questioning suddenly stepped up to machine gun speed.)

> Q. Who is Stanley Burke? Where can Burke be reached? What business is Stanley Burke in? Where did you meet Stanley Burke? Why did he call you?
>
> A. Mr. Payson introduced me to Mr. Burke. I also had dinner with him one night at Colonel Lindbergh's. He is a New York lawyer. He is in the telephone book, I believe. He had heard Colonel Lindbergh's testimony before the House Committee on Foreign Affairs and was greatly impressed by it. He felt as we did that the newspapers did not cover it fully enough. I understood that he and Payson and Stewart planned to pay the bills on a reprint of the testimony to be mailed out, using our lists.

> Q. Why did *Scribner's Commentator* participate in sending out Lindbergh testimony?
>
> A. Because Payson and Stewart thought it was good promotional material, and coincided with the policy of our magazine.

> Q. Who owns *Scribner's Commentator*?
>
> A. Charles S. Payson and Douglas Stewart.

> Q. Are you sure there is no one else?
>
> A. To my knowledge they are the stockholders.

> Q. Are you sure there is no other money in it? How about a New York lawyer?
>
> A. Mr. Stewart has borrowed some capital from his cousin, who is not a New York lawyer.

> Q. What is his cousin's name?
>
> A. Jeremiah Milbank.

> Q. Isn't he a New York lawyer in the firm of Milbank Hope and Tweed?
>
> A. No, I believe the lawyer Milbank is a cousin of Jeremiah Milbank.

> Q. Who is Jeremiah Milbank?
>
> A. Among other things he is treasurer of the Republican Party and owner of the Southern Railroad.

Q. How much money does *Scribner's Commentator* lose in a month?

A. I am in the editorial and not the financial end of the company, but I have been told *Scribner's Commentator* has been losing around $6,000 per month.

Q. Isn't that a lot of money to lose?

A. It is about half the amount the magazine was losing before I came on as editor. Mr. Payson had already invested more than a quarter of a million dollars in *Scribner's Commentator*. The left-wing tabloid *PM* loses $100,000 per month with their pro-war editorial program. Our mailing tests indicate that *Scribner's Commentator* will show a profit within the next twelve months.

Q. Do you know of any sums of money received from sources other than Payson, Stewart, or Milbank?

A. Mr. Stewart told me of an anonymous donation of $15,000 he had recently received.

Q. Of how much?

A. Of $15,000.

Q. Anonymous?

A. Yes.

Q. How did it come to you people?

A. It was left at Mr. Stewart's house in Lake Geneva.

Q. You mean to say it was just left on his doorstep?

A. He said he found it inside his front hall.

Q. What did it look like?

A. Stewart said it was a package of currency — all in twenty-dollar bills.

At this point Maloney turned to the jury and said: "I guess we had better get Stewart in here tomorrow morning. You are temporarily excused, Mr. Eggleston."

Mr. Maloney had seemed quite unimpressed by the testimony revealing that Mr. Payson had invested over $300,000 in *Scribner's Commentator*. But he acted greatly shocked by my testimony that Stewart had received an anonymous donation of $15,000. One can suppose that such a cash donation looked enormous to the members of the jury.

From the hearing room I went directly to Senator Nye's office. He and Bennett Champ Clark were chatting when I entered. When I told them how Maloney had gone after me as though I were guilty of treason, they said that was to be expected as routine practice under the present New Deal Justice Department. Maloney had been instructed by the White House to put *Scribner's Commentator* out of business, and he was out to do just that. Now that FDR was sending arms to Russia, all voices in any way critical of Communism must be silenced.

William Power Maloney was one of the group of young New Dealers and FDR worshipers who flocked into Washington in the late 1930's to find jobs in the proliferating bureaus. Maloney had graduated from Fordham Law School in 1925, and after a stint as an assistant in the U.S. Attorney's office of the Southern District of New York, he had served as a trial counsel for the Securities and Exchange Commission. In early 1941 he had joined the Department of Justice as a special assistant to Attorney General Biddle. In the bimonthly bulletin issued by the left-leaning Friends of Democracy Maloney was hailed as "a man well suited to the job of investigating the tangled skein of enemy propaganda in the U.S." The Friends of Democracy had a fixed policy of calling all conservative Republicans "fascists" while never printing a word critical of Communism.

When I assured the senators that we would continue publishing our point of view until FDR managed to get us into a shooting war, they said that a shooting war might come much sooner than anyone had expected — the Japanese were apt to start shooting at any moment. That very morning while I had been in the hearing room word had been leaked to Senator Wheeler that FDR had prepared an ultimatum to be handed to the Japanese ambassador demanding the withdrawal of all Japanese military forces from Indo-China and mainland China. Since the President had earlier cut off oil and metal shipments to Japan and by executive order frozen all Japanese assets in the U.S., this new threat by FDR was sure to compel Japan to move against the British-Dutch oil sources in Malaysia. To move into the South China Sea and protect her lines of supply and communication it was obvious that Japan's forces would first have to neutralize the Philippines. Senator Nye made the observation that the first bombs might be dropped on the Philippines, prime targets being General MacArthur's minuscule air force and the U.S. naval installations at Cavite.

What none of us knew at the time was that U.S. Naval Intelligence had broken the Japanese code, and all communications between Tokyo and Washington and Tokyo and Hawaii were decoded as received and put on the President's desk. Of the many messages decoded, one reaching the White House on September 24 was most revealing of Japanese intentions. This was a request from Tokyo to the Japanese consul general in Honolulu to report on the exact location of U.S. warships at Pearl Harbor:

WITH REGARD TO WARSHIPS AND AIRCRAFT CARRIERS WE WOULD LIKE TO HAVE YOU REPORT ON THOSE AT ANCHOR...TIED UP AT WHARVES BUOYS AND IN DOCK...WE WOULD LIKE YOU TO MAKE MENTION OF THE FACT WHEN THERE ARE TWO OR MORE VESSELS ALONGSIDE THE SAME WHARF.[1]

Secretary of State Hull actually delivered the Roosevelt ultimatum to envoys Nomura and Kurusu on November 26. The previous day Secretary of War Stimson, following a conference with FDR, wrote in his diary: "The question was how we should manoeuvre the Japanese into firing the first shot without allowing too much danger to ourselves." Since an earlier White House decision was to pass *none* of the decoded intelligence on to our commander in either Hawaii or the Philippines, Stimson should have known that the "danger to ourselves" in those areas was enormous.

The day after my appearance before the grand jury Stewart was grilled for several hours and plied with hundreds of questions along the same general lines of my interrogation. We were summoned back to Washington twice in the next fortnight to answer the same questions all over again.

It never occurred to us to use the Communist technique of refusing to answer. We had nothing to hide. We felt secure in our lifetime record of loyalty to flag and country. But perhaps the most naive thing we did was to state that our direct mail tests were bringing in a 20 per cent return (a fantastic figure) and that if and when we sent out a mailing of a million, our circulation gain of 200,000 readers would put the magazine well in the black. This innocently volunteered information induced Maloney to subpoena our mailing lists and thus cripple our entire promotion program. By shuttling us unexpectedly back and forth to Washington it was almost a miracle that we managed to put out the November and December issues of the magazine.

In the several months before Pearl Harbor it had become clearly apparent to us that the White House was using *The New Masses*, the *Daily Worker*, and *PM* as the basis of the attack upon us. The following statements appeared interchangeably in each of these three publications:

1. Lindbergh, Ford and *Scribner's Commentator*, unofficial organ of the America First Committee, have collaborated in secretly filing and coding — at Ford's expense — thousands of names of persons throughout the country. This is intended to be the basis of a fascist movement of menacing proportions.
2. The America First Committee has received a minimum of $1,000,000 from unidentified sources suspected of being channels for Nazi money.
3. The America First Committee is a nationwide conspiracy against our country's freedom and security.
4. The U.S. Department of Justice should do everything in its power to smoke out these fifth column appeasers who are trying to deliver this nation gagged and bound to Hitler.
5. The America First Committee is the most dangerous potential fascist body ever organized in the United States — and *Scribner's Commentator* is their mouthpiece.

We were appalled, as we faced the pugnacious Maloney in session after session, that he used the wildest statements of the Communist press as the basis of his questioning. Only the Communist press, with its new feeling of immunity from investigation, would have dared publish such outlandish lies about anyone. This was the press that had denounced Franklin D. Roosevelt as an arch-fiend and satanic warmonger up to the moment of Hitler's invasion of Russia. In this dark period of the perversion of justice by the White House we took solace from the words of a man also vilified by the Communist press, John Edgar Hoover. The FBI chief was on record with the statement: "Anyone who opposes the American Communist is at once branded a fascist or a Hitlerite or an anti-Semite, and becomes the object of a systematic campaign of character assassination. This is easily understood because the basic tactics of the Communist Party are deceit and trickery." Had we possessed a crystal ball we might have taken solace also from a development that lay some years ahead. William Power Maloney, far from being a noble champion of righteousness, possessed feet of clay. After the war he was hailed before a Federal court and charged with "willfully" failing to list taxable income of $71,570. By paying taxes due, plus penalties, he barely managed to avoid a jail sentence.

Why had Maloney been so intent in his pursuit of pre-war isolationists who had been America Firsters, while unconcerned about the Communist network that had sabotaged U.S. defense efforts prior to the recent embracement of Russia by FDR? The answer to this riddle was supplied in a book published in 1945 by an official of the leftish *Friends of Democracy,* Henry Hoke, who apparently had easy access to the highest echelons of the Administration.[2] Hoke wrote that at the close of a cabinet meeting in the White House in late June, 1941, President Roosevelt asked Attorney General Francis Biddle to stay on for a discussion of an important matter. Alone with Biddle, the President spread an assortment of reading matter on the table and said, "Francis, I want you to prosecute these people." On the table were a number of hate sheets put out by the pro-Nazi, crackpot fringe. Also included were issues of *Scribner's Commentator.* Not included were the hate sheets that had been put out by the Communists denouncing FDR prior to Hitler's attack on Russia.

Day after day, week after week, since the summer of 1940 Ingersoll's *PM* had been denouncing Charles Lindbergh as America's number one Fascist and *Scribner's Commentator* as the mouthpiece of American Fascism. Every anti-war statement by such noninterventionists as Herbert Hoover, Senator Taft, and a thousand other prominent citizens critical of FDR's motives, was branded in *PM* as "pro-Fascist."

Where had this blanket labeling of spokesmen for an America First policy originated? A very interesting clue to the mystery can be found in Joseph P. Lash's post-war memoir on Eleanor Roosevelt. In quoting a 1940 conversation with Mrs. Roosevelt he states:[3]

> She could not see how people could reconcile themselves to the spread of Hitler slavery. There must be an allied victory. I shared her sentiments, I said, and favored a pro-allied policy as long as a New Deal government was in power. But suppose the Republicans won and we went to war. Would it not mean Fascism here, I asked. She said she wondered whether under a Republican Administration we would escape Fascism even if we were not at war. Some people seemed to fear communism — while she thought the danger was from the right.

So, to my onetime friendly correspondent, the First Lady, and obviously to the Commander in Chief himself, the party of Abraham Lincoln and Theodore Roosevelt could from 1940 onward be suspect as a cover for what they called "Fascism."

This revelation by Mr. Lash of pre-war White House thinking was not from a man who was favored with a few moments of intimate exchange of thought with Eleanor Roosevelt. According to J.B. West, who served as chief usher at the White House for twenty-eight years, Lash was a "permanent guest" in the mansion for months at a time while she was there, with the Blue Bedroom on the second floor across from the President's study assigned to his exclusive use.

In his book *Upstairs at the White House* West has written:

> Joe Lash occupied a unique position in Mrs. Roosevelt's life during my years in the FDR White House. He was her closest confidant, her most personal friend. The two would sit in his room talking until late at night; she'd step across the hall to say good morning before breakfast and say good night after everyone had gone to bed. They often walked together around the sixteen acres of White House grounds. Mrs. Roosevelt was like an anxious mother. She was closer to him than she was to her own children. Later her great friend had been drafted after she had tried unsuccessfully to get him an officer's commission. He was, however, stationed in the air corps at Bolling Field near Washington and retained his room at the White House. He commuted to his post in Mrs. Roosevelt's official limousine complete with chauffeur and footman.[4]

There were several reasons why Joe Lash's application for a commission in Naval Intelligence was turned down even though he had been personally sponsored by Mrs. Roosevelt. In the late 1930's Lash had gone to Spain to join the Communists in the war against Franco. In 1936 he had been an active leader in the American Student Union, a Communist front and had at that time released the statement to the press: "The American Student Union states that we will not support any war which the U.S. Government may undertake, for we recognize that such a war would be imperialistic in character."

Lash had also perjured himself before the House Un-American Affairs Committee by denying he had ever been a member of the Communist Party. It was when Lash and several leaders of the American Youth Congress were invited to testify before the House

Committee in November, 1939, that Mrs. Roosevelt first became involved with the so-called "youth movement." Lash was thirty years old at the time. Instead of testifying civilly, the "young people" tried to turn the hearing into a circus. Lash stood up and delivered a bit of verse ridiculing the chairman and then caused to be read into the record a resolution "denouncing the Committee and urging its immediate abolition." This was the famous hearing where Mrs. Roosevelt turned up unexpectedly and sat with the testifying group and took them all back to the White House for lunch, dinner, and an overnight stay in the guest rooms. Lash wrote: "I was assigned to the Lincoln Room, never for a moment suspecting I would occupy the room quite frequently the next few years."

XV

Roosevelt Abandons MacArthur

ALTHOUGH MALONEY FAILED to induce the grand jury to indict any of us for the so-called "sinister" operation of *Scribner's Commentator*, he worked out a way to smear us from another direction. He discovered that back in 1939 Ralph Townsend had produced a booklet in San Francisco of which a quantity of copies had been purchased by the Japanese Information Service. The booklet was a condensation of his early books published by Putnam's arguing for peace between the U.S. and Japan.

Townsend was called before the same grand jury Stewart and I had faced. And an indictment was quickly handed down charging him with violation of the Foreign Agency Registration Act. Townsend was to spend several months in the Washington, D.C., jail before he was released thanks to the heroic efforts of Senators Taft, Wheeler, and Nye. The conviction of Townsend inspired stories throughout the press that a "writer for *Scribner's Commentator* was a convicted enemy agent." Townsend was no more an enemy agent than Bob Hope. But Maloney scored for the White House, and had exerted his best efforts to discredit our magazine by way of convicting an innocent man.

Upon our return to Lake Geneva after finally being excused by Maloney, Stewart and I prepared a "Win the War" issue of *Scribner's Commentator* with the expectation that America would soon be at war with Japan and her Allies. Germany and Italy were treaty-bound to declare war on the U.S. promptly upon Japanese involvement. We did, however, lay out the issue with emphasis on America's responsibilities in the Pacific, with Germany and Italy being of secondary importance. We had chosen General MacArthur to be our front-cover subject. We did not know at the time, nor did the commanders in the Philippines or Hawaii, that a secret agreement had long since been signed and sealed between Roosevelt and Churchill declaring that when war came with Japan, the Pacific would be at the bottom of the priorities list, while aid to Russia stood at the top of the list.

When the first news of Pearl Harbor reached us we immediately sent a wire to the Associated Press: "WE ARE IN IT — LET'S WIN IT — Payson, Stewart, Eggleston for *Scribner's Commentator.*"

America First headquarters announced to the press that in the interest of unity the committee was being dissolved at once. As predicted by General Wood, the President had got us into the conflict by the back door. The Hon. Oliver Lyttelton, Production Minister in Churchill's War Cabinet, was later to declare: "America provoked Japan to such an extent that the Japanese were forced to attack Pearl Harbor. It is a travesty of history ever to say that America was forced into war."

Although millions of unsuspecting Americans were surprised beyond belief by the Pearl Harbor disaster, the group around the President at the White House took the news in stride. Mrs. Roosevelt wrote: "December 7th was just like any of the later D-days to us. We clustered at the radio and waited for more details — but it was far from the shock it proved to the country in general. We had expected something of the sort for a long time." At a cabinet meeting that night Frances Perkins noted that "The President had a much calmer air than usual. His terrible moral problem had been resolved by the event."

Across the sea church bells rang in England and American flags were flown hailing America's entry into the war. In the Commons Mr. Churchill declared: "This is the object that I have dreamed of, aimed at, worked for, and now it has come to pass." Within the week Churchill had boarded the heavy cruiser *Duke of York* and was en route to Washington. In Churchill's *The Second World War* he notes that during the eight-day passage across the Atlantic he worked fifteen hours on a memorandum for FDR reemphasizing his conviction that the war in Europe required U.S. troops immediately, whereas the prosecution of war with Japan could wait. Churchill and his staff were worried that the impact of the U.S. disasters in Hawaii and the Philippines might focus American opinion on action in the Pacific rather than Europe. He was right about American opinion. But he needlessly worried about FDR's intentions. Churchill wrote:

Immediately broached my ideas to the President the first night of my arrival — December 22nd — on all points Mr. Roosevelt agreed. The President said that he was anxious that American land forces should give their support as quickly as possible wherever they could be most helpful and favored the idea of a plan to move into North Africa.

Mr. Churchill received the immediate approval of the President to his plan that the U.S. send to North Africa "not less than 150,000 men during the next six months, and it is essential that some American elements, say, 25,000 men, should go at the earliest possible moment."

Christmas Eve at the White House, as described by Churchill's physician, Lord Moran, found everyone in good spirits, especially the President. Following the singing of Christmas Carols, "they wheeled away the President in his chair, after he had waved a 'goodnight' to us. He had been like a schoolboy, jolly and carefree. It was difficult to believe that this was the man who was taking his nation into a vast conflict, in which, until Pearl Harbor a few days ago, she had no thought of being engaged."

Shortly after Mr. Churchill's arrival in Washington, as more detailed reports of the tragic happenings in Hawaii and the Philippines trickled in, we began to have misgivings about continuing *Scribner's Commentator*.

Over the radio and in the news came grandiose statements about the billions and billions of dollars worth of planes and arms promised to Russia. No news came through at all about aid to MacArthur. The *Washington Times-Herald* leaked a story from the archives of the Joint Chiefs of Staff that Roosevelt had plans to call up an American expeditionary force of five million men for a land offensive against Germany to relieve the pressure on Russia. There were no plans to send troops, or anything else, to MacArthur in the Pacific.

The Administration soon had the benefit of a tight wartime censorship of all news. The American people were allowed to know only the barest details of the Pearl Harbor disaster — 3,000 U.S. dead, several warships and planes destroyed, enough details for a proper background to amplify FDR's "Day of Infamy" speech.

Of the incredible situation faced by the 55,000 U.S. and Filipino troops on Luzon under General MacArthur's command, few details of their fate came to light until the General's book, *Reminiscences*,[1] appeared years later:

Although Admiral King felt the fleet did not have sufficient resources to proceed to Manila, it was my impression that our Navy deprecated its own strength and might well have cut through to relieve our hard-pressed forces. The bulk of the Jap Navy was headed south to seize Borneo, Malaya, and Indo-China. American carriers having escaped destruction at Pearl Harbor could have brought planes to the Philippines. The Navy fought the next two years and had great victories without any new ships.

But a top-level decision had long before been reached that the Atlantic war came first, no matter what the cost in the Far East. President Roosevelt and Prime Minister Churchill, in a Washington conference after the attack on Pearl Harbor, reaffirmed a policy to concentrate first on the defeat of Germany....Unhappily, I was not informed of any of these vital conferences and believed that a brave effort at relief was in the making.

Three weeks after the first Japanese bombs had fallen and Japanese forces in overwhelming numbers had begun to close in, MacArthur declared Manila an open city and moved his U.S. and Philippine forces to Bataan Peninsula and Corregidor to await the siege. As Japanese pressure on Bataan steadily built up, MacArthur sent a barrage of messages to Washington asking for help. General Marshall's first replies seemed to imply that help would soon be on the way. Then a later radiogram from Marshall stated that early help could definitely *not* be expected. It was now the end of December. MacArthur wrote:

At this time, despite my pleas to Washington, supplies of food and weapons were running dangerously low. On January 10th and January 17th I wired Washington explaining the seriousness of the situation. We had been on half rations for some time now and the result was becoming evident in the exhausted condition of the men.

The General described the sea blockade as only lightly held. In his opinion, ships carrying supplies could have easily got through to him.

It seemed incredible to me that no effort was made to bring in supplies. I cannot overemphasize the psychological reaction on the Filipinos. They were able to understand military failure, but the apparent disinterest of the United States was incomprehensible. Aware of the efforts the Allies were making in Europe their feelings ranged from bewilderment to revulsion.

By early February the food situation began to get really desperate.

> I was forced to cut the soldiers' rations not only in half but later to one quarter. The slow starvation was ultimately to produce an exhaustion, which became the most potent factor in the destruction of the garrison....Constantly fresh Japanese troops arrived by transport to replace the enemy's losses. But I could only bury my dead.

Malnutrition and malaria were taking a frightful toll. Radio news from America carried stories day after day telling of the enormous output of munitions and aircraft going to England and Russia. The only support received from FDR came in a series of telegrams of good wishes, of which this one is typical:

> GENERAL DOUGLAS MACARTHUR: MY PERSONAL AND OFFICIAL CONGRATULATIONS ON THE FINE STAND YOU ARE MAKING. ALL OF YOU ARE CONSTANTLY IN OUR THOUGHTS. KEEP UP THE GOOD WORK. WARMEST REGARDS.
> FRANKLIN D. ROOSEVELT

The FDR cables to the Philippines stand in odd contrast to the Presidential cables to Moscow, of which this is typical:

> TO MARSHAL STALIN — 9/10/42 — I AM NOW TRYING TO FIND ADDITIONAL PLANES FOR YOU IMMEDIATELY, AND WILL ADVISE YOU SOON. I AM ALSO TRYING TO ARRANGE TO HAVE SOME OF OUR MERCHANT SHIPS TRANSFERRED TO YOUR FLAG TO INCREASE YOUR FLOW OF MATERIAL IN THE PACIFIC. I HAVE JUST ORDERED AN AUTOMOBILE TIRE PLANT TO BE MADE AVAILABLE TO YOU. EVERYONE IN AMERICA IS THRILLED BY THE GALLANT DEFENSE OF STALINGRAD AND WE ARE CONFIDENT THAT IT WILL SUCCEED.

(In early March, 1942, FDR had written Churchill: "I know you will not mind my being brutally frank when I tell you that I think I can personally handle Stalin better than either your Foreign Office or my State Dept. Stalin hates the guts of all your top people. He thinks he likes me better, and I hope he will continue to do so.")

In mid-March General MacArthur received orders from Washington to leave his command and set up new headquarters in Australia. After he succeeded in making his escape by PT boat, the Philippine command became the responsibility of General Jonathan Wainwright, who had no choice but to surrender his starving troops on Bataan and Corregidor within the month after MacArthur's departure. The Japanese took in total some 45,000

Filipino and American prisoners. The Death March of Bataan claimed 25,000 casualties. Wainwright and his men who survived the march looked like so many skeletons.

Some further grim details of the final agonies of the besieged garrison were later supplied to Paul Palmer (and subsequently to me) by his friend Colonel Warren J. Clear, who served as an intelligence officer with General MacArthur on Bataan:

> This was the story of men who fought the most dismal, bloody, and hopeless campaign in the history of warfare. They were the only Americans in the world at this time who were fighting the enemy, yet the flood of weapons from their country's arsenals was being rushed to every other battle front but theirs. Anyway, they fought on, with the machine gun, the hand grenade, the rifle, and the bayonet against massed troops and massed artillery; fleets of bombing and strafing planes. Only the sheer weight of Japanese manpower finally over-whelmed the defenders of Bataan. Then the full fury of the enemy was turned upon Corregidor. Besides round-the-clock bombing from the air, 5,000 artillery shells a day pulverized the surface of the Rock.
>
> The day came when there was no more room to bury the dead, and what was the use when the great shells churned the tortured bodies up again to rot in the tropic sun? American soldiers, sailors, and marines, with their pride and spirit drowning in misery and mud, were obliged to eat, drink, and sleep amidst their own putrefactions. In the mo-ments of the final agony before the surrender, the last bandage had been used up, the last shot of morphine gone, almost all food gone, and no more ammunition for the last anti-aircraft gun. In all the thousands of years of human warfare, here was the only known example of a besieged army written off and deserted by fellow coun-trymen.

Fort McKinley, Manila, the largest U.S. military cemetery on foreign soil, lists 53,644 American service men who lost their lives in the Philippine disaster. The cemetery is unique, with 36,272 names chiseled on a "Wall of the Missing" honoring those battle dead whose bodies were never found or never identified.

Could anyone imagine the British, the French, the Japanese, the Germans, the Israelis, or the Americans of Theodore Roosevelt's time thus committing tens of thousands of their besieged fellow-countrymen to death and imprisonment? FDR's proud boast to the British, "Where thou diest will I die," did not apply here.

And in the meantime, during all of the hours of horror in the Western Pacific, the great liner *Queen Mary*, in gray war paint, was making weekly shuttle passages across the Atlantic carrying 15,000 G.I.'s to England on each trip. In recalling those hectic trips immediately following Pearl Harbor, Cunarder Commodore Harry Grattidge was greatly impressed by the prodigious appetites of the U.S. lads in uniform. Meats, vegetables, fruits, sweets, and ice cream — all were loaded aboard in lots measured in tons. The Commodore was most impressed by "The G.I.'s love for bacon and eggs. On occasions we used 35,000 eggs and 3,500 pounds of bacon at breakfast alone".[2]

As far as the future of our magazine was concerned, I can speak for every member of the staff and for publishers Payson and Stewart when I say that the long weeks of persecution by Maloney and Company brought a delayed reaction of disillusionment concerning the great American principle of freedom of speech. We could foresee that no matter how wholeheartedly we continued to publish, under the slogan of winning the war, if we so much as suggested that FDR send war planes across the Pacific to MacArthur as well as across the Atlantic to Stalin, a dozen more Maloneys would be set upon us. Freedom of speech was out for the duration. We decided to discontinue *Scribner's Commentator* with our WIN THE WAR issue of January, 1942. Payson and Stewart arranged to pay everyone two months' salary, and we were at liberty to go our separate ways. When we announced to our readers that our January issue was to be the last, we received hundreds of letters lamenting our demise. Subscribers were offered a refund of their money or the option, thanks to DeWitt Wallace, to receive the *Reader's Digest* for the unfulfilled numbers of future issues.

XVI

Hatchetman O. John Rogge

AFTER HAZEL AND I had said our goodbyes to our colleagues on the magazine and the many friends we had made in Lake Geneva and Chicago, we decided to visit my parents in California. And we chose a rather unorthodox way to get there. We purchased a heavy-duty, six-wheel trailer, which we hitched onto the rear of our three-year-old Packard. With the help of a derrick, our two-ton *Mai Tai* was loaded on the chassis of the trailer and secured in a special cradle. Our furniture was put in storage to be called for at some future date, and we were off on the 2,000-mile trek from Wisconsin to the West Coast. By going around, instead of over, so many high spots of U.S. terrain, we covered more like 3,000 miles between the icy February roads of Lake Geneva and orange groves of Santa Barbara. As an exercise in occupational therapy, we could not have made a better choice of activity. We both needed and welcomed the complete change of pace from the petty world of political controversy in which we had been entangled for so many months.

We had plenty of tire trouble along the way, and I became a master of the tire change. On many a hill I had to engage a tow truck, not only to help us up, but to hook on behind the boat and hold us back on the way down the other side. Our air brakes failed us once on a downhill bit near the Mexican border at Bisbee, Arizona, and only luck saved us from going over a cliff. I took some interesting pictures of *Mai Tai* crossing the Great Divide and later parked under pipe organ cactus in the Mojave Desert. One night in desert country we had a puncture in a God-forsaken stretch 50 miles from nowhere. On that occasion it was too dark to change a tire, so we slept in an abandoned adobe hut until daybreak. Several times when we stopped for gas or a tire change in remote country, locals gathered round and ogled the boat. Many had never seen a keel boat before, and one youth, pointing to the propeller, actually said: "I guess it's a boat, all right, but what is that little electric fan doing sticking out underneath?"

In California we motored up the coast from Santa Barbara and finally deposited *Mai Tai* in the water at the Palo Alto Yacht Club, located on an eastern bight of San Francisco Bay. *Yachting* Magazine published my account of the venture, "Cross Country Cruise," in two installments. At that time, when boat trailing was a rarity, we held the record for long-distance hauling of a keel boat.

In Palo Alto, after a few good sailing days in the brisk cool winds of San Francisco Bay, we decided that something needed doing to bolster our financial situation. To help restore our bank balance and at the same time contribute a bit to the war effort, I took a course in welding and after induction into the International Brotherhood of Boilermakers, Iron Ship Builders, Blacksmiths, Forgers and Helpers of America went to work at the yards of Western Pipe and Steel Company. Western Pipe was at the time busily engaged in producing baby aircraft carriers. Needless to say, I did not realize how soft my muscles had become during the years of desk work. Fifteen years had gone by since I had pulled an oar in a University of California shell. At the end of weeks of lugging a heavy welding cable up and down ladders inside and outside a steel hull, my back gave out. At age thirty-six I was definitely past my prime as far as day labor was concerned.

After a fortnight of bedrest I telephoned DeWitt Wallace and was immensely relieved when he promptly assured me that I could do some work for *Reader's Digest*. We had no trouble selling *Mai Tai* and the six-wheel trailer. Our remarkable Packard carried us once more across the United States, and we were able to re-rent our former house in Riverside, Connecticut, Shortly after our return the Wallaces had us for a weekend at "High Winds" in Westchester County, New York. The radiant warmth of their friendship helped us to forget the unpleasantness of the past year.

During the first afternoon of our visit Wally took me on a long walk in the woods, and I outlined some ideas I had for future articles in the magazine. None of my story ideas was even slightly controversial or political.

One of my suggestions is worth recalling as an illustration of how the Wallace editorial mind worked. I said that I had recently been reading a biography of Thomas Jefferson and was struck by the fact that the two-hundredth anniversary of our third President's birth was but a few months away. When we returned to the house, Wally telephoned Donald Culross Peattie in California and asked him to prepare a feature story on the life of Jefferson. When the Peattie piece ran as the lead story in the magazine, it inspired a flood of similar tributes to Jefferson in the U.S. press as well as a new play on Broadway. Our lunch with the Wallaces that day was an especially memorable one; we were told that the *Digest* had just passed another milestone. Latest worldwide circulation figures showed that readership had reached the ten million mark.

As was the arrangement with many other contributors to the *Digest,* I worked at home and sent my memos of ideas to DeWitt Wallace by mail. Over a period of months I sent in quite a stack of suggestions, all on Americana, and a fair percentage were used.

Then, about mid-year of 1943, with our finances once more in order, Hazel and I had a talk about the possibility of my enlisting in the service. At this time American participation in the war was just about to get into high gear on all fronts. I was still seething inwardly when I recalled that my patriotism had been questioned by the likes of William Power Maloney.

On my study wall, beside several autographed photos of Americans I admired, was a framed certificate I had especially cherished during the dark days of the Maloney harassment, a commission as a second lieutenant in the Army Air Corps. The commission had been awarded in 1928 following four years of ROTC at the University of California and training in aerial observation at Crissy Field, San Francisco. In 1939, after the outbreak of war in Europe, I had written to the War Department asking if my commission might be reactivated in the Air Corps Reserve, and was advised by the Chief of the 2nd Military Area that it could be by taking a course in the Military Area Extension School. I considered this, but then decided that the only branch of the service compatible with my love of boats and the sea was the Navy.

During another relaxing visit with the Wallaces, Hazel and I told them of our plans. Their reaction was that since I was in an exempt draft status as a married man with dependents, I had better think it over. They added that if I decided to go, the established practice of the *Digest* was to continue my salary. In addition, they offered Hazel a responsible position in the book department.

In our mail, a few days after seeing the Wallaces, were two unsolicited letters addressed to me, apparently because of my longtime interest in sailing. One was from the Coast Guard Recruiting Office, Boston, stating that "The U.S. Coast Guard is desirous of contacting yachtsmen who are experienced in the handling of sail, with the view of enlisting their services in the Coastal Picket Patrol, consisting of fishing schooners such as the *Gertrude Thebaud,* as well as the country's largest seagoing yachts." The other letter was from the Director of the U.S. Civil Service Commission, Brooklyn, stating that my name had been brought to their attention as a possible recruit for duty in the manning of small motorboats in the Southwest Pacific. "If you are interested in the possibility of an immediate appointment in this service please contact the undersigned." Both these letters suggested fascinating possibilities, but were not as tempting to me as the U.S. Navy.

The obvious thing I might have done, considering the friends I had on Capitol Hill and my former commission in the Air Corps, would have been to seek a commission in the air branch of the Navy. This could have been easily arranged through Senator Walsh's office. My preference, however, was for sea duty, and I decided not to make use of "connections," but to go instead to the nearest Naval Recruiting Station and offer my services cold.

About this time I had an amusing lunch with the *New Yorker's* star columnist, Lois Long, a good friend of ours and a fellow America Firster. Lois said that several of Ross's younger writers who had ardently favored the U.S. entering the war were now happily stationed at the Office of Flying Safety in Winston-Salem, North Carolina, writing flight manuals. They had quickly obtained lieutenants' commissions and desk jobs when the shadow of the draft hung over them.

When I went to the Naval Recruiting Station in nearby Norwalk, the officer in charge, after only a few moments of questioning, said: "Our orders are to send anyone in your age bracket who has a university degree to 33 Pine Street, New York City. When you call there, ask for Lieutenant Darling."

My visit to the Norwalk recruiting station was on a Thursday, August 26. The next morning, Friday, August 27, at 9:00 A.M. I was at 33 Pine Street being interviewed by Lieutenant Darling. He was most helpful and cordial in checking me through a mass of questionnaires covering everything I had ever done in my life, as well as information regarding my family connections and forebears. Lieutenant Darling then turned me over to the medical department, and I had a physical going-over that took up most of the day. With my physical fitness verified, I was advised I was to send in six testimonial letters. I was then asked if I had a preference as to what I hoped to do in the Navy. When I replied that I would like sea duty in some area where the action was, my interrogator said he would recommend that I be assigned to combat intelligence.

The following week the Office of Naval Procurement at 33 Pine Street received from me the required testimonial letters — letters representing a cross-section of close friends over many years: H.L. Curtis, assistant to the president, Shell Oil Company; R.K. Hines, chief legal counsel, Vick Chemical Co.; J.T. Moll, financial adviser to Jeremiah Milbank; Fred E. Dayton, sales manager, Condé Nast Publications; The Reverend John J. Hawkins, Rector, St. Paul's Episcopal Church, Riverside; DeWitt Wallace, owner-editor of *Reader's Digest.*

A couple of days later I received a phone call from Al Webb, a Riverside Yacht Club acquaintance, asking me to take on the job of air raid warden for my immediate neighborhood. The call took me by surprise. Webb surely knew that I had been an America Firster and that I believed Colonel Lindbergh was right in his prediction that there would be no enemy bombers over America. Also, everybody knew that bombs had long since stopped falling on Britain because the Germans were totally occupied in Russia. But I politely listened to Webb as he explained to me that the Office of Civilian Defense in Washington had asked him to head up an air raid warning system in the Greenwich, Riverside, Stamford area, and he was sorely in need of volunteers.

I might have told Webb that I had already signed up for active duty in the Navy. But my curiosity got the better of me, and I said all right, send me the necessary particulars. The very next day's mail brought me a large bundle of pamphlets, booklets, and memos. Three of the pamphlets totaled some two-hundred pages of directions and explanatory matter. Some of the most vividly worded stuff was dated six months prior to Pearl Harbor and signed by Mayor La Guardia, "U.S. Director of Civilian Defense."

A seventy-page booklet expensively printed with a brightly colored jacket was titled: "Air Raid Warden Service, Greenwich, Conn., January, 1942." The opening chapter declared:

> This is total war—a war in which the enemy attempts to disrupt the whole of civilian life as well as to destroy military targets.

You have been chosen as Air Raid Warden of your sector because you are known to be reliable and responsible and because you have the needed qualities to lead, direct, and help the people entrusted to your care.

Your equipment will be:

1. Arm Band
2. Steel helmet (when available)
3. Gas Mask
4. Gas-protective clothing (when available)
5. Flashlight
6. Notebook and pencil
7. Warden's whistle. (The whistle is attached to a metal chain. The end of the chain is to be hooked to the left lapel or other convenient buttonhole and the whistle carried in the left breast pocket.)

Page after page of the literature described "probable examples" of what was to happen:

A high explosive bomb has landed on the Post Road at Horseneck Brook Bridge. There are 20 casualties — 5 people are trapped under a bus. The bus is on fire. The electric light wires are down. The Post Road is blocked by a bomb crater. (Fill out your Air Warden's Report Form as follows.)

There were several essays explaining the characteristics of the many kinds of gas to be coped with. Included was a recent lecture delivered at the Greenwich Air Raid Center by a visitor from overseas, a Mrs. Humphrey Plowden, deputy chief warden of Oxford, England. After listing the various types of poisoned gas to be expected, Mrs. Plowden explained that raiding planes would also "undoubtedly use incendiary bombs," and "when you have several planes dropping them, as we did in the London blitz, it isn't very pleasant."

The most colorful passage in the lady's lecture had to do with the warden's behavior if and when caught in a situation where demolition bombs were falling all about. Her advice: If the warden was patrolling an open area, he was to lie down immediately in a handy gutter.

When you lie down keep your head down and put your arms around it, and push your helmet over the back of your head and keep your mouth open; thus you eliminate a great deal of risk. If you close your mouth you are not only going to have your teeth broken, but you are going to injure your hearing and your lungs. I would like to give you a hint that will help you. The simplest way to keep your mouth open is to take an India Rubber eraser and bore a hole through it, put a string in it, and wear it around your neck. You can bite it between your teeth and still have your mouth open.

A special bulletin signed by "Chief Air Raid Warden Alfonso J. Webb" carried the announcement that a practice statewide field exercise was to be announced soon "assuming that a large flight of enemy bombers with fighter escort were bombing the towns of Stamford, Danbury, Bridgeport, New Haven, Old Saybrook, New London, Waterbury, Middletown and Norwalk."

My routine duties consisted of visiting the homes of fifty or so neighbors and telling them to put pails of water and sand in their attics in case of fire, and to prepare all windows to comply with blackout regulations. I knew most of the people I called on, and had to turn down lots of drinks during my evening rounds. The neighbors tended to regard the whole business as pretty ridiculous, but everybody good-naturedly agreed to comply. In fact, anyone failing to comply with the blackout orders was subject to arrest by the police.

I spent several hours each night the next few weeks making the rounds and hobnobbing with fellow wardens. It was a very monotonous routine, except for one dark night when a curious coincidence occurred. I had been sent by headquarters on a special assignment which was to report at midnight to the grounds of a large estate in the Greenwich suburbs and relieve a watcher who was stationed atop a water tower on the premises. On arrival a gardener led me to the stairway of the tower, and I found my way upward with the aid of a flashlight. At the top my light picked out the man I was relieving. It was John Kobler, the *PM* reporter who had written the critical stories about me and *Scribner's Commentator* in 1940. The pitch darkness of the tower top was indeed an eerie place to encounter Kobler. But he soon relaxed the situation by saying that he had heard I was presently with *Reader's Digest* and he wondered if he could send me a couple of article ideas he would like to submit. We parted without referring to past differences of opinion.

While I was waiting to hear from the Navy several copies of a new book called *Under Cover* were received by the *Reader's Digest* book department. On one of my calls at the Digest a book editor handed me a copy and said, "There's some stuff in here about you; it seems to me you should sue somebody for libel."

The book was written by one "John Roy Carlson," and published by E.P. Dutton Company, New York. On the jacket in bold type was the statement: "The amazing revelation of how Axis agents and our enemies within are now plotting to destroy the United States. John Roy Carlson names names — from Congressmen, Senators, Industrialists to hatchet men. *Under Cover* exposes the wealth and power behind American Fascists." I was stopped by the words "now plotting." All the congressmen, senators, and industrialists I knew of had united in one purpose following Pearl Harbor—winning the war. A glance at the index showed me that the America First Committee was listed over a hundred times, with an entire chapter devoted to "revealing" that it was a pro-Nazi organization.

Again I pondered the words on the jacket "now plotting to destroy the United States." The America First Committee had ceased to exist immediately following news of the Japanese attack. There were presently several million former members of the America First Committee in uniform with the fighting forces. A further look at the index of *Under Cover* revealed listings of *Scribner's Commentator:* Charles S. Payson, Jeremiah Milbank, and George T. Eggleston. No mention was made that *Scribner's Commentator* came out with a "Win the War "issue and ceased publication immediately after Pearl Harbor. The book described *Scribner's Commentator* as "the American Nazi Bible."

Under chapter headings such as "Puppets of Adolf Hitler," "Grave Diggers of Democracy," and "Liberty's Hangmen" the book named sixty-five former isolationist senators and congressmen as the dupes of Nazi-Fascist agents. Senators Taft, Wheeler, and Nye were portrayed as saboteurs of U.S. defense. And of course General Wood, Colonel Lindbergh, and Henry Ford came in for a full share of smears.

In a typical quote from the book:

> America First Chairman General Robert E. Wood indicated his willingness to let Hitler plant his legions firmly on the Western hemisphere and place the Panama Canal at the mercy of the Luftwaffe. General Wood's Committee became polluted with Bundsmen, Silver Shirts, Klansmen and Nazi and Japanese agents.

Under Cover's reference to wicked industrialists was in line with its attacks on Henry Ford as an unrepentant isolationist. There is, of course, no mention in the book that at the very moment of its publication Ford's Willow Run plant was turning out the thousands of B-24 bombers that were to win the war. Or that Colonel Lindbergh was at Willow Run as chief adviser on design, production, and flight testing of the newest war planes. Neither I nor any of my friends had the time or the stomach to become involved in a suit for libel. But several people took the author and the publisher of *Under Cover*, E.P. Dutton and Company, to court, and in every case the jury brought in a verdict sustaining the charge of libel.

Federal Judge John P. Barnes said following one verdict: "I think this book was written by a wholly irresponsible person who would write anything for a dollar. I wouldn't believe this author if he was under oath. I think he and the publisher are as guilty as anyone who was ever found guilty in this court."

Author John Roy Carlson was to be later thoroughly exposed in a series of columns by Westbrook Pegler. Pegler discovered that Carlson, an Armenian immigrant whose real name was Avedis Derounian, had been for several years employed as a stool pigeon by the outfit called Friends of Democracy. That group, as previously noted, specialized in smearing only conservatives—never Communists or left-wingers. This was the slant of *Under Cover*. In the entire 520 pages of the book there was not one word critical of Communism or Communists.

As the weeks went by with no word from the Navy I began to think my offer to serve had been pigeonholed. Then, in late November, 1943, I received an unpleasant surprise in the mail, a subpoena to appear before another Washington grand jury. My troubles weren't over, it seemed. A newspaper story had recently appeared stating that Mr. Maloney had been relieved of the job of prosecuting suspected pro-Nazis, and the new man taking his place was one O. John Rogge of the Justice Department.

Thirty-nine-year-old O. John Rogge was one of the many graduates of Harvard Law School who joined the Washington bureaucracy in the 1930's. He was appointed to the Department of Justice following service as Assistant General Counsel of the Securities and Exchange Commission. Author Albert L. Kahn has described him as a man "who thought in terms of the New Deal and talked enthusiastically about the prospect of 'Democratic Capitalism' in the United States."

Thanks to another column by Westbrook Pegler I learned something about Mr. Rogge that was an eye-opener. Pegler revealed that the author of *Under Cover*, John Roy Carlson, was functioning as an informer for Mr. Rogge in the pursuit of pro-Nazis in America.

I had earlier thought William Power Maloney was one of the most obnoxious characters I had ever met. But after a session in the grand jury room presided over by O. John Rogge I could think of Maloney as almost a gentleman. Rogge, red in the face and with the veins in his neck bulging, railed at me as though I were the devil incarnate. Wildly gesturing, he went over all the old stuff. His questions made it very evident to me that he had collaborated with the professional liar Derounian, alias Carlson, in the writing of *Under Cover*. *Under Cover* was *his* Bible.

Back home in Connecticut after this new ordeal in Washington, I found a letter from the Navy saying I had been appointed a lieutenant (j.g.) in the U.S. Naval Reserve. On December 8 I went to 33 Pine Street, and, after taking the oath of allegiance, received a certificate of commission signed by Navy Secretary Frank Knox. A few days later I received Navy orders to purchase all uniforms and equipment and report for duty at Officers' Training School, U.S. Naval Air Station, Quonset Point, R.I., on January 4, 1944.

XVII

Commissioned in the Navy

AFTER A FINAL QUIET weekend at home, Hazel saw me off on the train to New London, and I arrived at the air station as the Eastern Seaboard was experiencing the worst snowstorm in years. The Quonset training course was as one would expect in wartime, a sort of shock-treatment routine designed to keep one off balance and under pressure. There were 256 men in my class, all in their thirties and all college graduates. Nearly all had been deskbound executives prior to joining the service. Some sixty were lawyers. Other categories included bankers, architects, university professors, and a superior court judge.

For a group of men used to giving orders to others and used to leisured living the novel situation of drilling to barked commands, hurrying on the double to lecture classes, living in barracks with only iron double-deck bunks and foot lockers for furniture, was a bit flabbergasting. Each trainee was issued eighteen books to be studied and digested in preparation for the dozens of written examinations that followed. Since there was never any privacy, and never much time to study between drilling, gunnery practice, lectures, pistol shoots, and workouts on the track, it was not surprising that after lights-out each night the latrines were full of men cramming for next day's quizzes.

The other 255 men in my class were fortunate. They had only the Quonset crash course to cope with. I had the wild inquisitor Rogge again on my trail.

I shall never forget that cold early dawn of February 6. After the usual run around the track, the shower, and the singing interlude in the assembly hall, which always began with "Oh, what a beautiful mornin'," I paused to reflect that I had just about recaptured the glow of health of my undergraduate days.

"I got a beautiful feelin' everything's goin' my way." As I left the hall humming these last lines of the Quonset theme song, I was informed that a long distance call was awaiting me. It was Hazel. She said that Rogge had called her from Washington and asked where he could reach me. She told him that I was at Quonset and soon to be in the midst of final examinations, and added: "Surely, Mr. Rogge, if you need to see him again, can't you make it two weeks from now so he can complete his training course." This was just what Rogge wanted to hear. He replied that he needed me in Washington immediately.

So I found myself reporting to the grand jury again at 10:00 A.M. on February 9. This time Rogge tried a clever series of ploys. Upon my arrival outside the court room a clerk informed me that my hearing was postponed and I was to "come back tomorrow." Next day the same thing, "Come back tomorrow." Next morning I was told, "Come back this afternoon at 2:30."

That afternoon, after an hour-long wait in the antechamber, I was finally called before the grand jury. This time Rogge took a new tack. Scowling at me and slowly looking my uniform up and down, he pointed to some copies of *Scribner's Commentator* on the table and said the magazine had carried several cartoons by me that were highly critical of President Roosevelt. I tried to tell the jury that the drawings were done, of course, very much prior to Pearl Harbor and prior to my enlistment in the Navy and were in the same vein as dozens of cartoons appearing in the *Chicago Tribune* at the time. Rogge did not let me get anywhere with my explanation. He merely sneered that "an officer in the Navy had criticized his Commander in Chief." When I said I was told that I was to be assigned to a combat unit, he sneered again.

Before I left Washington Rogge asked me to call at his office in the Department of Justice. There, with no witnesses present, he gave me a piece of his mind, while I, self-conscious in my U.S. Naval officer's uniform, didn't feel I dared talk back. This is what he finally said to me: "Eggleston, I am going to have you down here forever until you tell me where Stewart got that $15,000. By God, if I had you in Russia I would find a way to make you talk." Rogge apparently didn't seem to grasp — or didn't want to grasp, after all the thousands of words of testimony — that I had nothing to do with the finances of *Scribner's ·Commentator* or any of its promotion efforts. I was concerned with editor's duties only, and my salary was paid by two prominent patriotic Republicans, who were each known to be millionaires.

I arrived in Quonset with five days of the hardest book work of the course to make up. I had taken a few books with me to Washington and done some memorizing in my hotel room and on the train going and coming. But under the distracting harassment of Rogge it was difficult to concentrate on anything. My superior officers were all very understanding upon my return and advised me to try to forget it. Several were admirers of Lindbergh and had been members of the America First Committee themselves. The morning I arrived back on the station I took part in the final pistol competition and won it, which cheered me. Rogge's tactics hadn't rattled me as much as I thought. I somehow survived the barrage of final examinations with satisfactory grades in every category.

Then, on the Sunday evening prior to graduation ceremonies, a bizarre incident took place. As our class members were now about to be assigned to active duty, we were allowed as a special privilege to stay on at the officers' club after 9:00 P.M. About five minutes past nine, as we were enjoying our drinks and the background music of Guy Lombardo over the radio, someone switched the dial, and suddenly the air was filled with the rasping voice of Walter Winchell. Someone shouted, "Turn that son of a bitch off — and get some more music." But before the music resumed I heard some bits of stacato chatter that made me wonder if Rogge himself was speaking: "In a German newspaper there is a cartoon...a bitter attack on Mr. Roosevelt....It was drawn by a person now being investigated by the Department of Justice....He is a famed magazine editor who tells people he has been commissioned in the U.S. Navy. How do you like that?...Write to Secretary Knox." (Apparently a German paper had reproduced a cartoon of mine that had appeared in *Scribner's Commentator* before America got into the war. Winchell made it seem I had done the cartoon that week.)

It so happened that of the hundred and fifty men in the room nobody knew what Winchell was talking about. But I felt I had been most unfairly betrayed as I realized that Rogge had been passing the secret grand jury records to the gossip columnist, who was supposed to have millions of readers.

I should, of course, have expected a blast from Winchell. We had been highly critical of his tactics in several *Scribner's Commentator* pieces in 1940. Following Pearl Harbor Winchell had continued to rail vociferously at such pre-war isolationists as Senators Taft, Wheeler, and Bennett Champ Clark, as well as numerous congressmen. He called Congress "Washington's Rogue's Gallery and House of Reprehensibles." In 1942 he wrote: "While the noose is being tightened around the necks of Quislings in Europe and Asia it would be folly and a betrayal of our heroic dead if we let bygones be bygones for Quislings here — whether they are street-corner Hitlers...or congressmen."

Winchell was the embodiment of lasting hatreds and lifelong feuds. For example, he literally hounded Harold Ross right up to death's door. And all because Ross had run à profile in the *New Yorker* calling Winchell "an odd little ex-vaudevillian, a product of New York's East Side, vain, hard, ambitious, with little education, no taste, and no respect for accuracy." Three days before Ross died of terminal cancer in Boston, Winchell was trumpeting that the *New Yorker* editor was faking his illness to avoid divorce proceedings in New York. He said Ross had gotten out of town because he was a coward.

Winchell had been described in a *New York Times* article as a close friend of FDR who was often invited to the White House for a private session with the President. During these conversations FDR and the columnist exchanged information about persons pro and anti the Administration.

Back in 1941, when Maloney was in pursuit of *Scribner's Commentator*, Winchell ran several barbs in his column about our magazine. At that time we predicted in print that despite his warlike words, if war came he would be found sitting it out at the Stork Club (which turned out to be what he did).

At any rate, after Pearl Harbor, with the President's blessing Winchell got himself a commission as a lieutenant commander in the Naval Reserve and continued his vindictive columns and broadcasts in uniform. By early 1943 the senators and congressmen he castigated had had enough. On February 13, 1943, his friendly editor at *PM* headlined a front-page story: "WINCHELL PUT OUT OF SERVICE."

> Yesterday the Navy stripped Walter Winchell of his Lt. Commander's uniform to appease the onetime isolationist bloc in Congress.

That same day Congressman Hoffman called a press conference and announced that he had the "Secretary of the Navy's assurance that Walter Winchell will not be recalled to active duty, which will prove a boon to Navy morale. No longer will Navy men wince at the spectacle of a Broadway gossiper sporting a lieutenant commander's stripes while he snoops about in search of sexy tidbits."

All this was the background for the bizarre radio bulletin received in the Officers' Club at Quonset, Rhode Island, at our pre-graduation party with drinks and music.

Graduation exercises took place on February 18. Our diplomas were handed out by Admiral Pye. My orders were to report to the Bureau of Aeronautics, Washington, D.C., on February 28, with time in between to be used as leave at home.

Then came the big day. At 11:00 A.M. on February 28 I was "welcomed aboard" at the Bureau of Aeronautics in Washington by a Lieutenant Armstrong and asked if I wanted more insurance and if I needed help to find a temporary place to live before being sent overseas. Lieutenant Armstrong then took me down the hall to another office and introduced me to an Ensign Richie. While I was chatting with Armstrong and Richie another ensign appeared and handed me a paper signed by a Commander Shanklin directing me to report to his office. I was ushered there and shook hands with Commander Shanklin and a Captain Baber, who shared the desk with him. These officers and gentlemen then proceeded to inform me as politely as they could that orders had just come down from above to separate me from the service. I said that in a situation like this there was supposed to be a hearing, when I believed I could easily prove that I was being victimized. They replied they understood there had already been a hearing. I replied that I had never had the slightest opportunity to refute the lying charges the Communist press had made against me. I asked for forty-eight hours to contact the influential people who had endorsed me in the first place. The officers agreed I could have the time requested. They also pointed out that perhaps the simplest thing for me to do would be to resign. They noted that Lindbergh had done just that when he felt the wrath of the White House focused on him.

Yes, Lindbergh had resigned his commission when, in peacetime, he wanted freedom to speak out as a civilian against FDR's policies. But for me to resign with the war raging full blast would have been unthinkable. Lindbergh, by the way, had immediately volunteered for active duty when Pearl Harbor struck. The Army high command had welcomed him, but FDR refused to allow him to serve. When Curtis Wright, Pan American, and United Aircraft asked the Colonel to work for them, Roosevelt had stepped in and advised them not to employ him. Finally Henry Ford asked him to come to Willow Run and help with flight testing and bomber production, and refused to clear it with the White House. Lindbergh worked at Willow Run for no salary, and contributed enormously to the production of bombers and fighter aircraft. Nothing better illustrates the petty vindictiveness of FDR than his vengeful pursuit of Lindbergh. I, being only a lowly lieutenant (j.g.), found it hard to figure why I was worth White House hounding, except perhaps by way of trying to intimidate the prominent Republicans whom I numbered among my friends.

After I left the Aeronautics building I walked around the historic streets of Washington for an hour thinking and wondering why I had allowed myself to get into such a predicament when I might have so easily taken my deferment and sat out the war in comfort, as Maloney and Rogge intended to do. I rested for half an hour in the lobby of the old Willard Hotel and glanced at a copy of the *New York Times*. A story on the front page was headlined: "35,000 OFFICERS NEEDED BY THE U.S. NAVY."

From a phone booth at the Willard I called Pleasantville and reached Al Cole, the *Digest*'s general manager. As I related in some detail what had happened to me, Al grew more and more indignant. He said he would get in touch with the Navy Secretary's office at once and was sure I would get a hearing from Mr. Knox. He was positive that a full-dress hearing would clear up the matter once and for all. There was no need for me to call anyone else.

When I reported back again to officers Baber and Shanklin, I was able to tell them that I had received the assurance that a proper hearing would be arranged, and soon. Meantime I would go back to my job at *Reader's Digest* and await further word. As Ensign Richie walked with me down the corridor again, he said: "A great many of us here in the bureau are with you. The Navy has had nothing to do with this."

After leaving Richie I walked over to the office of David I. Walsh, Democratic senator from Massachusetts and Chairman of the Senate Naval Affairs Committee. There I spent an hour with Captain Saunders, liaison officer for Senate Naval Affairs. Senator Walsh was in Florida on holiday, but the Captain was sure he would help me when he returned. He said I was lucky I hadn't been shipped off to the Aleutian Islands for the duration of the war. Several former America Firsters in naval uniform had already been sent to that God-forsaken outpost by White House decree. "Look at what happened to FDR's former friend and crony, General Hugh Johnson," said the Captain. "The War Department welcomed the General's request for active duty, but quickly received a White House directive that on no account should Johnson be allowed to serve." He added that Senator Walsh had recently been very upset about White House pressure to admit Communists into the Navy. Columnist George Sokolsky had written a revealing article about this, stating that in May, 1942, a distinguished group of admirals met with Secretary Knox to view with alarm the penetration of Communist Party members into the communications branches of the Navy. Knox answered the admirals in these words: "The President has stated that considering the fact that the United States and Russia are allies, and that the Communist Party in the United States is now bent on winning the war, the United States is bound *not* to oppose the activities of the Communist Party, and specifically *not* disapprove the employment of Communists in the armed services. The President further stated that this is an order and must be obeyed without mental reservations." Had I known what was going on behind the scenes in official Washington at the time, I would not have been even slightly surprised at what was happening to me.

According to James Burnham in his book *The Web of Subversion*[1] Washington during the war years was riddled with Communist agents who had infiltrated the government. The New York *World Telegram and Sun* said of Burnham's book: "Mr. Burnham, holding himself scrupulously to proven fact, shows how the agents of Moscow penetrated 44 key U.S. departments."

As I walked the streets of the capital and passed the imposing facade of the U.S. Treasury Building, I would have been profoundly shocked had I known what was going on inside. At that very moment Assistant Treasury Secretary Harry Dexter White — the man FDR appointed to the post of passing out billions of lend-lease credits to Russia — was operating as Moscow's top spy chief in the U.S. White's guilt was not to be officially announced until 1953, when Attorney General Herbert Brownell declared: "Harry Dexter White was a Russian spy. He smuggled documents to Russian agents for transmission to Moscow. He was known to be a Communist agent by the very people who appointed him to the most sensitive position he ever held in government service."

In his book Burnham names names and spells out the treasonous activities of scores of people in dozens of sensitive agencies of government. White's betrayal of his country was certainly the most brazen. One of White's most spectacular jobs for the Soviets was brought off when the U.S. Occupation Army entered Germany and a special invasion currency was printed for our troops. Acting on orders from Moscow, White sent the U.S. engraving plates to Russia, resulting in the Red Army being supplied with $270,000,000 of invasion currency at the expense of U.S. taxpayers.

During subsequent numerous hearings before Congressional investigating committees the sworn statements of dozens of witnesses supplied this picture of what had been going on:

Immediately upon the heels of the German invasion of Russia in June, 1941, the top Soviet spy boss in New York, Jacob Golos, received orders from the NKVD to set up a courier service in Washington to gather and relay to Moscow all information pertaining to war plans obtainable in the various bureaus where comrades had been placed during the pre-war years. Harry Dexter White at Treasury, Alger Hiss at State, and Lauchlin Currie as special adviser to FDR in the White House were key figures in this operation. The prime courier who deserted the Communist Party and whose testimony first exposed the wholesale treason, was, of course, Whittaker Chambers. Another courier, less publicized, was Elizabeth Bentley. The Chambers-Hiss story has been told many times. The full Bentley story came to light more recently in a book about Harry Dexter White, by David Rees.[2]

Elizabeth Bentley, a Vassar College graduate, had served as both mistress and secretary to Jacob Golos prior to his death in 1943. Her contact in Washington was one Nathan Gregory Silvermaster, whose cell boss was Harry Dexter White. White and Silvermaster had contacts in the War Production Board, the Office of Strategic Services, and the Army Air Corps headquarters in the Pentagon.

Bentley testified that by the spring of 1943 she was delivering forty rolls of 35 mm. film, containing sensitive military and political intelligence, to Golos every fortnight. The microphotography was all done in a photo laboratory located in the basement of Silvermaster's house at 5515 30th Street, N.W., Washington. Bentley said that she called regularly on Mr. and Mrs. Silvermaster, often dined with them, and sometimes helped with the processing of the film.

Silvermaster had come to Washington in 1935 and had worked in such varied New Deal agencies as the Resettlement Administration, Maritime Labor Board, Farm Security Administration, and finally the Treasury Department until he resigned in 1946. When in 1942 the Office of Military Intelligence sought to have him fired from the Board of Economic Warfare as a security risk, Presidential aid Lauchlin Currie intervened and had him transferred to the Farm Security Administration "without prejudice."

The file on Silvermaster in Military Intelligence (G-2) states:

> Overwhelming testimony from many sources indicates beyond doubt that Nathan Gregory Silvermaster is now, and has for years been, a leader of the Communist Party and very probably a secret agent of OGPU.

(In Washington in those days as fast as a Red was fired as a security risk in one department, he was quickly rehired by a comrade in another.)

Silvermaster could claim the world's record for refusing to answer questions. In one short hearing before the Internal Security Subcommittee he declined to answer some 250 questions with: "I claim my privilege of refusing to answer this question under the Fifth Amendment."

One of the oddest things about the White, Currie, Silvermaster trio was that the latter refused to acknowledge knowing his colleagues, whereas White and Currie readily claimed Silvermaster as a close friend, and each recalled sessions of Ping Pong in the basement rumpus room at 5515 30th Street, N.W. But they claimed that at no time did they notice a photographic lab on the premises. And they told the Security Committee they were positive that Silvermaster was not even slightly pink.

Although Silvermaster refused to answer all questions concerning a photo lab in his basement, he ran this advertisement in the *Washington Star* in May, 1947, describing his house for sale: "Contains nine rooms and three baths. In the basement an excellent photographic room...."

Alger Hiss turned out to be the only Washington subversive caught red-handed and punished. White glided through the war years in high office, unpunished, even though Whittaker Chambers had disclosed his secret operation to two special agents of the FBI in early 1941. White was to die of a mysterious heart attack in 1948 between appearances before a new Internal Security Committee. Lauchlin Currie made a brief appearance before a committee before moving to Colombia, South America, and beyond U.S. jurisdiction. Gregory Silvermaster's insistence on silence apparently paid off. He too went unpunished and was last heard of as living in the small town of Harvey Cedars, New Jersey.

So I was back at the *Digest* on civilian status for a period I estimated would be a month or less. Soon after my return Al Cole showed me a letter he had received from Secretary Knox, in which he promised that the Eggleston case would soon come up for a thorough hearing. In the letter Knox said: "While Eggleston is not guilty of any wrongdoing the Justice Department files show that there were things going on out in Lake Geneva which I am certain will raise your eyebrows." (Of course the Rogge-John Roy Carlson lies would raise anybody's eyebrows.) The Navy Secretary's letter concluded with this paragraph: "I also want to acknowledge your letter of March 16 containing the list of men who have endorsed Eggleston's application for a commission. It is certainly a strong list of names."

Curiously enough, there was a period a few years earlier when Mr. Knox was on record as criticizing FDR far more vehemently than anything any of us had printed in the pages of *Scribner's Commentator*. In the 1936 campaign, when Alf Landon was running against Roosevelt, Knox had been Landon's ticket mate as Vice-Presidential nominee. Knox had only recently switched his allegiance from the Republican to the Democratic Party upon being handed the cabinet post by FDR. This is what Knox said when he was a Republican:

> Mr. Roosevelt was a member of the memorable Wilson Administration, which, in trying to keep us out of war, got us into it. It is bad enough to have for President, in time of peace, a man who is overconfident, incautious, self-willed, uncertain, and unreliable. In time of war it would be disastrous. Mr. Roosevelt is a strange figure in the American scene. He has broken practically every pledge he has ever made to the people of the United States....Collectivists of every sort support Mr. Roosevelt. That is natural. For at the root of his philosophy lies the view, shared alike by Communists and Fascists, that individual liberty under democracy as hitherto practiced in this country is no longer desirable or feasible.

Alas for Mr. Knox. He died of a heart attack shortly after writing to Al Cole of his willingness to arrange personally for the hearing I requested. Al and I had lunch together the day news of Knox's death came through on the radio. In speaking of Knox Al said: "He was a decent man. There is no question in my mind but that had he lived, you would have been assigned to duty overseas in short order. But now that fate has stepped in — perhaps saving your life — I would suggest you stay on the job at R.D. and the hell with the hearing. Wally feels the same way about it." Next time I saw Wally, he smiled and said: "I'm glad to see they didn't put you in jail. If they had, I was going to ask for a cell next to you."

Shortly after my return to civilian status Hazel and I attended a dinner dance at the Riverside Yacht Club, and I was furnished with a footnote to my Navy experience that eased the pain somewhat. While chatting with Mrs. Paul Phoenix, wife of the Commodore of the club, she suddenly said to me: "I hope you won't let what happened to you worry you too much. My brother suffered through quite an ordeal himself, thanks to the long arm of the White House." Her brother, Donald C. Starr, a successful lawyer in Boston, had been a prominent member of the America First chapter there prior to Pearl Harbor. Then in 1942 he had volunteered for sea duty in the U.S. Navy, was given a lieutenant's commission, and promptly assigned to a shore post at Reykjavic, Iceland.

His orders to this out-of-the-way spot were a slap in the face, but worse was yet to come. The day before he was to embark for Iceland a fresh Navy directive came from Washington ordering him to stay in Boston and report to a captain there, twice daily. After six weeks of this charade, he was given the choice of resigning his commission or being handed a discharge. After he took the discharge, scores of his friends wrote to Washington in his behalf, with no results. One friend got as far as the Assistant Secretary of State, Adolf A. Berle, Jr. and was bluntly informed that Starr should not have expected to "hunt with the hounds and run with the hares." Considering the Navy's drive to add thousands of officers to its ranks, it would seem the verdict was particularly vindictive in Starr's case. An outstanding yachtsman, Starr, with a party of friends, had sailed his 85-foot schooner *Pilgrim* on a 28,500-mile East-to-West voyage around the world in 1932-34, an adventure duly serialized in *National Geographic Magazine*. Later he served as Vice Commodore of the Cruising Club of America. Starr's wife had been very vocal in America First affairs in Boston, and although she was the daughter of a former dean of the Harvard

Law School, the Starrs learned to their dismay that the mischief they encountered resulted from several letters denouncing Starr, written to the White House by two of Harvard's so-called "liberal professors." Starr and his wife and family retired to farm life for a year before returning to his Boston law firm, but he nursed a painful duodenal ulcer, thanks to the shattering experience with the Navy.

A couple of months later, on one of my visits to Pleasantville, Wally called me into his office and said he had a special job he thought I might like to tackle. To cope with its huge growth in circulation, the magazine was ordering several million dollars worth of new presses designed to print the magazine in full color. Specifically he wanted me to take a current issue of the *Digest*, and, using the same text material, redesign the whole thing to produce a single copy of the magazine as I thought it should look. He explained that I would be taking on quite a challenge. Already two teams of New York art directors and typographers had been at work on the same project. I would be getting a late start. The end product I delivered would be judged against the others by a final vote of the senior staff of the magazine. The identity of the designer of each entry would be kept secret. I immediately responded that I would like to enter the contest. He then said I could go about it any way I pleased, hire what help I needed, and spend as much money as I felt necessary. The deadline was sixty days hence.

My first move was to line up the services of a typographer in New York City, one that could not only set type, but had facilities to print color and put together an entire magazine of 138 pages. I soon discovered that the two outstanding houses I had used in my experimental work at Condé Nast had been engaged by my two competitors. I was fortunate that I found a third, which had all the facilities I needed. Shortly after my talk with Wally I was sending pages through the typographic shop of Fred A. Schmidt, with Schmidt personally taking an interest in the race to redesign and produce half a dozen copies of a complete magazine in the time allotted.

From my Condé Nast days I remembered a free-lance designer, C.O. Woodbury, who had excellent taste in layout, as well as a good color sense. His small apartment studio was a short walk from the Schmidt shop. I believed that he and I could produce the magazine with the new look before the deadline. But we would have to work days, nights, and weekends to do it.

Woodbury, known to his friends as "C.O.," was typical of many New York commercial designers with a fine arts background. He was not a reader of magazines. In fact, he was totally unfamiliar with the *Reader's Digest*. It was my job to analyze the stories, decide on the appropriate type faces to be used on the title pages, select the proper art work, and suggest the proportion of decoration to text. From here on layout pages meticulously calculated to a fraction of an inch flowed from C.O.'s drawing board to the Schmidt composing rooms.

For the ensuing eight weeks before our deadline was reached I saw very little of Hazel or anyone else but C.O. and Schmidt. Happily for our team, when the three competing copies of the redesigned magazine were finally circulated through a dozen top editors of the *Digest*, our presentation won all the votes. Incidentally, the total cost to produce our entry for the competition was but a fraction of the cost of the others.

From this beginning the large *Reader's Digest* art department came into being, permanently located in New York. To cope with art direction, not only for the U.S. *Digest*, but for foreign editions around the world, plus promotion and book projects, I engaged several more designers to back up Woodbury. I also engaged a photographic team whose ultimate assignment was to travel to the foreign offices and supply color photography for a schedule of *Digest* covers required in a dozen countries abroad. With the whole operation functioning smoothly, my name suddenly appeared on the masthead as an associate editor.

Two weeks after my name appeared in the line-up of editors Al Cole dropped by my office with the news that the Friends of Democracy were after me again. They had issued a special bulletin repeating all the smear stuff that had earlier been in *Under Cover* and *PM* and announced that they were "launching a project" to have me discharged from the *Digest*. In addition, the head of the outfit, the Reverend L.M. Birkhead, had written Wally a long letter requesting that one G.T. Eggleston be summarily fired. The gist of the letter was that GTE was an unrepentant, dangerous fascist.

The July, 1943, issue of *Reader's Digest* had featured as its opening article a long essay by Max Eastman, "To Collaborate Successfully We Must Face the Facts about Russia," which upset all the left-wingers and Communists, as well as some well-meaning Democrats. The *Digest* had also carried several articles suggesting that Germany could be forced to surrender by intensive bombing attacks rather than a bloody assault by U.S. invasion forces. As the slogan of every left-winger in the U.S. at the time was "We demand a second front NOW," these *Digest* pieces advocating winning the war by air power were infuriating. Most infuriating to the Friends of Democracy had been the Eastman piece, because it dared speak realistically about Russia. Although I had nothing whatever to do with the article, the Friends of Democracy were wild with indignation when they read it, and there is no doubt at all that it sparked their campaign to have me fired.

The main theme of the article was that while we Americans admired the heroic fight the Russian armies and people were putting up against Hitler it was time we stopped heaping praise on the Stalin dictatorship. Eastman wrote:

> An astonishing number of our influential men and magazines and newspapers are fawning on Russia. Recently at a Soviet Friendship Rally Vice President Henry Wallace actually praised what he called Stalin's practice of "economic democracy."...
>
> There are presently 10,000,000 prisoners living, or rather dying, at hard labor in Stalin's concentration camps. These slaves are the bottom layer upon which the whole edifice of so-called "economic democracy" rests....
>
> It is well known that Stalin has two foreign policies: one conducted by his diplomatic corps, the other by his secret agents. The former is a facade — in the latter Stalin talks his own language of "World Revolution," and "overthrow of Imperialism" (by which he means primarily England and the U.S.). We must stop kidding ourselves about Russia's democratic war aims when Stalin's inflexible purpose is to destroy democracy everywhere. Yet American Communists denounce any word written or spoken by Americans in honest criticism of the Russian dictatorship as outright "fascism." They will so denounce this article and the *Reader's Digest* for printing it.

As predicted, the day after the Eastman piece appeared in R.D. the left-wing press came out in its full fury of indignation. On the front page of *PM* in red ink was the headline: "ANSWERING MAX EASTMAN'S ATTACK ON RUSSIA IN READER'S DIGEST." In a two-thousand-word essay on page two Max Lerner denounced Eastman for questioning Russia's motives. He argued: "If you look at the record of Russia's deeds you find that under Stalin Russia abandoned the tactic of world revolution and used the Comintern mainly for its own safety. And if you look at the record, you know that Russia's so-called plotting has not caused us in a quarter-century to add a single soldier to the American armies."

While the left-wingers were still seething over the Eastman article, the *Digest* came out in the very next issue with an opening article especially painful to the Friends of Democracy and a body blow to FDR himself. This piece, called "Boondoggling on a Global Basis," was written by ace war correspondent Henry J. Taylor. Taylor did not beat around the bush. He came right out with the first honest appraisal of FDR's Four Freedoms to appear in the U.S. press: "The whole conception of giving or infusing the Four Freedoms universally is preposterous. It is not idealism. It is sheer political buncombe."

Al Cole said he had taken the chore of dealing with the letter from the Reverend L.M. Birkhead about firing me off Wally's hands. But instead of throwing the diatribe into the wastebasket, he had answered it in detail, pointing out that the Friends of Democracy were totally misinformed and ill-advised in their project. To this Al received a reply repeating the same lies and renewing the demand that I be immediately dismissed. Al said he didn't quite want to tell the good Reverend what he thought of him, but he did sharply inform him that it was "high time this persecution of George Eggleston should stop." The Birkhead reaction to this was to cause about 500 irate letters from members of the Friends of Democracy to be addressed to the *Reader's Digest*. These five hundred letters, among the million pieces of mail arriving at Pleasantville each week, of course cut little ice. But each was answered politely, as was R.D. custom.

John T. Flynn did some research on the Friends of Democracy and wrote a memo, revealing their technique of character assassination:

I have in my possession a document issued by the Rev. Birkhead entitled: "Report on the status of the Lindbergh Project." It went out from the Friends headquarters to persons who were asked to put up the money for the purpose of destroying various reputations. The document concluded:

It will take time and money to *destroy Lindbergh* politically. But it will take only a little of your time to write a check or money order to the Friends of Democracy....The Lindbergh project is only one of several projects now under way.

Al Cole had had the benefit of reading the Flynn memo and also talking with Flynn about Birkhead's long reputation for smearing conservatives while coddling Communists and left-wingers. Apropos of all this, I showed Al a recent clipping from the New York *Herald-Tribune* quoting Birkhead as setting up a $250,000 budget to carry on his "fight against Fascism in America." Said Al: "This fellow seems to spend his time scaring money out of people for his hatchet jobs. I wonder what will happen next time on Project Eggleston?"

XVIII

The "Hate Machine" and a Dying President

IN EARLY 1943 the Reverend Birkhead's Friends of Democracy had made news with the announcement that its chairman, mystery novelist Rex Stout, had been appointed to head up a new propaganda bureau called the Writers War Board. Stout, with a staff supplied by Birkhead and expenses paid by the Government, soon had the new bureau operating in high gear. In news releases sent daily to 1,500 newspapers, plus radio scripts sent to 500 local stations, Stout ground out his twin themes: hate for the Germans — praise for the Russians. I must have benefited indirectly from Birkhead's preoccupation with the new quasi-government bureau — he had less time to devote to Project Eggleston.

A piece of news that the Stout bureau received with joy was the announcement that FDR planned to make a harsh peace if and when the war was won. During the recent Anglo-American summit meeting at Casablanca FDR had told reporters that in any future peace negotiations with the Axis Powers *no terms* would be granted — there would be Unconditional Surrender.

On the spot in Casablanca FDR's surprise announcement immediately sent shudders through the ranks of the Allied military strategists. They knew that any such ultimatum was certain to stiffen the backs of the enemy and needlessly sacrifice millions of lives. The comment of Churchill's Chief of Staff, Major General Ismay, was typical:

Everyone will agree that it is unwise for great men to give vent to public announcements without having their implications examined with scrupulous care. Everyone will agree that the cheapest and quickest way of winning a war is to make your enemy realize that nothing is to be gained by further fighting, and that the only sensible course is to sue for peace. A man robbed of hope will fight to the bitter end, and it is defeating your own object to let him think that terms of surrender will be utterly merciless.

There was nothing remotely resembling the wisdom of Ismay's remark in the flood of propaganda that now poured forth from Stout's hate bureau. Promptly upon receiving the news of FDR's Casablanca statement Stout wrote an article for the *New York Times Magazine* entitled "We shall Hate or We Shall Fail." In it he put forth the thesis that only by hating *all* Germans as evil beasts could we be uncompromising in the job of destroying them.

The immediate reaction to the Stout piece was a deluge of letters to the *Times* denouncing Stout. The paper published a collection of the letters, noting that the writers had "almost unanimously opposed Mr. Stout's views."

The rebukes to Stout's views published in the *Times* brought no noticeable change in the hate output. In an America's Town Meeting of the Air broadcast on January 31 Stout's colleague, Quentin Reynolds, declared: "We must go to the peace table with hatred in our hearts. The mental disease of Germany cannot be cured—we must kill."

In other Town Meetings, and on America's Forum of the Air, as well as on innumerable talk programs, the hate theme reached ever wider audiences. Louis Nizer's proposal to execute thousands of Germans after the war and send hundreds of thousands to labor camps in Russia was given a glowing presentation. Likewise columnist Dorothy Thompson's recommendation that with the signing of a peace "at least 150,000 Germans should be executed as war criminals." On the same program another speaker argued that to prevent future breeding in the Reich all German males between the ages of twenty to forty be shipped to Russian labor camps. The plans went on and on. For a time the scheme FDR most favored was the "Morgenthau Plan," which called for stripping Germany of all industrial potential and reducing her to a nation of small farms.

In no instance did the Stout propaganda hint that there might be a "good German" in Germany. One was to assume that if there were no "good Germans" in the Germany of 1943, there had probably never been any good Germans. Thus the heads of our three armed services — Eisenhower, Nimitz, and Spaatz — should have viewed their Teutonic ancestry with shame. Not to mention such titans of America's growth as the pioneer in building suspension bridges, John Augustus Roebling, and the inventor of the linotype, Otthmar Mergenthaler. Or optical wizards Bausch and Lomb, steelmakers Schwab and Frick, pharmaceutical pioneers Merck and Pfizer; Westinghouse, Chrysler, Steinway, Knabe, Wurlitzer. Were these and vast numbers of Americans of like background to revile their German blood? Americans can count themselves fortunate indeed that Napoleon Bonaparte, conqueror of Prussia and Austria in 1806, did not order extermination of his beaten enemies after their surrender!

As the all-out participation in the war by the U.S. made Germany's ultimate doom certain, there were constant rumors that a clique of German generals planned to kill Hitler and sue for peace. The Stout bureau warned that any such peace plan was a scheme to cover up the fact that these same generals were planning World War III. And later, when Hitler narrowly escaped assassination at his staff headquarters, the Stout propaganda machine proclaimed that the incident was merely another Nazi trick to get easy peace terms preparatory to starting another war.

During the spring months of Presidential election year 1944 there was much speculating in the press about whether Mr. Roosevelt would run for a fourth term. My interest in politics had dimmed considerably following my long grillings by the White House-sponsored inquisitors. I just wanted to pursue running the *Digest* art and graphics operation, insulating myself as much as possible from anything resembling political controversy. But when in July FDR won the Democratic nomination to run again — and rumors were rife that the nominee was in fact a very sick man — my curiosity as an innocent bystander was aroused. A photo taken at the Democratic Convention and widely distributed by the Associated Press revealed a haggard President, with eyes dark sockets and mouth hanging listlessly open. Stories began to appear in the Luce press hinting at the fragile health of the President. Luce directed both *Time* and *Life* to plug unabashedly for Republican nominee Thomas E. Dewey.

Speaking of pictures, at the height of the campaign Luce was called upon to make a personal decision that was to have great impact on the outcome of the election. In early October my friend Dan Longwell, who was then managing editor of *Life*, called Henry Luce into the picture room and asked him to make a selection of Roosevelt photos to be run in upcoming issues.

Luce was later to comment on this incident:

> The big irresponsibility—or big failure — of the American press came when we did not indicate, especially in *Life*'s pictures, that Roosevelt was a dying man. Longwell showed me, oh, a hundred pictures of Roosevelt — two hundred. In about half of them he was a dead man. We decided to print the ones that were the least bad. And thereby — by trying to lean over backward being fair or something, or kind — we infringed our contract with readers to tell them the truth. Actually the truth *was* in the pictures.

It was not until many years later that the whole truth about Roosevelt's physical condition in 1944-45 was revealed in Jim Bishop's painstakingly researched *FDR's Last Year*.[1] The medical details were as follows:

> In March of 1944 a checkup on the President at Bethesda Naval Hospital confirmed indications of "hypertension, hypertensive heart disease, failure of the left ventricle of the heart, and fluid in both lungs. FDR had a persistent cough, a grayish pallor on his face, a noticeable agitation of the hands, a blue cast to lips and fingernails."
>
> Blood pressure was 186 over 108. In sum, he had a severe heart condition as well as a hardening of the arteries. The President's personal physician, Admiral Ross McIntire, ordered that the results of this examination be kept secret. When a reporter from Time, Inc. called the Admiral in April, he was told that the President was in good health. "Considering the difference in age, his recent physical examination is equally as good as the one made on him twelve years ago."

Two weeks before election day Admiral McIntire was again queried by reporters regarding FDR's health. "The President's health is perfectly okay," he said. "Absolutely no organic difficulties at all." About this statement Bishop comments: "The Admiral lied arrogantly. His duty was to keep his medical puppet alive and in office."

The deception worked. But this time around there was no Roosevelt landslide. The popular vote was FDR, 25,602,505 *vs.* Dewey, 22,006,278. Roosevelt had enjoyed a more comfortable margin in his 1940 victory over Wendell Willkie. In that election

FDR's great deception was the promise to keep American youth out of the war. In 1944, with the President running as the Commander in Chief of millions of young Americans on the battlefronts of the world, it was imperative that his doctors lie about his health if he was to be elected.

On January 6, 1945, the President's State of the Union Message was sent to Congress to be read. The President stated to friends that he could not stand on his feet long enough to deliver even three thousand words. Later in January, immediately after the inaugural swearing in, the President confessed to his son James that he had suffered severe chest pains and feared he might have collapsed in the middle of the ceremony. When James wheeled him from the portico to a secluded room the President asked for and drank a half tumbler of straight whiskey to ease the pain.

In February the President went to Yalta for a summit meeting with Stalin and Churchill. Close friends and members of the family were fearful that he might not last out the trip, which was a strenuous one. There was the long first leg of the voyage by warship to Malta. Then the flight by plane to the Crimea. Then a series of exhausting talk sessions with the principals and their small army of advisers. There were social demands as well: A typical Yalta dinner party, with the Russians as host, consisted of twenty courses and as many as forty-five separate toasts with vodka. No one should have been surprised that the Free Polish Government in London was sold down the river at Yalta, along with millions of anti-Communist Eastern Europeans.

In describing the final banquet of the conference, with again the innumerable toasts, Churchill noted that "The President seemed very tired," but that "Stalin was in the best of tempers." He had reason to be. The Russian leader would return to Moscow with everything his heart (or lack of heart) desired. Russia could now officially absorb the eastern half of Poland. The Poles under a Communist government would be compensated for their loss of land to Russia by absorbing territory to the West, "including the free city of Danzig, the region of East Prussia west and south of Konigsberg, the administrative district of Oppeln in Silesia, and the lands sought by Poland to the east of the line of the Oder." Poland's total land grab of ancient German territory was to result in "the displacement of some 16 million Germans from their homes in central and Eastern Europe, a process by which over 2 million did not survive."[2]

Churchill did manage to inject into the proceedings the thought that, after all, Britain had gone to war to guarantee a free Poland, and the British people expected that at some future date free elections would be possible in the new Polish State. Stalin assured the Prime Minister that this was his intention also, but he knew full well that with all the anti-Communists disposed of, any "free election" would be similar to an "election" in the USSR.

No knowledge of the Yalta settlement was of course permitted to leak to the press of America and reveal the enormity of the sellout.

There were, however, high hopes in the U.S. that this meeting of the Big Three would bring an early peace and an end to the bloodshed. Victorious Allied armies were fast closing in on Germany from the West; the Russians were closing the pincers from the East. The U.S. Bomber Command controlled air space over all of Germany. It was only FDR's threat of Unconditional Surrender that kept the German armies in the field fighting the hopeless cause.

Just a week before FDR left the U.S. for Yalta a White House press release pointedly revealed that the President had taken the Oath of Office with his family Bible opened to First Corinthians, chapter thirteen: *And now abideth faith, hope, and charity, these three; but the greatest of these is charity.*

Editorial comment in the press at the time suggested that FDR might just possibly be relaxing his Unconditional Surrender demands. It soon became evident that a spirit of revenge, not of charity, was the ruling emotion of the gathering at Yalta.

The conference had barely got under way when British Air Marshal Sir Robert Saundby received an order from the War Cabinet to bomb the city of Dresden.[3] Since Dresden was an open city, unfortified, and by no means a military target, Saundby thought that the order was in error, and immediately cabled Churchill for clarification. Churchill's reply was to destroy the city at the earliest opportunity.

Not only was Dresden naked to attack, without a single antiaircraft weapon, but the city had for centuries been considered a museum piece, second only to Vienna in the splendor of its ancient buildings and collection of art masterpieces, plus a million-volume library dating back to the sixteenth century. The normal population of Dresden was 600,000, but at the hour of Churchill's order the city was swollen by the influx of some 200,000 of the millions of homeless refugees fleeing the Russian advance from the East.

Capt. Sir Liddell Hart described the destruction of the ancient city in a single sentence: "Dresden was subject to a devastating attack with the deliberate intention of wreaking havoc among the civil population and refugees."

The British writer David Irving cites British Official History in describing the destruction of the city. The first wave of Allied bombers, according to plan, "raised a gigantic fire storm" in the heart of the city. The second attack came three hours later "so fire-fighting brigades and relief crews from other towns would themselves be victims." At least 10,000 civilians died in these two raids.

The next day there was abundant proof that Roosevelt had been a party to the Churchill decision when some 1,200 U.S. Flying Fortresses attacked the city and left tens of thousands of dead and dying, men, women, and children. The two Allied leaders who, in 1940, had warned that the downfall of Western Civilization was at hand were now in full partnership with the Asiatic power bent upon destruction of the West.

Following the devastation of Dresden there was speculation in the Allied command that the decision at Yalta was taken at the behest of Stalin. This was denied by the Russians, and today one may visit the Communist-controlled city and view a large photo mural in the reconstructed museum: a view of the terrible devastation after the bombing. A descriptive placard on the photo attributes the square miles of destruction to "the terror-bombing by American and British aircraft."

Benjamin Colby, following a study of British Official History of the War, flatly stated in his book, *Twas a Famous Victory*[4] that the bombing of civilian centers was a tactic instigated by Winston Churchill. Four months before any bombs fell on London the Prime Minister had ordered a series of bombing raids on Berlin for the specific purpose of enticing the Germans to attack London. It seems rather obvious that by this maneuver he hoped to get America in the war. FDR had promised the King in 1939 that if London were bombed we would be in.

George H. Crocker, in *Roosevelt's Road to Russia*,[5] states:

> Craftily, Churchill provoked the Germans to bomb England. In an early period of the war Churchill fumed, not because Hitler dropped bombs on English cities, but because he did not. General de Gaulle, in his memoirs, describes Churchill's frustration:

"I can still see him at Chequers one August day, raising his fists toward the sky as he cried: 'So they won't come!'"

"Are you in such a hurry," I said to him, "to see your towns smashed to bits?"

"You see," he replied, "the bombing of Oxford, Coventry, Canterbury will cause such a wave of indignation in the United States they will come into the war."

Allied bombing attacks on German cities finally accounted for over 500,000 civilian dead and over 800,000 wounded. In reprisal German bombs killed some 60,000 British civilians and wounded an estimated 80,000.

As the Yalta Conference came to a close, Lord Moran, Mr. Churchill's physician, penned an amazingly prophetic note in his diary: "To a doctor's eye the President appears a very sick man. He has all the symptons of hardening of the arteries of the brain in an advanced stage. I give him only a few months to live."

Just two months later, on April 12, 1945, at 3:25 P.M., Franklin Delano Roosevelt died of a massive cerebral hemorrhage while resting at Warm Springs, Georgia.

XIX

The Ultimate in Perjury

*We Democrats have always believed that men
ought to be free to speak, to read, to write, to
listen, and to unburden their innermost
thoughts to their neighbors without fear.*
— ADLAI STEVENSON

FOLLOWING PRESIDENT ROOSEVELT's death and Harry
Truman's accession to office events on the world scene moved
rapidly to the conclusion of the war on all fronts. In the spring of
1946 the mood of the American people was to honor the heroism of
our million war casualties and return to peacetime pursuits. There
remained some people in government, however, legacies from the
FDR White House, who thought otherwise.

Under the dateline of March 31, 1946, wire services across the
U.S. announced the news from Washington that Department of
Justice prosecutor O. John Rogge was off to Germany with a team
of assistants to interview imprisoned Nazi war criminals. Rogge
declared that the object of his mission was to seek out, by interrogation and by delving into captured enemy files, evidence to prove
that certain prominent Americans had been used as "pipelines of
Nazi propaganda." He swore he was going to expose "American
fascists — Americans with Nazi ties who are trying to destroy the
United States."

After Rogge and his team had been in Germany about two
months, the left-leaning *New York Post, PM,* and the Communist
press began running stories to the effect that his interrogations
were turning up some shocking revelations that would come to
light when the interrogators returned to the U.S. Rogge an-

nounced in a Nuremberg press release on June 3 that evidence obtained from Germans in prison camps and from the files of Ribbentrop, Goebbels, and other top Nazis would reveal definite links with citizens in the U.S.

Upon Rogge's return to Washington he immediately leaked a story to the left-wing press naming his choice of public enemy number one. The issue of the *New York Post* for August 15, 1946, announced in large black headlines across a full page the startling scoop:

MAGAZINE EDITOR ACCUSED OF PREWAR NAZI DEALINGS

Washington, Aug. 15. O. John Rogge, special assistant to the Attorney General, has urged the Justice Dept. to institute Grand Jury proceedings against an associate editor of the *Reader's Digest* he accuses of prewar dealings with the Nazis, the *Post* learned today.

Key target of Rogge's attack is George T. Eggleston, formerly a major figure in *Scribner's Commentator* magazine.

In the six-hundred-word story Rogge is quoted as promising that the "case against Eggleston will be fought to a finish on the basis of testimony received from Germans now in Allied hands. This testimony, Rogge's report will assert, establishes a direct link between Eggleston and the Nazis and reveals how Nazi money backed *Scribner's Commentator*."

The writer of the *Post* piece, James A. Wechsler, had an interesting background. At the mature age of twenty-one he had joined the Young Communist League and was editor of its official organ, *The Student Advocate,* named by Congress as a Communist-financed publication. In an editorial at that time Wechsler had penned a call for "a Nationwide Student Strike for Peace to dramatize the firmness of those who declare that no war undertaken by American Imperialism can be a just or fruitful venture for the majority of the American people." Wechsler, of course, claimed he later disavowed his Red ties. But anyone who had been reading the *New York Post* could have easily noted that the paper followed the Rogge left-wing line that America First Republicans were "dangerous fascists" while the Reds in government who had been exposed by Congressional committees were in fact perfectly harmless liberals.

G.T. Eggleston was not for long the single person named by O. John Rogge. Shortly after he gave the story about me to the *New*

York Post, he gave syndicated columnist Drew Pearson some "secret testimony" concerning my friend Paul Palmer, then a senior editor of *Reader's Digest.* Obviously the leak was planned to attempt to smear the good name of the *Digest.* This new attack claimed that

> The amazing thing about Nazi propaganda before Pearl Harbor was the Nazi ability to suck in certain high-placed and supposedly intelligent Americans. The *Reader's Digest,* largest circulating magazine in the world, was one of them. The report on Nazi activities in the U.S.A. prepared by John Rogge of the Justice Department after weeks of interviewing top Germans shows that one editor of *Reader's Digest,* Paul Palmer, was often in consultation with Hans Thomsen, Hitler's personal ambassador in Washington; also with Manfred Zapp, head of the official Nazi propaganda agency, Trans Ocean News Service.

This leak by Rogge was a perfect example of establishing guilt by innuendo and another example of Rogge's willingness to spread lies. After this column appeared I spoke to Paul on the telephone, and he said: "Hell, the last contact I had with the Germans was when I was with the U.S. Marines fighting the Kaiser's troops in 1918."

In his attack on Palmer, Rogge managed to drag in the names of DeWitt Wallace and Senators Vandenberg, Bennett Champ Clark, Robert Reynolds, and Harry Byrd of Virginia, implying that all these men were dupes of the Nazis.

Although the left-wing press and columnists Drew Pearson and Walter Winchell had a field day leaking out material supplied by Rogge, the prosecutor evidently felt he needed still more publicity. So he appeared for a lecture at Swarthmore College in Pennsylvania repeating much of his early material and adding Senator Burton Wheeler, ex-President Herbert Hoover, and United Mine Workers chief John L. Lewis to his list of "dupes of the Nazis." Rogge denounced John L. Lewis "for making a pre-Pearl Harbor appeal to the White House for a negotiated peace and suggesting Hermann Goering as the man with whom FDR could do business." Lewis was hated by the White House because he had been an ardent supporter of America First and had made an angry speech denouncing FDR during the 1940 election campaign.

The Swarthmore attack on John L. Lewis at last landed Rogge in the headlines of the *New York Times* and the respectable press across the nation. Following his Swarthmore appearance Rogge took a plane for Seattle, where it was his announced intention to make another address along the same line. When his plane made a landing en route at Spokane, to his surprise he was met by a special agent of the FBI, who handed him a letter from Attorney General Tom Clark worded as follows:

> On the day before your speech at Swarthmore, Pa., you stated to me that you had no intention of using the text or substance of your report in such speech and that it would be highly unethical to do so. Having been in the Department of Justice for over five years, you are conversant with the laws and rules of the Department which make such reports confidential and not for public disclosure.
>
> It therefore appears that you have willfully violated the longstanding rules and regulations of the Department of Justice and your services therefore are dispensed with as of the close of this business day, Oct. 25, 1946.

Rogge's prompt reaction to his firing was to call a press conference and declare that he not only intended to deliver his lecture in Seattle, but was also booked to speak in San Francisco, Los Angeles, and a number of other cities before returning to Washington. He said his avowed purpose was to awaken America to the menace of a fascist plot to destroy the United States. I could not believe my eyes when I read the last paragraph of the AP dispatch from Seattle, in which Rogge said:

> I and my assistant Mr. Raymond Ickes have been urging the Department of Justice since July to prosecute George T. Eggleston of *Scribner's Commentator,* the magazine the Nazis sponsored. Why has this investigation not been authorized? Is it because Eggleston is at present an editor of *Reader's Digest?*

Rogge's name soon dropped out of the headlines of the legitimate press after his ouster from any official connection with the Government. But in such papers as *PM,* the *New York Post,* and the *Daily Worker* he was hailed as a martyr who had been victimized "to appease the isolationist bloc of senators and congressmen who were fearful of being exposed." *PM* devoted most of an issue to praising Rogge and condemning President Truman and Tom Clark for the firing.

Walter Winchell promptly jumped into the act with such venomous remarks about President Truman and Tom Clark that many

"Fathers and mothers, I give you one more assurance. I have said this before, but I shall say it again and again. Your boys are not going to be sent to any foreign wars."

—Franklin D. Roosevelt
October 20, 1940

Cartoon by the author in *Scribner's Commentator*, January, 1941, a year before Pearl Harbor.

America First Rally, Madison Square Garden, New York, October 30, 1941, at which Lindbergh and former U.S. Ambassador to Belgium, John Cudahy, spoke to a capacity audience.

America First Rally, June 20, 1941. Largest attendance in the history of the Hollywood Bowl, with 80,000 in the Bowl and 10,000 on the hillside above.

(top) Platoon 3, Quonset Graduation Class, February, 1943. Author first row, extreme left.

(bottom) Author upon award of commission in U.S. Navy.

FDR at Yalta Summit meeting, with Stalin and Churchill, February, 1945, two months before Roosevelt's death.

(top) Charles S. Payson, founder of *Scribner's Commentator*.

(bottom) William R. Hearst, Jr. (right) with Major General Quesada, Commander of the 9th Army Tactical Air Force in Europe.

Paul Palmer, Executive Editor of the *Reader's Digest*.

A.L. Cole, General Manager of the *Reader's Digest*. Former President Hoover framed above.

Lila and DeWitt Wallace at dedication of *Reader's Digest* building in Tokyo, May, 1951. At right, Premier Yoshida.

Lila and DeWitt Wallace, Founders, Editors, and Publishers of The *Reader's Digest*.

of his paragraphs were killed by editors of the papers receiving his syndicated columns. Here are a few typical excerpts:

> Attention Mr. and Mrs. United States! As Jefferson's administration was magnificent, as Lincoln's administration was noble and as FDR's administration was exalted, the present Truman administration is ridiculous. Its latest scandal is the discharge of prosecutor O. John Rogge....Just whose Department of Justice is it?...Does it belong to the American people — to whom Rogge told the truth — or to some slimy senators who engineered the firing of this honest prosecutor?...When the Dept. of Justice fired Rogge it blew out its brains.

A contrastingly quiet month went by following the Rogge firing. Hazel and I enjoyed some invigorating days of fall sailing before we had our final weekend across the Sound and back, and put the boat up for the winter. I had rather thought that with Rogge out of the picture his repeated requests for my prosecution would be forgotten. I wondered if Rogge's man Raymond Ickes was still in the Department of Justice, and I wondered just which Ickes this Ickes was in relation to the Harold Ickes of FDR's Cabinet. I was to be enlightened on my birthday, November 21, 1946, at 10:00 A.M., before another grand jury.

The subpoena was delivered to my home on November 18. Next day, when I drove to Pleasantville and told Wally and Al Cole the galling news, they found it hard to believe that I was still being hounded for having edited the anti-war *Scribner's Commentator* way back before the war. I also told them that I had talked to Charley Payson on the phone and been advised that he and Jeremiah Milbank had already engaged a law firm in Washington for consultation. I was to confer with one Alfons B. Landa before making my appearance before the grand jury. Wally and Al were rather puzzled, as was I, by the political makeup of the proposed legal talent—the prestigious firm of New Deal lawyers, Davies, Richberg, Richardson and Landa. Joseph E. Davies, head of the firm, had been FDR's ambassador to Russia. He had also authored *Mission to Moscow*, a book favorable to the Soviet regime under Stalin. Both Richberg and Landa had been top officials of the Democratic National Committee. We knew nothing about Richardson. Perhaps with Roosevelt and Rogge no longer on the scene, Milbank and Payson had reasoned that New Deal lawyers would be the most effective in defending *Scribner's Commentator* against the preposterous accusations Rogge had made.

Alfons B. Landa was the very archetype of the successful Washington lawyer. Meticulously dressed, calm, totally self-assured, he gave me the impression that my troubles would soon be over. He exuded an air of knowing everybody of any importance in Washington. He had, in fact, been in charge of two of FDR's inaugural celebrations.

After a friendly greeting he handed me a clipping from page one of the Washington *Times Herald* and asked,"Did you know these guys?" The article was indeed a shocker. It said that two high-ranking Nazis had been brought over from Germany to testify in the investigation of two Americans who had allegedly perjured themselves before a grand jury in 1944. Both Nazis had been top-ranking officials in the German Embassy in Washington before Pearl Harbor. They had testified at the Nuremberg war crimes trials that they had given money to an American magazine. The Nazis were named as Hans Thomsen, former chargé d'affaires of the embassy in Washington, and Herbert von Strempel, its former first secretary. The Germans, under military guard, had appeared that morning before the grand jury for questioning by Raymond Ickes, son, as it turned out, of former Interior Secretary Harold Ickes.

After I had scanned the clipping for a couple of minutes, Landa said with a grin: "Those two Americans that Ickes is after are you and Douglas Stewart. Stewart is still living in Chicago and hasn't as yet been subpoenaed. I talked to him on the phone this morning, and he said he never laid eyes on either Hans Thomsen or Strempel. I assume you, Eggleston, will have the same answer?"

"Of course. Happily for me, I never knew any foreign nationals — German, Italian, Japanese, or what have you."

"I'm taking you over to Ickes' office tomorrow morning for a private session. He has agreed to check some things out with you before he gets you in the grand jury room."

Landa went on to tell me that in the view of Ickes anyone who had ever disagreed with Roosevelt's foreign policy was per se either a Nazi or a Fascist sympathizer. Raymond Ickes, like his father, was a rabid New Dealer. He had stated to Landa in so many words that he was convinced that "The owners and editors of *Scribner's Commentator* had tried to sell their country down the river before Pearl Harbor."

Next morning, promptly at 10:00, Landa accompanied me to Ickes office, 3511 Department of Justice Building. Upon being introduced to the prosecutor and his assistant, I received a couple of very half-hearted handshakes. Seated next to Ickes' desk and not introduced to me was an unsmiling well-tailored man who stared straight ahead as though in a trance. As Landa and I were seated, the unsmiling man was told to step into the next room and wait for further orders. The mysterious man was unmistakably German. The dueling scars on his cheek were most pronounced. Obviously he was one of the two diplomats mentioned in the press.

After an exchange of pleasantries between Landa and Ickes, Landa left, saying he would see me back at his office later. Now began a rapid-fire series of questions. Ickes was not nearly as fierce as Maloney and Rogge had been. But the interrogation was any- thing but pleasant. It became apparent to me that Ickes was trying to prove that the $15,000 anonymous donation Stewart found in his hall and took to New York for deposit had in fact been received in another way. I was later to learn that his case was built upon the assumption that Stewart and I had gone to New York together and met a German in a New York hotel room.

Q. Did you accompany Stewart when he claims he took that $15,000 to New York?
A. No. I was in California at that time.
Q. What were you doing in California?
A. Visiting my mother and father.
Q. Whom else did you see in California?
A. My aunt and uncle, Mr. and Mrs. William Chamberlain.
Q. Did you make regular trips to California.
A. No.
Q. Did you make other trips to New York?
A. Yes.
Q. Why?
A. To see Mr. Payson and various contributors to *Scribner's Commentator*.
Q. Do you know two Germans in Chicago?
A. No, I never knew anyone with foreign connections.
Q. Do you know the man that was sitting here when you came in?
A. I never saw him before.
Q. We know a lot you think we don't know.
A. I have told all I know to the grand jury many times over. I am tired of this five-year persecution.
Q. Some people haven't been persecuted enough. If I had my way there would be more persecution.
A. I'd like to stay here this time until the thing is cleared up once and for all. I'd like to get it over with.

Q. I know, I know, you've said all that before. That stuff you were printing was very bad.

A. That's funny. A great many senators and congressmen were our subscribers, and thought *Scribner's Commentator* an excellent magazine.

When I described the encounter to Landa later, he said it was just about as he expected. Ickes had been greatly put out when he discovered that I was in California at the time Stewart and I were supposed to be in contact with the Germans in New York in the summer of 1941.

As Landa handed me a new subpoena to appear before the grand jury on November 26 he said: "Don't worry too much about it. I have the feeling that Ickes is going to bypass you and try to get the jury to indict Stewart. Ickes is desperate to justify the vast amount of money he and Rogge spent in Europe this year."

As we were talking a tall, dignified-looking older gentleman came into the room. Landa introduced him to me as Seth Richardson, a senior partner in the firm. Mr. Richardson immediately put me at ease by remarking that he had been a reader of *Scribner's Commentator* and an admirer of Colonel Lindbergh. When I asked if he could explain why the persecution of us had been so everlasting and malicious, he said: "Eggleston, the people who are after you and your friends hate anyone who ever disagreed with our late President. They hate with a bitterness that is almost diabolical." Here Landa spoke up and said he had once overheard Rogge remark that the best way to check the drift to fascism in this country would be to have a lot of U.S. dissidents shot by a firing squad.

I said it seemed curious to me that so many of these diehard worshipers of Roosevelt lived by a credo of hatred, while the objects of their hatred such as Stewart and Eggleston and all the people we had met in the America First movement had wished no one ill, gone in for no name-calling, and had but the one objective before Pearl Harbor — that a well-armed U.S. stay out of the European war.

Most Washington law partnerships made a point of having both Democrats and Republicans listed on their letterheads. It seemed evident to me that Seth Richardson was the Republican in the firm.

My session before the grand jury on November 26 was apparently just a token affair. I was in the jury room less than ten minutes. The questioning was polite and soft-spoken for a change. I felt that Ickes had indeed given up hope of indicting me and was instead about to go after Stewart. With this in mind, I emphasized the fact that Stewart was as loyal an American as I had ever met; and certainly, since he had the backing of Payson and Milbank, two of the wealthiest men in the United States, he had no need to solicit foreign funds. I also pointed out that in our many hours of questioning over the years, neither Stewart nor I had ever refused to answer a question.

At the end of my brief examination Ickes told me I was free to leave Washington, he didn't need me for further questioning.

Two days later in New York I read this item in the *New York Times*:

> Douglas M. Stewart of Chicago, former publisher of *Scribner's Commentator*, pleaded innocent today to an indictment handed down by a Federal Grand Jury charging him with perjury in connection with receipt of alleged Nazi propaganda money. Trial was set for January 2.
>
> Following his arraignment Stewart gave out a statement saying he "welcomed the chance at long last to prove the falsity of the accusations. The indictment was clearly the result of political persecution by radical and communistic elements in the government, including the Justice Department."

At the time Stewart did not realize how right he was in charging Communist infiltration in the Government. A Congressional committee was soon to discover that the Alger Hiss ring in the State Department had passed copies of hundreds of top-secret documents to Colonel Bykov, Soviet Intelligence chief in the U.S. At the same time, as we know today, the Harry Dexter White espionage ring in the Treasury Department had continued to operate unexposed. In addition, during the years the New Deal Justice Department was relentlessly pursuing Stewart, Eggleston, and *Scribner's Commentator* the Klaus Fuchs-Harry Gold ring had been quietly stealing atomic bomb secrets from Los Alamos and passing them to Jacob Golos, the New York-based Soviet agent. The FBI was later to call this treachery "the Crime of the Century."

The indictment of Douglas Stewart prompted Walter Winchell to go on the air with a five-minute denunciation of "the pro-Nazi Stewart and *Scribner's Commentator*," as well as a denunciation of President Truman and the Justice Department for failing to indict "George T. Eggleston, presently an editor of *Reader's Digest*." Winchell had at last come to realize that with his friend FDR no longer in the White House, he was not welcome there. President

Truman thoroughly detested him. From then on Winchell's popularity waned steadily. He began to lose the newspapers that subscribed to his column. During the next dozen years he lost 700 of his 800 newspaper outlets, and his radio contract as well. He died a disillusioned recluse on February 20, 1972. He was buried in Phoenix, Arizona, with one mourner present, his daughter.

The trial of Douglas Stewart opened in Washington March 11, 1947, with Alfons Landa in charge of the defense, assisted by Warren Magee, the well-known Washington trial lawyer. Hazel and I flew to Washington to attend the trial, I being called as a witness for the defense.

A new prosecutor, John S. Pratt, appeared in place of Ickes, and as the trial opened he promised to prove that "Baron Herbert von Strempel, former first secretary of the German Embassy, met Douglas M. Stewart at a New York hotel in the summer of 1941 and gave him a $15,000 contribution to his magazine, *Scribner's Commentator.*"

Warren Magee, in outlining the defense, stated that "Charles Payson, worth $40,000,000, had backed Stewart, as had also multimillionaire Jeremiah Milbank, in producing *Scribner's Commentator*, a pre-Pearl Harbor publication aimed at keeping the United States out of the war." Magee promised to demolish the Government's case through its own two German witnesses. He was as good as his word. During hours of cross-examination Magee extracted the following story:

Strempel testified that O. John Rogge had threatened him with death unless he signed a statement that he had given $15,000 to Stewart and George T. Eggleston in a meeting at the Hotel Pennsylvania in New York in the summer of 1941. He said that following the German surrender in 1945 he had been arrested and after several weeks in an American interrogation center had been transferred to a detention camp, where he was locked up and questioned by a team of fifteen interrogators over a period of seven months. He said the questioning was so intense that he felt as though he had been hypnotized. He became so weak after a loss of forty pounds that he spent most of every day in bed. He was finally put in solitary and his shoelaces and necktie removed, with the implication that he was ready to commit suicide. In solitary he was often questioned all day without food or water. Strempel testified: "When Rogge gave me the paper to sign, I was told if I did not cooperate I would never see my family again — I would be shot as a spy."

The testimony of Dr. Hans Thomsen, the former chargé d'affaires in the German Embassy, was very much along the same lines as Strempel's. He had been jailed and interrogated time after time by Rogge. He said that in at least six interrogations Rogge had suggested to him that two Americans, Douglas Stewart and George Eggleston, now a *Reader's Digest* editor, received $15,000 from the embassy. Dr. Thomsen said he had never heard these names "until Rogge and his assistants coached me for quite a time." He too had been constantly under duress. During his months in prison he had suffered a serious loss of weight and impairment of health.

The summing up for the defense, as prepared by Landa and Magee, was short and to the point:

1. The prosecution had failed to produce the two material witnesses necessary in a perjury case. Dr. Thomsen's testimony was only hearsay.
2. The prosecution had failed to produce any evidence whatever.
3. The prosecution had forced the Germans to make statements against the defendant while under duress and death threats in Germany.

In short, the Justice Department was guilty of attempting to build an entire case on a tissue of lies.

The story in the *New York Times* next day summed up the acquittal in these words:

> A Washington jury yesterday did not take long to free Douglas M. Stewart from allegations that he testified falsely regarding the source of $15,000 he admitted receiving in 1941. The nine men and three women retired for consultation at noon, went out to lunch, and returned with a verdict of "not guilty" at 2:30 P.M.

The most incredible thing about the whole affair was that the Justice Department had pressed on with the case despite the fact that Rogge and his assistants failed to find one single shred of evidence against *Scribner's Commentator* or Stewart or Eggleston during all the months they spent sifting German files.

An editorial in the *Chicago Tribune,* deploring the tactics used by the prosecution in the trial, ended with this paragraph:

> The conduct of the government lawyers, Rogge and Ickes, should be investigated searchingly. If charges that the court record contains against them are substantiated, they should receive long terms in the penitentiary.

A week after Stewart's acquittal this paragraph appeared in the New York *Daily News*:

> And where is Rogge now? He has popped up as defense counsel for a group cited for contempt of Congress for refusing to allow examination of its books. The present clients of ex-U.S. prosecutor Rogge are officials of the Joint Anti-Fascist Refugee Committee, an organization whose activities have brought it under the scrutiny of the House body charged with exposing Communism in the U.S.

Rogge henceforth appeared regularly in the news as spokesman for convicted U.S. Reds. When a jury found eleven U.S. Communist party bosses guilty of plotting the overthrow of the U.S. Government by force, and Judge Harold Medina sentenced them to heavy fines and jail terms, Rogge called a news conference and declared the Communist plotters innocent. He said: "Every American must now ask himself who is next. Until this verdict is reversed no one who holds new or unorthodox ideas can be safe." He also declared: "The Communist scare is a tremendous hoax behind which looms the threat of the American police state and the third world war."

Rogge soon became openly affiliated with an assortment of such Communist fronts as the National Lawyers Guild, the International Workers Order, and the Committee for Peaceful Alternatives to the Atlantic Pact. In 1949 he attended a Communist-sponsored "World Peace Conference" in Warsaw, and attended a similar conference in Moscow in 1950, when he became the first American to address the Presidium of the Supreme Soviet of the USSR.

A final word on Rogge: It is interesting to note that while he and his team were searching the German files in vain trying to find evidence that pre-Pearl Harbor American noninterventionists were collaborators with the Nazis, a team of U.S. State Department experts found the most startling evidence of collaboration of the decade. Captured German documents uncovered in Frankfurt revealed that six months before Pearl Harbor Stalin had offered Hitler a total military alliance against the West in return for further Communist expansion westward.[1] Stalin was fortunate that Hitler turned the offer down. He was later to receive much more at the hands of Churchill and Roosevelt than he had ever hoped to gain from Hitler.

So, at long last, with Stewart and *Scribner's Commentator* declared not guilty by the jury — and with the ousted O. John Rogge devoting himself full time to Communist causes — we had our tormentors off our backs. After five years of harassment by *PM*, the *New York Post*, Friends of Democracy, the *Daily Worker*, and *The New Masses*, the campaign of character assassination had drawn to a close.

XX

Sailing Interlude

MY NEXT FEW YEARS, in charge of the *Digest's* rather large and complicated art and graphics operation, were. as rewarding and tranquil an interlude as one could hope for. When the first issue of the redesigned magazine appeared, the art department received a telegram cheering the new look, signed by both the Wallaces. Henceforth, scarcely an issue went by without some message of encouragement from one or the other of the Wallaces.

I was continually pleased by the personal interest Lila Wallace took in the selection of art for the magazine. We had frequent review sessions, sometimes in Pleasantville, sometimes at my New York office, selecting covers and possible art features for months in advance. Her smiling, inspiring presence in any of the offices gave all who came in contact with her a special lift. The magazine was officially honored in 1949 with an award for excellence in design by the American Institute of Graphic Arts.

It was because of the portraits we ran in the magazine that I had a memorable first visit with former President Hoover in March, 1951. I had been following with interest the *Personal Memoirs of Herbert Hoover*, which had been running serially in *Collier's*, and when Wally scheduled a large portion of the story to run in the *Digest*, I commissioned the artist William Oberhardt to do a portrait of the author.

My friend Frank Mason arranged for the sitting, and when the charcoal drawing was completed, he phoned to say that Mr. Hoover liked it very much and asked if he could have some photo copies made to autograph for friends. With the photo copies in hand, Frank suggested I pick him up at the Hotel Marguery and we deliver them to the Hoover suite in the Waldorf Towers.

Mason, a former president of International News Service, had long been close to Mr. Hoover. He had accompanied him on his round-the-world fact-finding mission as Coordinator of the European Food Program, an assignment set up by President Truman. During our walk to the Waldorf he remarked that the ex-President followed an amazingly busy schedule for a man of seventy-seven. "He is active on all sorts of Government committees and keeps three secretaries occupied answering his mail," said Frank. Our visit would be warm, but probably short, he warned. Because of a recent fishing holiday Hoover had taken in the Florida Keys a lot of desk work had piled up to attend to.

I said I would be pleased just to shake the hand of the man who through all his years of public service had never drawn a salary from the Government. The Hoover *Memoirs* reveal that after receiving his degree in engineering from Stanford University in 1895, his first job had been pushing a lower-level rubble cart in a California mine at two dollars a day. He wrote that he didn't know there was a depression on in 1898 "because the Government didn't tell us those things then."

Prior to our visit I had noted this paragraph in the *World Almanac*:

> Mr. Hoover, as a mining engineer in Asia, Europe, and Africa, early in his career became a millionaire and director of numerous mining corporations. He gave his official salaries to charities and to underpaid officials.

Frank remarked that back in 1921 the Guggenheim brothers, owners of the largest mining and metallurgical company in the world, had offered Hoover a full partnership and a guaranteed minimum income of $500,000 per year. He had turned it down to be Secretary of Commerce, which paid a salary of $15,000 per year, which he never took for himself.

At the Waldorf I followed Frank to the basement and, accompanied by a security guard, stepped into an express elevator that quickly whisked us to the thirty-first floor. The elevator opened on a small reception room, where we were met by a secretary and led to an office annex. There we were soon joined by Hoover's private secretary, Bernice Miller, who shook our pale hands with her bronzed one and smiled, "Florida sunshine." She said, "Mr. Hoover is expecting you, come right in." We followed her down an inner corridor and emerged into a large, richly furnished drawing room with many lamps lighted. On our left, across the room behind a large desk, was our host, partially obscured behind a stack of books. As he started to rise, Miss Miller took the photostats to him and said, "Chief, I thought you might sign this one now for Mr. Eggleston." After he signed, I could see that he was writing something more. He had personalized the autograph "with appreciation" to me. As Miss Miller left, he joined us, shook our hands warmly, and showed us to a divan. After seating himself facing us, he lit his pipe with a large kitchen match and motioned to Frank to open the conversation.

"George here has always been an ardent Republican, Chief," Frank began "so ardent that the Roosevelt crowd tried to put him in jail for his stand before Pearl Harbor. He edited the *Commentator* for Jerry Milbank and Charley Payson, and the crowd actually brought two Germans over under threat of death unless they testified that Eggleston was a Nazi agent."

Mr. Hoover nodded, puffed a couple of times on his pipe, and said: "Nothing would surprise me about the tactics they used to shut up critics. Those were the days when only left-wing liberals and Communists were entitled to free speech in America with no fear of harassment." He added that Lindbergh's position and his — that the United States stay out of the war and allow Russia and Germany to maul each other to exhaustion — was being further vindicated each day.

I said that my wife and I had listened with interest to his recent broadcast and admired his forthright stand against sending a land army to Europe. (In 1951 the West enjoyed the advantage of having sole possession of the atom bomb.)

He struck another kitchen match and puffed vigorously on his pipe as his eyes moved back and forth to meet Frank's and mine.

"That bunch — those infantry generals — they think only of an infantry war," he said. "And to conduct one successfully they need to build up a tactical air force as cover for their huge land army for Europe. They will spend countless millions of dollars on tactical planes to support and cover infantry in a hopeless assault on Stalin's inexhaustible supply of troops.

"If those billions were spent on heavy bombers we could build two-three thousand that would level off Joe at home or on any front he chose to move. How much more logical this would be than a bogged-down effort in Europe, where we would lose our boys, lay Europe in waste, and fight a stalemate war — to further wreck our economy here at home. It is only the threat of our strategic air power that has kept Stalin quiet so far.

"My air general friends in the Pentagon all agree with what I have just said; they agree violently and off the record. But the infantry generals have Truman's ear. They are in control and won't listen to anything that even faintly obscures the ancient infantry approach to battle."

At this point I could sense that Frank wondered whether we were overstaying our visit, and he made a move to go. Whereupon our host waved his hand, gently indicating that we remain seated. He went on:

"Speaking of infantry, why, when I was in the White House I looked at the cavalry—the First Division—horses ridden by officers wearing spurs in the tradition of ancient warfare. I called a young cavalry officer to my office and asked him to mechanize the cavalry — he was Douglas MacArthur. He did it so well I made him Chief of Staff. But the old traditions still linger on. You remember, Frank, when we were in Tokyo watching that review. The officers of that First Division still wore their spurs with their dress parade outfits. Remember that, Frank?"

Mr. Hoover voiced his long-range hopes for the U.S. political system. "Let us keep a two-party system, " he said. "To the right for Republicans, to the left for Democrats. We should not tolerate a diffusion of left and right, we should keep them separate. Much of Europe has been wrecked by the mischief of too many splinter parties, leading almost invariably to dictatorship."

Some forty-five minutes had sped by while we visited with our host. As we rose to leave, I referred to his current memoirs. To this he laughingly replied: "That Collier's editor doesn't seem to want to run my views on economics or war and peace. He says he wants to run only stuff that will humanize me. He's been talking about humanizing me for fifteen years."

He walked to the office door with us and said "Goodbye, and thank you for coming." Miss Miller accompanied us to the elevator. On the street again, Frank remarked that it had been an unusually long visit, and he could tell that the Chief enjoyed it as much as we did. I was to meet Mr. Hoover again on a few later occasions when two or three of us Digesters accompanied DeWitt Wallace to the Waldorf Towers for lunch. But this first occasion was the most unforgettable.

In the spring of 1949 Hazel and I had succumbed to that weakness of all yachting enthusiasts—we bought a larger boat. *Musketeer* was every yachtsman's dream of a seagoing ketch. She was 45 feet overall, designed by Furnans, and built by Casey of Fairhaven, Massachusetts. The yacht was fifteen years old, but had been kept in immaculate condition. She had been active and successful in the racing circuit before the war. I had often admired the half model of her that hung on a wall of the New York Yacht Club lounge bar.

Musketeer had for me the main essentials for some exceptional sailing — a beautiful and sound hull, excellent spars and rigging and an enormous inventory of sails. For Hazel the yacht had two commodious cabins handsomely finished in teak and mahogany, an ingeniously equipped galley, plus such extras as cork tile flooring throughout and a full-length mirror in the main cabin.

I knew when we purchased *Musketeer* that we were no longer sailing a one-couple boat. On several trial spins across the Sound and back we were grateful that our friends Selwyn and Fran Eddy were aboard. But the Eddys had a new 35-foot sloop of their own and were understandably just as attached to their craft as we were to ours. As nearly all of our Riverside friends owned boats, we began to face the problem of finding a crew each time we went off for a day or weekend on *Musketeer*. Hazel and I, without help, once took *Musketeer* up the Sound for a weekend at Port Jefferson. That excursion brought a firm declaration from Hazel that I was tempting fate, just asking for a severe back strain by handling the heavy anchor alone. So from here on we always dropped our mooring with another pair of hands aboard. But we believed firmly in the amateur sailor's slogan — no yacht is big enough for more than two couples.

The one time we ignored this firm dictum we found ourselves in about as much trouble as possible. July 4, 1949, will for us, and for many others, always be a day to remember. The sailing couple we invited for that day, our rector, the Reverend John Hawkins, and his wife Jane, had done a lot of dinghy racing in Riverside and also in Maine. We looked forward to an idyllic several hours of heading up the Sound and picnicking along the way. But just before we were to meet at the yacht club Jack Hawkins phoned to say they would be a little late. A pair of his Greenwich parishioners were on the way to the rectory to pay a call. I asked, "Do they know anything about sailing?" Jack answered, "I think so." I said, "Bring them along."

Hazel and I had just finished readying *Musketeer* to take off when the club launch pulled alongside, and the embarrassed Hawkinses made the introductions. The couple from Greenwich were indeed happy to be welcomed aboard. Then to our surprise two more people came aboard from the launch — the mother and father of the Greenwich man, both in their seventies. The elderly folk said they had never been on a sailboat before. As Hazel conned *Musketeer* out of the narrow club channel under power, Jack and I hoisted the working sails, main, mizzen, and jib. I looked at the weather and noted there was a heavy and rather odd overcast to windward. The breeze was so light I considered putting on our big genoa, but thought better of it with so many people aboard. An hour of sailing in the light air brought us to the middle of the Sound. Hazel served a lunch of cold consommé, sandwiches, date cake, and coffee. The middle of Long Island Sound on this day was fairly empty of pleasure craft. Back along the Connecticut shore, as far as the eye could see, small craft were massed in racing competition while larger boats were standing by, watching.

Our four unexpected passengers were pleasant people and most appreciative of the novel experience. After the lunch things were cleared away and as the boat continued to ghost along, our two oldsters remarked on the great peace of mind one enjoys in such surroundings. "I can now understand why so much has been written of the joys of sailing," said the older man.

He had hardly spoken these words when it hit. Within seconds and without a warning gust, a gale force blast of total fury knocked *Musketeer* over on her beam ends and blew out the jib with the sound of a shotgun blast. As I threw the wheel hard down, the boat spun like a top to help me, and Jack sprang to the main halliard to get the mainsail down in a flash, just as the mizzen blew out. In those few seconds, as *Musketeer* cut through a sudden fierce chop, I spotted three dark objects in the water almost in the path of our bow. I touched the starter button, and the engine responded instantly to hold us in position heading into the wind. In the one pass *Musketeer's* bow rose and fell within a foot of the bobbing objects — three strangers in the water. *Musketeer's* bow plunged deep, then rose, and I saw six hands grasping the forward gunwale. In another matter of seconds, Hawkins, lying flat on the foredeck, managed to pull a man and two very frightened youngsters aboard. The three new passengers were immediately hustled below, where our elderly couple administered skillful rubdowns and wrapped them in warm blankets. The Weather Bureau was later to report that the first gusts that hit us topped 90 m.p.h. Our motor packed up and quit within five minutes after the rescue. The wind continued with such force that we blew before it across the Sound to Huntington Harbor — nine miles—under bare poles at about *Musketeer*'s maximum hull speed. After we were towed to a dock inside Huntington, we discovered why our motor quit. The small sloop that had capsized and sunk under the rescued three had left lines trailing, which could not be seen, but which wound themselves around our propeller until it could turn no more. The sloop had been manned by its owner, Carl Chadsey, a Greenwich realtor, his son, and a young friend. When Chadsey reappeared on *Musketeer*'s deck, after a short warm-up below and a shot of whiskey, he told us that their life jackets had gone down with their boat and if we hadn't happened along at the precise moment we appeared, they were finished. Newspaper reports next day stated that because so many fleets of racing craft were under sail when the freak blow hit, over seven hundred boats capsized in the western end of Long Island Sound alone.

A couple of weeks after this epic experience a piece of silver from Cartier arrived at our house. It carried the inscription: "Thanks, George. Bless you and the *Musketeer* — Carl and the boys. July 4, 1949."

In August we had a month's holiday on *Musketeer*. Aboard, with only Jack and Jane Hawkins for crew, we touched all the old familiar ports en route to Nantucket and return. Every day and night of the cruise was marked by perfect weather. We enjoyed breezes that made the ketch perform at her very best. When we at last picked up our mooring at Riverside and went ashore with our gear to resume land living, Hawkins said: "Now don't ever again quote that old saw — that a preacher aboard jinxes a boat. You can bury that one for good."

But could we? At 3:00 A.M. next morning we were awakened by a howling wind and a ringing telephone. We were advised to come right down to the yacht club. "Is *Musketeer* all right?" I shouted into the phone. "No boat down here is all right," said the voice as the phone clicked off. We found the yacht basin a shambles. Some thirty boats had gone adrift in a series of squalls of such cyclonic intensity that mooring pennants had parted all over the place. A dragging yacht had evidently hooked onto our mooring line and sawed it off near the bow chock. *Musketeer* lay on her side full of water, holed by the one and only boulder at the harbor's edge.

Hazel said, "I think I feel too crushed to cry." *Musketeer* was well insured, however, and was soon given a temporary patch, pumped out, and towed around to the the New England Shipyard, where she was to be restored to perfect condition, including the installation of a new engine. But our pride and joy was definitely out of commission until the following season.

As the lovely September sailing weather came along we did some **sailing** with friends and also did some driving about the countryside to while away our shorebound weekends. Frequently on our Sunday drives we dropped by the Norwalk Yacht Club and had sundowners with the editor of *Yachting* magazine, Bob Rimington, and his wife Jay. One evening as we sat chinning with the Rimingtons on their sloop *Water Gypsy* I pointed to a large Victorian house perched on a bluff just above the Norwalk Yacht anchorage. "I'll bet the view from the tower room in that house is superb. I wonder if the place is for sale, not saying we could possibly afford it if it were."

"I can tell you what I know about it," said Bob. "It was originally the home of a president of U.S. Steel, John Farrell. He sold the house to a close friend when he built the enormous fieldstone mansion next door. The million-dollar stone castle presently houses the executive offices of IBM."

Next weekend we called at a Norwalk real estate office and inquired about the house. We were told that the place had never been on the market. But the realtor said there was a rumor about that Hickory Bluff might be for sale. "Let's drive over and ask," said the salesman. As we drove in past the gate house and tennis court and parked in a turnaround next to a large curving veranda, Hazel and I each experienced a distinct feeling of chill inside our shoes. We knew we deserved cold feet; our mission was brash and out of character. To our surprise we had a warm welcome. Two charming ladies, one in her seventies, one in her eighties, were in residence — the last remnants of a once large family. They said they were about to put Hickory Bluff up for sale; they just could not cope with walking up and down so many stairs. As we had imagined, the third-floor tower room commanded a sweeping view of the Sound over Green's Ledge lighthouse to the south, and, to the east, the lovely pattern of the Norwalk islands.

The fifteen-room house proved to be much more livable than we had hoped for. The four acres with fifty hickory shade trees and a winding walk down to the yacht club was to us the answer to our dreams. When the spring weather arrived and the restored *Musketeer* was moored below, the picture was complete. But we enjoyed only a couple of good sailing weekends on *Musketeer* before I disregarded Hazel's warning and handled the heavy anchor once too often. I threw my lower lumbar disk so far out of line that I had to spend two months in Presbyterian Hospital in New York before the back specialists put me on my feet again. We were at last forced to admit that *Musketeer* was too big for us. Regretfully we sold the lovely ketch and bought a 34-foot Alden sloop, which we named for the flower of Tahiti, *Tiare*.

Once we were settled in at Hickory Bluff I dusted off my notes of our South Seas cruise and completed the long-delayed manuscript. I also sorted out the photographs I had made with my trusty Rolleiflex. After Hazel had put my sixty thousand words through her typewriter, Devin Garrity of the Devin-Adair Company brought out the book under the title *Tahiti, Voyage Through Paradise*. The book was enthusiastically reviewed in the *New York Times, Washington Star, Chicago Tribune, San Francisco Chronicle,* the *Los Angeles Examiner,* and a hundred other newspapers. Gilbert Highet in *Harper's Magazine* went all out about the pictures: "Clearly and gaily written, full of good native talk and the chat of sailors and old residents — with some of the finest travel photographs I have ever seen."

After a piece from *Tahiti* appeared in *Reader's Digest* and its fifteen foreign editions — and a London publisher produced a British edition of the book—Hazel and I found we had quite a lot of fan mail to answer. After such an experience one is bound to become very book conscious. I asked DeWitt Wallace if I could come to Pleasantville and be a book editor, and he said yes.

XXI

DeWitt and Lila Wallace

WHEN I BEGAN DRIVING the thirty miles from Hickory Bluff to the *Digest* each weekday it was mid-spring, and the gardens and landscaping around the office buildings were at their glorious best. Rows and rows of pink and white dogwood trees were in blossom; great beds of white tulips were in bloom near a reflecting pool. Masses of purple pansies were contained in patterned borders of yellow pansies in an acre of garden where many employees spent their lunch hour.

The main office bulding, approached from a tree-shaded stretch of road off N.Y. Route 117, reminds one instantly of Colonial Williamsburg. This impression of the stately three-storied red brick building with its white cupola is valid, for Mrs. Wallace had long admired the Georgian architecture of Williamsburg and wished to reflect it in the *Digest*'s home office. At the base of the cupola are four bronze figures of Pegasus, the symbol of the magazine, especially sculpted for Mrs. Wallace.

The lawns, grounds, sunken gardens, planting, and landscaping all directly reflected the taste of Lila Wallace. Under her supervision dozens of full-grown oaks and other shade trees had been moved onto the grounds. An entire bearing apple orchard was transplanted to the *Digest* without losing a tree. An eighteenth-century pillared Colonial mansion was remodeled into a guest house near the entrance gate, to be used to accommodate visiting authors, editors, and *Digest* personnel from overseas.

Every detail of decor and furnishing inside the buildings was the inspiration of Lila Wallace. When I once took a prominent New York book publisher on a tour of the premises and he noted the selection of fine paintings from the *Digest's* collection of Impressionists — all selected by Mrs. Wallace — that decorate many of the rooms and hallways, and the twenty-five handsomely furnished lounges for employees, the piped-in music, and the flower arrangements everywhere in evidence, he said, "I should think that in such an environment one would find it difficult to get any work done."

Quite the contrary. In the editorial wing of the building fifty editors and readers were at the moment carefully sifting through over five hundred magazines, periodicals, and newspapers received each month, searching for material. Of the twelve thousand new books then published each year in the U.S., several hundred nonfiction volumes required scanning for possible condensation in the *Digest.*

In another department, separate and apart from the magazine operation, an editorial staff had since 1950 been producing Reader's Digest Condensed Books. Each of these hardcover volumes, issued quarterly, contained five condensed books, nearly all of them fiction, an ingredient rarely found in the magazine. In its first year the Reader's Digest Book Club attracted more subscribers than any other in existence.

In the large complex of business offices a thousand clerical assistants, with the aid of every mechanical and electronic device known, were taking care of over 150,000 pieces of incoming mail daily. Twenty million pieces of direct mail were going out yearly, after being carefully checked to avoid duplication. Of the U.S. *Digest's* circulation totals in the early 1950's some 2,000,000 copies of the magazine were sold on newsstands, over 7,000,000 subscribers were serviced from Pleasantville. (The offices are actually seven miles north of Pleasantville, but the original post office address was retained.) Total world circulation at the time, in a dozen languages, amounted to more than 15,000,000 copies per month.

When I paused to contemplate the bare statistics of the Pleasantville operation, I marveled that the two most modest, natural human beings Hazel and I had ever known had sparked the idea that brought the whole thing about. And I marveled again that the sweep of Lila Wallace's imagination was so wide that besides her deep involvement in the Pleasantville operation, she found time to contribute her ideas and millions of dollars in such other directions as the Metropolitan Museum, the Metropolitan Opera Company, the New York Zoological Society, and to hospitals, colleges, schools, and numerous charities.

In 1951, when portraits of DeWitt and Lila Wallace appeared on the cover of *Time*, a lengthy article about them declared: "By world circulation standards DeWitt Wallace, the *Digest's* founder and owner, is the most successful editor in history. Wallace and his wife Lila Acheson Wallace, the *Digest's* co-editor, between them seem to have discovered a magic formula." The *Wall Street Journal* later carried a long and searching feature article about the magazine under the headline "BIBLE'S RUNNER-UP — Reader's Digest is Top Publishing Success Since The Scriptures."

With the publication of the February, 1952, issue, the *Digest* celebrated its thirtieth anniversary and received birthday greetings from President Truman, Dwight Eisenhower, General MacArthur, and leaders of every branch of American life. From around the world came messages of congratulation from prime ministers, kings, and princes.

Some time later Hazel and I were among a group of *Digest* people invited to a dinner at the Theodore Roosevelt House, New York City, when the Wallaces were presented with the Theodore Roosevelt gold medal for public service. Although the Wallaces were to receive many awards over the years, including the Medal of Freedom, America's highest award for civilian achievement, we thought the wording of one paragraph in the Theodore Roosevelt citation the perfect tribute to them:

> An American couple, filled with the conviction of the fathers of the Republic that the American conception of life and government is the most precious resource that America has to export, they have interpreted their country to the world in terms so simple, humble, and sincere that, listening to these twain, millions, frightened of American power, skeptical of American wisdom, have given America their hearts.

That DeWitt and Lila Wallace founded the magazine and brought it through its early issues to financial stability by their single-handed efforts is one of the most incredible success stories of all time.

DeWitt Wallace was born in St. Paul, Minnesota, November 12, 1889, the fifth child of Janet Davis Wallace and Dr. James Wallace, a professor at tiny Macalester College. In 1907, when DeWitt entered Macalester as a freshman, Dr. James Wallace, Ph.D., LLD., was president of the struggling Presbyterian institution. It is of record that DeWitt took little interest in impressing his father with his scholarship. Young Wallace was far more interested in baseball, football, and hockey. He had, however, an early avid interest in reading magazine articles — and in saving and cataloguing pieces that held for him a special interest. When he found after two years at Macalester that he wanted a change, with his father's permission he went to the West Coast and enrolled at the University of California. There he spent two rather relaxed years, including many happy hours in the Psi Upsilon fraternity house. He dropped out of Berkeley before finishing and returned to St. Paul and a job writing sales promotion letters for the Webb Publishing Company, publisher of *The Farmer* and *The Farmer's Wife*. During his four years with Webb the idea of producing a magazine composed of condensed articles of lasting interest from leading magazines gradually took a firm hold on his imagination, and he would have done something about it in 1917 except for a new development on the world scene.

Simultaneously with the U.S. declaration of war on Germany, Wallace volunteered, and served in France with the 35th Infantry Division. During the Meuse-Argonne offensive half of his company were killed or wounded, and the survivors were about to be relieved when a sudden burst of shrapnel hit Wallace in the abdomen and neck. Splinters also entered his lung and pierced his nose. The fragment that entered his neck just barely missed severing his jugular vein. The date was October 1, 1918 — just a month before the armistice. Wallace spent four months convalescing in the army hospital at Aix-les-Bains. The hospital was handsomely supplied with magazines from the U.S., and Wallace whiled away the hours selecting and condensing articles he considered outstanding. Before he was discharged from the hospital, he had a skeleton copy of a complete issue of the *Reader's Digest* in hand.

Back home in St. Paul, he borrowed some money and produced a printed dummy of his brainchild, which was in every way a prototype of today's *Digest,* except that it carried no advertising or illustrations. The subject matter of the selections included articles on world affairs, health, spiritual uplift, the art of living, self-improvement, and politics. Also included was a generous supply of short quotes and humor. Wallace's only problem was that as he made the rounds showing his product to a series of publishers, he was turned down flatly by everyone. One and all agreed with the editor of *Woman's Home Campanion* that a magazine without fiction could not succeed. Wallace's offer to *give* the idea to any publisher who would retain him as editor enticed no takers.

James Playsted Wood has described what happened next in his book, *Of Lasting Interest: The Story of the* Reader's Digest:[1]

> In the midst of his depression Wallace found a convert and ally. While an undergraduate in California, DeWitt Wallace had spent a Christmas vacation in Tacoma, Washington, at the home of Barclay Acheson, a Macalester college mate whose father also was a Presbyterian minister. In Tacoma he had met and been attracted to Acheson's sister, Lila, who had already announced her engagement. In January, 1920, Wallace met Acheson, by now a Presbyterian minister with a relief organization, who told him that his sister was now neither married nor engaged. Lila, who had graduated from the University of Oregon, was doing social work among working women in New York.
>
> Though he had not seen slight, blue-eyed, delicately featured Lila Bell Acheson in eight years, DeWitt Wallace immediately dispatched a telegram:
>
> CONDITIONS AMONG WOMEN WORKERS IN SAINT PAUL GHASTLY URGE IMMEDIATE INVESTIGATION.
>
> A week later, by coincidence, not collusion, Lila Bell Acheson was sent to Minneapolis to establish an industrial YWCA.
>
> Where DeWitt Wallace was still struggling toward his start, Lila Bell Acheson was already active and successful in a busy career. The young woman who came to Minneapolis already had three jobs, and she was being lent from one to the other. Before she left Minneapolis, she had accepted both DeWitt Wallace and the digest-periodical idea which every publisher had rejected. From that point the *Reader's Digest* was a joint venture of DeWitt Wallace and Lila Bell Acheson.

Next followed a period of several months during which the engaged couple were to be some 450 miles apart. Lila Acheson returned to her work commitment in New York, and Wallace went to Pittsburgh to take a job in the publicity department of Westinghouse. When the depression of 1921 hit, Wallace was told by his boss that since he had been the last man hired, he was to be the first man fired. This turned out to be the best thing that could have happened to DeWitt Wallace. He immediately collected a stack of college catalogues and sent out a series of test mailings to faculty members describing his proposed publication and soliciting subscriptions. He sent other test mailings to lists he obtained of doctors, teachers, and women's professional groups. His tests brought such an encouraging response that he hurried to New York to rejoin Lila. Their marriage took place in Pleasantville, Westchester County, New York, October 15, 1921, with Barclay Acheson conducting the church service.

They next rented a garden apartment in Greenwich Village, Manhattan, and a basement office and storeroom nearby. Then, before leaving for their honeymoon in the Poconos, they took several large bundles of subscription appeal letters to the post office and crossed their fingers.

When they returned to New York, they were thrilled to find that receipts from the new mailings, added to Wallace's earlier orders, plus a loan they negotiated for $1,300, paid for the first edition run of 5,000 copies of the *Reader's Digest* for February, 1922.

The reader response to the magazine was such that by the fall of 1922 the Wallaces felt financially solvent enough to consider a move out of Manhattan to the country. They had an especially soft spot in their hearts for Pleasantville, New York, where they had been married. An ad describing a garage apartment near the small Westchester village attracted their attention sufficiently that they journeyed to Pleasantville and rented the offering on sight. The fieldstone quarters over a two-car garage consisted of a large, beam-ceilinged room with a fireplace at one end and a bath and kitchen off the other end. The Wallaces' main possessions at the time amounted to a Spartan minimum of furniture and a huge accumulation of files, bundles of letters, and stacks of magazines. Thanks to Lila Wallace's flair for decoration, the place was soon made attractive despite its limitations.

In the early years, as the magazine made monthly gains in circulation and profit figures, the entire editorial burden was carried by the two Wallaces. An early worry that as the *Reader's Digest* grew the cooperating publishers might withdraw reprint rights failed to materialize. Most of the magazine editors to whom Wallace wrote for permission to reprint considered the additional circulation of their material a valuable publicity plus.

The growth of the magazine in the mid-1930's was such that the *Digest* editorial, business, and circulation department found it almost impossible to function in the little village of Pleasantville. All the available office space over stores, shops, and bank buildings was by then full to the bursting point with *Digest* personnel. The move to the nearby location between Chappaqua and Mt. Kisco and the new spacious buildings and grounds was a great relief to all concerned.

XXII

Inside the Reader's Digest

WHEN I BEGAN WORK at *Digest* headquarters, the only working editor I knew well was Paul Palmer. I hadn't seen Paul, except for a couple of brief encounters at *Digest* parties, since he did the piece on Colonel Lindbergh's mail for me in the *Scribner's Commentator* days. Coincidental with my arrival in the book department, Paul had been appointed to the post of executive editor. When I dropped by his office to congratulate him and tell him I was glad to see he had survived the attacks of the left-wingers who were after his scalp, he laughed heartily. "That damned bunch of character assassins sure worked like hell to have you and me sacked."

I soon came to know many of the *Digest* editors-in-residence, and the contributing editors and writers as well. They were a unique band chosen from all sorts of backgrounds. Curiously enough, the two top editors, who had served the Wallaces as the magazine's circulation grew to be the largest in the U.S., were former editors of two of America's smallest magazines — Ken Payne had edited *McClure's* and Fritz Dashiell had edited *Scribner's*. Many of the talented people listed on the masthead had come to the *Digest* with no previous experience in journalism whatever.

The head of the book department, Maurice Ragsdale, was one of the latter group. Ragsdale (called Raggy by everyone) had been successfully running the *Reader's Digest* book department for several years when I appeared on the scene. The R.D. book department was staffed with a team of junior readers, whose job it was to search through hundreds of submitted books and pass along likely candidates to Raggy and me. There were also several part-time readers in the New York office, plus others scattered across the country who sent in regular reports to Pleasantville. I found it especially cheering, after selecting a book, condensing it, and seeing it published, to receive a note from the author praising the end result.

One pleasant aspect of the work was that our book offerings were not required to run the gauntlet of editors (Murderers Row), whose duty it was to tinker with, okay, or kill material. We were fortunate that both Wallaces took a personal interest in the quality and variety of the book sections we produced. In fact, during my tour of duty several books that proved outstanding successes were discovered personally by Mrs. Wallace after having been over-looked by our entire staff.

In the pursuit of books I made regular trips to New York to call on publishers and learn about upcoming manuscripts that might be optioned for future issues of R.D. I made my New York trips on Tuesdays to coincide with the weekly luncheons of the Dutch Treat Club, gatherings always well attended by prominent publishers and writers. As publishers, editors, and authors realized that any book condensed in the *Digest* enjoyed a wider general sale in the book stores than usual, I found that I was often buttonholed by Dutch Treaters bent on telling me about some new opus, "a natural for R.D."

One author who especially amused me was Homer Croy, a member of the club's board of governors. Croy had written many novels, including a onetime best seller, *West of the Water Tower*. He had just completed *Wheels West,* the saga of the Donner Party. Croy was convinced that *Wheels West* was the best book he had ever written. He told me he was equally convinced that any mail he sent to a *Digest* editor was unopened and unread. At one Dutch Treat lunch he sat next to me and informed me that he was no longer going to lobby me in person about his book (thank goodness), he was going to try a new approach.

Croy's new approach was definitely ingenious. A couple of days after seeing him I received, in a pile of mail, a very official-looking tan envelope with my typed name and address in the see-through oval, and in the upper corner the imprint: Citizens' State Bank, Marysville, Mo. Naturally it was the first thing I opened. In the envelope was a folder from Croy's publisher, Hastings House, describing his new book. A note on an elaborate piece of stationery from Shepheard's Hotel, Cairo, stated:

> George —
> This is the dangdest story of courage that ever took place in America. The *Digest* should use it.
> > Yours, H. Croy, a good man and a just man.
> > Champion of Virgins and All other
> > Underprivileged Peoples.

Croy went to an incredible amount of trouble putting together eye-catching, amusing, faked mail. I received envelopes from him labeled the State Highway Patrol, the Tennesse Valley Authority, the Metropolitan Police Dept., the Senate, and the House of Representatives. Heavens knows how Croy obtained his variety of envelopes and letterheads, ranging from the Hudson's Bay Company to Madame Tussaud's Waxworks. It was good fun, but, sadly, *Wheels West* never quite got rolling as a *Digest* condensation.

In James Playsted Wood's history of *Reader's Digest* the statement appears:

> Editorial communication at the *Digest* is carried on largely through osmosis and contagion. There are no stated staff meetings or scheduled planned sessions. There is no taut chain of command. An article idea may originate with DeWitt Wallace, with the executive editor, or any one of the senior editors. A staff editor may propose it to a roving editor or an outside writer, or a roving editor may suggest it to Wallace. An author or a literary agent may approach the *Digest* with an article or an article idea at an informal luncheon.

On occasion, when a prominent *Digest* writer came for a visit — John Dos Passos, John T. Flynn, Hanson Baldwin, W.L. White, Max Eastman — there was an editorial lunch in the Wallace private dining room with D.W. presiding. Conversations at those luncheons usually resulted in an article, or even a book, being assigned.

Often, when I was involved in a complicated book condensation, I brought my lunch and ate in my office. A large well-run cafeteria also afforded a chance for a quick meal with no time wasted. If you felt a bit gregarious, there was an editor's dining room called the Pegasus Club, where a $1.50 steak lunch could be enjoyed in friendly company. I recall one particularly amusing

Pegasus Club luncheon that well illustrates the "communication by osmosis and contagion" mentioned by author Wood:

> EDITOR A: "Did you see the final press proofs on the "Snail King" that came through this morning?"
> EDITOR B: "I saw the Snail King thing several times coming and going. But not the proofs this morning. Frankly, there was more in that piece about snails than I cared to know."
> EDITOR A: "The proofs were on my desk when I arrived — and with a note from the boss across the title page saying the piece was not worth five pages. He said it should have been cut to what it was worth."
> EDITOR B: "I guess Wally just doesn't like snails."
> EDITOR A: "When I saw first proofs I thought Wally was probably crazy about snails."

The article had originally appeared in a West German magazine under the title "Snail King of the World." It was about a German lumber magnate who had lost his fortune when the Russians came and, after a spell in a prison camp, managed to build up a successful business raising snails for export to Paris. The piece had somehow passed uncut through a dozen editors before it reached D.W.'s desk. The Wallace notation caused the piece to be promptly cut to two pages and retitled: "Who'd Have Thought of Starting a Business Like This?"

The *Time* cover story on the Wallaces, in typical *Time* style, contained, besides the mass of complimentary copy, a few digs. Wally was good-naturedly annoyed at the reference to his driving "an old battered Chevrolet." His favorite car was indeed a ten-year-old Chevrolet, but far from being battered, it was kept in mint condition. A most inaccurate *Time* barb was the statement in the story:

> Memos have been known to molder in a sprawling mountain of manuscripts on his desk for years before Wallace gets around to scrawling in the margins "sure — go ahead. Wally."

Now, it so happened that of the whole staff of seventy-five editorial people who were listed on the masthead in my time, not one was known to answer a memo with the promptness of DeWitt Wallace. Typical was a junior editor's complaint: "That guy (editor X) has had notes from me on his desk since last year — and never an answer. But if I send anything to Wally I get it back with a comment in twenty-four hours."

I recall the experience of another junior editor who came into my office a few days after he had been hired. He was beaming. He had sent a memo to D.W. containing a dozen suggestions for various types of quizzes to be run as filler material in the magazine. D.W. had turned down all the suggestions, but the chap was beaming because the boss had taken the trouble to fill five pages of yellow foolscap with penciled notes explaining why each of the dozen ideas was not right for the *Digest*. "Gosh," said the young man, "all he had to say was 'thanks, not usable' and I would have understood. Now I'll work my tail off to follow his suggestions." On his next try the junior ed had four of his contributions out of five accepted.

Both Wallaces were meticulous about promptly answering all office communications addressed to them, and Wally even took a delight in answering his own telephone, often to find himself talking to a total stranger.

Beginning with the first issue of the *Digest* in 1922, every issue had carried one or two articles on the Golden Rule — the practice of thoughtfulness and kindness in one's dealings. The Wallaces lived by this rule, and hundreds of examples of their thoughtfulness could be cited. Here is one I vividly recall. On a very cold February afternoon, as I joined the four o'clock exodus of hundreds of employees pouring out of the office buildings and trudging to the snow-covered cars, I saw, coming out of the farthest end of the parking area, a heavy Cadillac sedan moving forward with a series of jerks, indicating it was being pushed from a car behind. As I got into my car, the sedan, carrying several female clerical assistants, suddenly leaped into motion as its motor started. Off it went with a roar as its occupants waved "thank you" to the man in "the old battered Chevrolet" who had come to their aid. It never failed to amuse me that Wally often parked in the farthest parking lot, while certain of his high-paid executives parked daily in the "No Parking" area in front of the entrance to the main building.

Another of the many examples of Wallace empathy occurred during my art department stint. When I mentioned to the Wallaces that one of our artists had suffered a light heart attack and his doctor pronounced his condition not at all serious, D.W. immediately sent off this note:

Dear Mr. B ——,
   Lila and I are distressed to hear about the condition of your heart. We like that heart and we want you to take care of it!

It is our desire that you and your wife take a month's vacation in the south at R.D. expense. We feel sure this is what you should do, and we do not want the trip to occasion any financial concern on your part.

Please let us know promptly that you will comply with our wishes.

Have a complete rest, an enjoyable time, and, we hope, a marked recovery.

With all best wishes,

Sincerely yours,
WALLY

Probably no head of a large organization ever showed more consideration for employees at all levels than DeWitt Wallace. And his patience with some obviously slack individuals on the editorial team was legendary.

In all the years I was associated with R.D. the nearest thing to a cross word from the boss came in a memo to twenty-five top editors in the fall of 1953. He was annoyed that on several successive closing dates, prior to going to press, there had been a last-minute crush of articles requiring final editing. With a total of some forty working editors listed on the masthead and scores of secretaries, and typists to back them up, it was in fact incredible that such a last-minute crisis should ever occur.

The memo is unique in that it is the one and only time D.W. ever referred to the early efforts of himself and Lila Wallace.

Editorial Staff:

Isn't it a mistake to accept the inevitability of a spate of articles going through the last two or three or four days before closing an issue? With our inordinately large staff of highly competent editors, it should not take a week or ten days, or even longer, for an article to meander leisurely through the editing process.

Perhaps a personal reference will be pardoned — one that some of you may have heard mentioned. After the Christmas rush in 1923, '24 and '25, LBW and I allowed ourselves precisely ten days in which to do all the editorial work of the month. Lila would read the magazines and discuss the articles. Often I would check-read several pieces in a magazine before deciding which one to use. (Articles ran longer in those days than at present.)

It is a fact that in each of the three months referred to we finished the editorial job in exactly the allotted ten *consecutive* days. I had to condense (doing my own typing) an average of three articles daily. My record was cutting and typing five articles in one day.

We *should* be able to lick the last-minute jam through better planning and teamwork.

There is not the slightest suggestion here that we want any editor or typist to be less of a perfectionist — to be less exacting in doing the best possible job. The whole point of this memo is that we should be able to effect a considerable saving of time by simply eliminating most of the hours, and even days, when an article is merely lying untouched on someone's desk.

Let's demonstrate that we have the will and intelligence to solve a problem that has been with us a long time.

DW

Wally sometimes liked to surprise his colleagues with an unexpected display of informality. One occurred during the 1951 Wallace visit to Japan for the dedication of the new *Reader's Digest* building in Tokyo. During the visit, as the Wallaces were being driven around the countryside by the magazine's Tokyo publisher, the latter proudly pointed out a stack of Japanese *Digests* on sale in front of a village bookstall. With mock seriousness Wally ordered the car halted, told his astonished host that he was shocked to see that the magazine was not selling, and proceeded to stand behind the counter waving a *Digest* while delivering a selling spiel in English, to the amusement of the passersby.

Because of the Digest's many editions overseas, every so often an interesting person from a remote part of the world came to call. One especially memorable visitor was the ruler of the Obibis of Nigeria, Oxford-educated Eze A. Oqueri II. The Obibi word for King is "Eze." This luncheon, in the R.D. guest house, was hosted by D.W.'s brother-in-law, Barclay Acheson, director of all *Digest* foreign editions. Barclay had, before coming to the *Digest*, been responsible for saving millions of lives in the Levant, where he headed the Near East relief operation. He was a charming man and an accomplished host. Under his genial prodding Eze Oqueri told us several eye-opening things about his country. "We Obibis," said he, "are a proud people. Although we have never had a written language, our culture goes back three thousand years. I remember well the wise sages of the tribes coming to my grandfather's house and talking for hours at a time about ways to live better together. Thus they fashioned the rules of life of the community." Commenting on this statement, senior editor Charley Ferguson remarked: "With all due respect to our craft, we may discover that the written word has really been a detour on the long road to culture."

When asked about his personal family life, the Eze smiled and said that from his impressions of American family life, as gleaned from the press, our two cultures were miles apart. He said that his family and all of the first families of the Obibi would not consider a marriage possible until the backgrounds of both the prospective bride and groom had been studied back ten generations, with careful attention to health, character, and status of all ancestors. This sparked a lively discussion among the several editors present. One Digester of liberal leanings ventured the opinion that this was, of course, quite an undemocratic point of view. The king smilingly replied that the Obibi sages had found that over the many centuries this attention to heredity had been the *one* most important factor in the stability of his country.

Shortly after I began commuting to Pleasantville the decision was made that the *Digest* would accept advertising. This major policy change was quite a surprise to the staff. Over the years D.W. had turned a deaf ear to hundreds of suggestions by eager ad men that the magazine carry advertising.

During the many years that the *Digest* declined to consider taking advertising, the power of the magazine's appeal to sell products was proven over and over again. One of the most spectacular examples of reader response came on the heels of a short two-and-a-half-page article about a new product called Adolph's Meat Tenderizer. During the six months following appearance of the article the manufacturers received an average of ten thousand letters a day with a grand total of over two million inquiries! So many orders came in by Western Union that the company had to install a direct wire. The single plant housing Adolph's Meat Tenderizer had to be expanded to six plants. *Reader's Digest* articles appraising other worthy products brought similar results.

When the decision was finally reached to accept advertising, the following announcement was prepared for release to the press:

> Although the *Digest* circulation is the largest in history—over 10,000,000 copies in the United States alone — costs have now reached a point where a deficit in the magazine's operations is faced unless new revenue is found.
>
> Polls of readers indicate an overwhelming preference for inclusion of advertising rather than an increase in the price of the magazine. Therefore, a limited amount of the highest grade advertising will be accepted. For at least one year not more than 12 pages of advertising will appear in any issue. There will be no alcoholic beverage or tobacco advertisements. The advertising should be of high reader interest.

There will be no reduction in the number of editorial pages, and the budget for editorial material and new talent will continue to be increased from year to year. Under the new program it will be possible to give readers more for their money than ever before.

The press release was never published. By the time it had been set in type the news had somehow leaked out to Madison Avenue and orders were already pouring in. Orders for over a thousand pages of advertising were received within ten days of the leak, more than six times the number of pages that could be accommodated during the next twelve months. Before any issue of the *Digest* containing advertising appeared, eleven million dollars in space had been purchased. On the first day of the leak one New York agency executive phoned to place an order for twelve full-color pages. As an afterthought he asked, "By the way, what's the price on that?" Informed that the price was $31,000 per page, he replied, "That's fine — thank you." Although the advertising costs per page were the highest in U.S. magazine history, they were low on the basis of cost per page per thousand readers.

The free-spending advertisers were soon to find that their money was well spent. Several were to report results just as spectacular as the Adolph experience. To cite two typical examples: An insurance company credited its *Digest* advertising with bringing in three-quarters of a million customers and increasing their business by twenty-five million dollars within the year. After the Libby canning company ran a coupon-clipping ad in the *Digest* to introduce a new minted pineapple product, Libby's president reported that fourteen freighters were required to bring the newly ordered shipments of pineapple to the U.S. in direct response to the R.D. ad.

The decision to carry no liquor or tobacco advertising meant a deliberate sacrifice of millions of dollars in advertising revenue per year, a policy that no other general magazine in the world would have considered for a moment. Because the *Digest* was owned outright by the two Wallaces — and they cared nothing for pyramiding their fortune — this ruling was final.

Another ingredient conspicuous by its absence from *Digest* pages was the exploitation of sex. As, year after year, standards of taste dropped ever lower on the U.S. publishing scene, the *Reader's Digest* became more and more conspicuous for what it *did not* print — and circulation gains rose to ever more dazzling heights to attain a readership, worldwide, larger by millions than that of any other magazine.

XXIII

Herbert Hoover's Warning

ALTHOUGH MY MAIN OCCUPATION at the *Digest* was in finding, cutting, and editing material for the book section of the magazine, I was by no means confined to this. At odd periods in between a heavy book schedule I often worked on articles I managed from time to time to turn up, and on subjects of special interest that caught my eye.

I had absorbed with great interest a speech former President Hoover delivered on August 11, 1954, in West Branch, Iowa, the town where he was born. He had come to Iowa at the invitation of the governor and state legislature to join in the celebration of his eightieth birthday. A condensation of the speech ran for five pages in the *Digest*. Mr. Hoover's central message for his fellow Americans was wonderfully refreshing to those of us who had suffered through the years of FDR's worldwide "Four Freedoms" policy. It seems fitting that a few paragraphs from Mr. Hoover's original speech and the condensation appear in the final chapter of this book. Mr. Hoover's total and prime concern was for the preservation of freedom in the United States.

The progress of freedom is a never ending struggle to prevent the abuse of power whether by individuals, by groups, or by government. Our Founding Fathers created unique restraints on power by the Bill of Rights and a structure of built-in checks and balances. Among those concepts was a division of power between the three branches of government. I don't need to tell you that. But what I have to tell you is that these separations of power became seriously confused, corroded, and weakened during the twenty years before this Administration.

During the last war we witnessed a special encroachment of the Executive upon the Legislative branch. This has been through a new type of commitment of the United States to other nations.

I am not going to argue legalisms, for they do not go to the center of the issue. The real issue is whether the President, through declaration or implication or by acquiescence, or by joint statements with foreign officials, can commit the American people to foreign nations without the specific consent of the elected representatives of the people.

There has been a grievous list of such commitments. Our tacit alliance with Soviet Russia spread Communism everywhere. Our acquiescence in the annexation by Russia of the Baltic States and the partition of Poland at Teheran extinguished the liberties of tens of millions of people.

Worse still was the appeasement and surrender at Yalta of ten nations to slavery. And there was the secret agreement with respect to China which set in train the communization of Mongolia, North Korea, and all of China.

These unrestrained Presidential actions have resulted in a shrinking of human freedom over the whole world. From these actions came the jeopardies of the "Cold War," and as a by-product, these actions have shrunk our own freedoms by crushing taxes, huge defense costs, and inflation.

We must make such misuse of power forever impossible, and let me say I have no fears of this evil from President Eisenhower. But he will not always be President.

To me and to the millions of Americans who had opposed FDR's plan to send a U.S. invasion army to Europe, the following words of Mr. Hoover were particularly gratifying:

I opposed and protested every step in the policies which led us into the Second World War.

Especially in June, 1941, when Britain was safe from a German invasion due to Hitler's diversion to attack Stalin, I urged that the gargantuan jest of all history would be our giving aid to the Soviet Government. I urged that we should allow those two dictators to exhaust each other. I stated that the result of our assistance would be to spread Communism over the whole world. I urged that if we stood aside the time would come when we could bring lasting peace to the world.

With these words of Mr. Hoover ringing in my ears, the most unexpected person imaginable came to Pleasantville and paid me a visit. A phone call from D.W.'s secretary had me guessing. "A friend of yours whom you haven't seen for years is on his way to your office. Mr. Wallace would like you to look over some ideas the gentleman wants to submit to R.D."

My visitor was Daniel Longwell, who almost two decades before had welcomed me at Time, Inc. and taken me "upstairs" in the Chrysler Building to meet Mr. Luce, whom he was privileged to address as "Harry." Beyond my surprise at suddenly seeing my old boss, I was greatly shocked by his physical appearance. During the interim since I had last seen Dan Longwell he had become a frail, little old man. He easily sensed what I was thinking, and quickly told me that the jobs he had been holding down on *Life* had literally worn him out. As managing editor of *Life* and later as chairman of *Life*'s board of editors he had occupied the two most ulcer-producing posts in the publishing business. He had retired in 1953.

I had a tremendous impulse to ask him how he felt now, in hindsight, about *Life*'s loud pro-war, pro-Russian jingoism of the early 1940's. But I couldn't bear to touch on the subject in the face of Dan's fragile state of health.

Dan spread two sets of pictures on my desk. One was of a civic beautification program recently launched in Tulsa, Oklahoma. The other illustrated a similar program he and his wife had launched in Neosho, Missouri, just across the border from Tulsa. He said that he didn't get very far trying to convince Mr. Wallace that each of these was worth a color feature section in the *Digest*. What did I think? I felt a little foolish being asked such a question by a man who had selected more pictures for publication than probably any other editor in the history of the world. I simply said that the idea of civic beautification was a natural for the *Digest*, but I would predict that the boss would prefer to run the stories as text with one picture illustrating each. This is how the Longwell stories eventually appeared.

Dan went on to tell me that he and his wife had bought a home in Neosho. They had chosen it for their retirement years because they had always liked the small-town atmosphere of the peaceful community in the Ozark foothills. Dan explained that he had lived there as a boy and had many old friends there.

"You probably never heard of Neosho," he said.

"Well yes, it rings a bell," I answered.

But again I couldn't bear to say what was really on my mind. Of course it rang a bell. Neosho, Missouri, was the town that Senator

Bennett Champ Clark's wife had written about for *Scribner's Commentator*. This was the town where *Life* had conducted the phony "poll" that purported to show that the 3,500 residents of Neosho (typical Middle-Western folk) were all-out for intervention in the war. Mrs. Bennett Clark's article pointed out that an official poll, conducted later by local newspapers, showed that the citizens of Neosho were overwhelmingly *against* U.S. entry into the war.

In January, 1956, Hazel and I had a holiday in the southern Caribbean, and among the several islands we visited we thought the little-known (at the time) island of St. Lucia the loveliest. We purchased six acres of shore property just outside the capital port of Castries. We thought that some day we might have a retirement home there. Meanwhile, we contracted to have a small shorefront cottage built on the property for our future holiday use.

Retirement came far sooner than we expected. In the fall of 1956 I had another bout with my slipped disk and was bedbound for two months. When I was walking again, the doctors said that the best way to cure my back condition was to swim a couple of hours every day. When we heard this advice, Hazel and I said at once: "Ah, St. Lucia!"

After fifteen very happy years with the *Digest* I was eligible for early retirement with a generous pension. When Hazel and I told the Wallaces of our plans to move to the Caribbean, they suggested that we try it for a six months' leave of absence — and, if we didn't like it, we would be welcomed back.

We had not the slightest intention of settling down on a tropical island and allowing ourselves to vegetate. As word of our plans got around, I soon had book contracts with three publishers — and an assignment to do book reviews on seagoing and tropical island subjects for the *New York Times Book Review*.

I had one very special book I wanted most to write, but I knew I would have to wait many years before I could attempt to work on it without upsetting my peace of mind. The tentative title of the book was *FDR and the Four Freedoms*.

Notes

FOREWORD

1. Gen. Albert C. Wedemeyer, *Wedemeyer Reports!* Old Greenwich CT.: The Devin-Adair Company, 1958; quoted also in Maj. Gen. J.F.C. Fuller's *A Military History of the Western World*. London: Eyre and Spottiswoode, 1956.

CHAPTER VII

1. Caroline Guild, *Rainbow in Tahiti*. New York: Doubleday, 1948.

CHAPTER VIII

1. A.J. Sylvester, *Life with Lloyd George, 1931-1945*. London: Macmillan, 1975; New York: Barnes & Noble, 1975.
2. W.A. Swanberg, *Luce and His Empire*. New York: Scribner's, 1972.
3. Basil Henry Liddell Hart (1895-1970) was wounded in the First World War and invalided out of the army with the rank of captain. He served as military editor of the *Daily Telegraph* 1925-35, and in the same capacity on the *Times* of London 1935-39. He was also military editor of the *Encyclopedia Britannica*. In 1937 he was appointed special adviser to the War Ministry. He was the author of a score of books on war and military tactics. He was knighted following the Second World War.
4. A.J. Sylvester, *op. cit.*

CHAPTER IX

1. *The Wartime Journals of Charles A. Lindbergh*. New York: Harcourt Brace Jovanovich, 1970.
2. Arthur Bryant, *The Turn of the Tide*; a history of the war years based on the notes of Field-Marshal Lord Alanbrooke, Chief of the Imperial General Staff. London: Collins, 1957; Garden City, N.Y.: Doubleday, 1957.
3. In the Franklin D. Roosevelt Library, Hyde Park, New York.
4. Duff Cooper, *Old Men Forget*. London: Rupert Hart-Davis, 1953; New York: Dutton, 1954.

CHAPTER XI

1. Stephen Becker, *Marshall Field III*. New York: Simon & Schuster, 1964.
2. Anne Morrow Lindbergh, *The Wave of the Future*. New York: Harcourt Brace, 1940.
3. Whitney Griswold became president of Yale University in 1950, to be followed in 1963 by Kingman Brewster. In 1977 Brewster was appointed Ambassador to Britain by President Carter.

CHAPTER XII

1. John Colville, *Footprints in Time – Memories*. London: Collins, 1976.
2. *The Memoirs of Lord Ismay*. London: Heinemann, 1960.
3. *Lord Moran, Churchill – taken from the Diaries of Lord Moran*. Boston: Houghton-Mifflin, 1966.
4. Ronald Lewin, *Churchill as Warlord*. London: Batsford Ltd. 1973; New York: Stein & Day, 1973.
5. Winston S. Churchill, *The Second World War*, Vol. II, *Their Finest Hour*. London: Cassell, 1949; Boston: Houghton-Mifflin, 1949.
6. *Ibid.*
7. Stephen Roskill, *Hankey: Man of Secrets. 1972*. London: Collins, 1971; New York: St. Martin's Press, 1972.
8. William Stevenson, *A Man Called Intrepid, The Secret War*. London: Macmillan, 1976; New York: Harcourt Brace Jovanovich, 1976.
9. H. Montgomery Hyde, *Cynthia*. New York: Farrar, Straus and Giroux, 1965; paperback, Ballantine, 1977.
10. David Ogilvy, *Blood, Brains and Beer* (an autobiography). New York: Atheneum, 1978.
11. Charles A. Beard, *President Roosevelt and the Coming of the War, 1941: A Study in Appearances and Realities*. New Haven, Conn.: Yale University Press, 1948; Hamden, Conn.: The Shoe String Press, 1968.
12. Merle Miller, *Plain Speaking: An Oral Biography of Harry S. Truman*. New York: Putnam's, 1974.

CHAPTER XIII

1. SCRIBNER'S COMMENTATOR is happy to be here and takes this opportunity to thank those residents of Lake Geneva who have so graciously helped us manage a complicated move with a minimum of effort. In approximately two weeks our new quarters on Main Street

will be completed and we hope that all members of the community will feel at liberty to call and see us and if they so desire avail themselves of sample copies of the magazine which will be obtainable in the reception room.

Among the nationally known people who have appeared in SCRIBNER'S COMMENTATOR during the past year were the following:

Fred Allen
Gov. Raymond E. Baldwin
Sen. Arthur Capper
James B. Carey (Gen. Secty, CIO)
Sen. Bennett Champ Clark
William Chamberlain
Sen. D. Worth Clark
Alan Devoe
Dr. Raymond L. Ditmars
John T. Flynn
Henry Ford
Rev. Harry Emerson Fosdick
Lillian Gish
Gen. Johnson Hagood
Don Herold
Rev. John Haynes Holmes
Sen. Rush D. Holt
Frazier Hunt
Robert Maynard Hutchins
Gen. Hugh S. Johnson
Sen. Hiram W. Johnson
Brig. Gen. George C. Kenny
Hon. Philip LaFollette
Stanton B. Lees
Col. George Chase Lewis
Fulton Lewis, Jr.

Col. Charles A. Lindbergh
Phillips H. Lord
Col. Robert McCormack
J.P. McEvoy
Graham McNamee
Robert A. Millikan (Nobel Laureate)
Rep. Karl E. Mundt
Albert Jay Nock
Sen. Gerald P. Nye
William Lyon Phelps
Amos R. Pinchot
Walter B. Pitkin
Nina Wilcox Putnam
Surgeon Gen. Thomas Parran
Ivan T. Sanderson
Monsignor Fulton T. Sheen
Jesse Rainsford Sprague
Alex Templeton
Lowell Thomas
Col. Roscoe Turner
Sen. Burton K. Wheeler
Frank Lloyd Wright
Maj. Malcomb Wheeler-Nicholson
Maj. Al Williams
Gen. Robert E. Wood

In our inspiring new environment here in Lake Geneva we hope to put out an ever better magazine and continue our steady growth this coming year.

SCRIBNER'S COMMENTATOR
Lake Geneva, Wisconsin

2. Robert Conquest, *The Great Terror: Stalin's Purge of the Thirties*. New York: Macmillan, rev. ed. 1973.
3. Peter Rowland, *David Lloyd George;* a biography. London: Barrie & Jenkins, 1975; New York: Macmillan, 1976.
4. Elliott Roosevelt, *As He Saw It*, with a foreword by Eleanor Roosevelt. New York: Duell, Sloan and Pierce, 1946.
5. Harold Nicholson, *The War Years, 1939-1945*. London: Collins, 1967.

CHAPTER XIV

1. Rear Admiral R.A. Theobald, *The Final Secret of Pearl Harbor*. Old Greenwich, Conn., The Devin-Adair Company, 1954.
2. Henry Hoke, *It's A Secret*. New York: Reynal and Hitchcock, 1945.
3. Joseph P. Lash, *Eleanor Roosevelt: A Friend's Memoir*. New York: Doubleday, 1964.
4. J.B. West and L. Kotz, *Upstairs at the White House.* New York: Warner Paperback Library, 1974.

CHAPTER XV

1. General Douglas MacArthur, *Reminiscences*. New York: McGraw-Hill, 1964.
2. Commodore Harry Grattidge, *The Captain of the Queens*. New York: E.P. Dutton, 1956.

CHAPTER XVII

1. James Burnham, *The Web of Subversion*. New York: John Day, 1954.
2. David Rees, *Harry Dexter White: A Study in Paradox*. New York: Coward, McCann & Geoghegan, 1973.

CHAPTER XVIII

1. Jim Bishop, *FDR's Last Year: April 1944-April 1945*. New York: William Morrow, 1974.
2. Alfred M. de Zayas, *Nemesis at Potsdam*, with foreword by Robert Murphy. London: Routledge & Kegan Paul, 1977.
3. David Irving, *The Destruction of Dresden*, with a foreword by Air Marshal Sir Robert Saundby. London: William Kimber, 1963.

4. Benjamin Colby, *Twas a Famous Victory: Deceptions and Propaganda in the War with Germany*. New Rochelle, N.Y.: Arlington House, 1974.
5. George N. Crocker, *Roosevelt's Road to Russia*. Chicago: Henry Regnery Company, 1959.

CHAPTER XIX

1. *The New York Times*, March 19, 1946.

CHAPTER XXI

1. James Playsted Wood, *Of Lasting Interest: The Story of the* Reader's Digest. Garden City, N.Y.: Doubleday, 1958.

Index

About the Author

Although he comes from an early New England background, a descendant of Bagot Eggleston, one of the founders of the First Congregational Church in America at Windsor, Connecticut, in 1630, George Eggleston is a native son of California. In 1929 he was graduated from the University of California at Berkeley, where he edited the monthly *Pelican*. Arriving in New York, he became a contributor to the old *Life* magazine. Before he was twenty-five he was the magazine's editor in chief. When Henry Luce launched the big weekly *Life*, he appointed Eggleston to the first board of editors of that magazine. From 1941 to 1957 he was an associate editor and department editor of *Reader's Digest*.

For many years an ardent Long Island Sound sailor and a member of the New York Yacht Club, he and his wife now reside in St. Lucia, West Indies, where the occupation of book writing combines felicitously with Caribbean blue-water sailing.

DATE DUE

GAYLORD			PRINTED IN U.S.A.

WITHDRAWN